MIDDLE EAST INDUSTRIALISATION

THE ROYAL INSTITUTE OF INTERNATIONAL AFFAIRS is an unofficial body which promotes the scientific study of international questions and does not express opinions of its own. The opinions expressed in this publication are the responsibility of the authors.

The Institute and its Research Committee are grateful for the comments and suggestions made by Mrs Miriam Camps and Dr Robert Mabro, who were asked to review the manuscript of this book.

To Jean
In memory of Mary E. and Milton M.

Middle East Industrialisation

A Study of Saudi and Iranian Downstream Investments

LOUIS TURNER
and
JAMES M. BEDORE

Published for
THE ROYAL INSTITUTE OF INTERNATIONAL AFFAIRS
by
SAXON HOUSE

Published by

SAXON HOUSE, Teakfield Limited,
Westmead, Farnborough, Hants., England

British Library Cataloguing in Publication Data

Turner, Louis
    Middle East industrialisation.
    1. Saudi Arabia — Industries
    2. Near East — Industries — Case studies
    3. Iran — Industries
    I   Titie
    II Bedore, James M
    III Royal Institute of International Affairs
    338'. 0953'8   HC497.A6

ISBN 0-566-00276-0

Contents

Tables

Figures

Acknowledgements

It is impossible to thank all the people who have helped with this book. As well as talking extensively to people in West Europe, we have visited and interviewed in places as far removed as Tokyo, San Francisco, Teheran and Riyadh. Everywhere, we found government officials, company executives and individual specialists unfailingly kind and helpful. In the typical Chatham House style, the authors were helped by a supporting study group with a floating population of around 30 people. As we finished each draft chapter, we sent copies to some 20 people who we felt were most concerned with the particular issues raised in it. The comments we invariably received back were frank, penetrating and stimulating.

Even if they were all willing to be acknowledged by name (and some are not, due to the delicate state of various negotiations), it would be difficult to list all those who have helped us, and totally invidious to present a partial list. Instead, to the 150 or so people whose comments and help have vastly improved the quality of this book, we would like to say 'Thank You'. We have done our best. It would have been far worse without you. Otherwise, thanks to the Ford Foundation, without whose financial backing the project culminating in this volume would not have existed.

L.T.
J.M.B.

Abbreviations

ALBA	Aluminium Bahrain
ASEAN	Association of Southeast Asian Nations
BP	British Petroleum
BTU	British Thermal Unit
CEFIC	European Council of Chemical Manufacturing Federations
CFP	Compagnie Française des Pétroles
CPE	Centrally Planned Economies
DR	Direct Reduction
EC	European Community
EEC	See 'EC'
ENI	Ente Nazionale Idrocarburi
GATT	General Agreement on Tariffs and Trade
GDP	Gross Domestic Product
GSP	General System of Preferences
hdPE	High Density Polyethylene
ICI	Imperial Chemical Industries
IDCAS	Industrial Development Centre for the Arab States
IEA	International Energy Agency
IIP	Index of Industrial Production
IJPC	Iran—Japan Petrochemical Company
INPC	Iran-Nippon Petrochemical Company
IRR	Internal Rate of Return
LDC	Less Developed Countries
ldPE	Low Density Polyethylene
LPG	Liquefied Petroleum Gases
MFA	Multi-Fibre Arrangement
MITI	Ministry of International Trade and Industry
NGL	Natural Gas Liquids
NIGC	National Iranian Gas Company
NIOC	National Iranian Oil Company
NPC	National Petrochemical Company (Iran)
OAPEC	Organisation of Arab Petroleum Exporting Countries
OECD	Organisation of Economic Co-operation and Development
OPEC	Organisation of Petroleum Exporting Countries
PBO	Planning and Budget Organisation (Iran)

PDRY	People's Democratic Republic of Yemen (South Yemen)
PVC	Polyvinyl Chloride
QAPCO	Qatar Petroleum Company
QASCO	Qatar Steel Company
SABIC	Saudi Basic Industries Corporation
SAFCO	Saudi Arabian Fertilisers Company
SBR	Styrene-Butadiene Rubber
UAE	United Arab Emirates
ULCC	Ultra-Large Crude Carriers
UNCTAD	United Nations Conference on Trade and Development
UNIDO	United Nations Industrial Development Organisation
VCM	Vinyl Chloride Monomer
VLCC	Very Large Crude Carriers
VLPC	Very Large Product Carriers

1 The noble hydrocarbons

It is quite understandable that the oil producing nations want to be more than just exporters of crude oil. Their citizens travel throughout the industrialised world, and see there the refineries and chemical plants which depend on the crude from oil wells back in their home countries. Why should the industrialised world monopolise these processing industries? Surely, these citizens argue, national pride and economic logic dictate that the oil producing states should process an increasing amount of their own crude oil and natural gas. Can OPEC's oil price revolution of the early 1970s be complete until OPEC members are in full control of what happens to crude oil after it has been pumped from the ground?

These demands are not peculiar to the oil industry, but reflect a growing expectation within the Third World that rich nations should allow the poorer ones to push ahead with industrialisation. At the UNCTAD III Conference at Santiago in 1972, Third World groupings were calling for a 'more rational' division of labour within the international community – in other words for 'more industry for the Third World'. By 1975, which saw the peak of the Third World's euphoria after the OPEC successes of 1973-4, this call was voiced in a more concrete manner by the United Nations Industrial Development Organisation (UNIDO)'s 'Lima Declaration', which specifically called for the Less Developed Countries (LDCs) to be allowed to increase their share of world industrial production from the current seven per cent to at least twenty-five per cent by the end of the century.

Already by 1975, there were some Third World countries which were clearly on the way to becoming industrial powers in their own right. In East Asia there were the 'miracle' economies of South Korea, Hong Kong, Taiwan and Singapore, emulating the earlier Japanese example. In Latin America, Mexico, Brazil and Argentina were already considerable industrial powers – as was India, in Asia. But if any one group of Third World countries had the chance to catapult itself out of the non-industrialised ranks, it was the oil producers which, as a result of oil price increases culminating in the massive rises of 1973-74, had the financial resources to invest, the raw materials on which to base such industrialisation, and the self-confidence to insist that the industrialised world make way for their products.

1

This, then, is a book about the decision of the two leading members of OPEC, Iran and Saudi Arabia, to become world forces in the oil refining and petrochemical fields. We have sometimes wandered away from these narrow cases to consider, for instance, the parallel plans of other Middle Eastern and North African oil producers, or the plans of Saudi Arabia and Iran for other industries, such as steel and car production. In general, though, we have concentrated on refining and petrochemical industries because, if these two countries cannot make a success of these industries, then many other Third World countries have little chance of improving their lot in the international economic order. Again, by going deeply into the politics and economics of two narrowly focused cases, we intend to pin-point issues, problems and opportunities which may be relevant to other LDCs which want to introduce other industries. In fact, this book is to some extent a re-action against the high level of rhetoric and generalities in the 'New International Economic Order' debate. We ask our readers to forget the lofty goals of the Lima Declaration for a while and to concentrate on the problems surrounding Saudi Arabia's and Iran's attempt to shift the centre of gravity of two key industries toward the Middle East. If they, with all their apparent advantages, cannot succeed, then the Third World is condemned to a permanent role as 'hewers of wood and drawers of water' for the industrialised world. If they can succeed, we shall want to see what effect this will actually have on the established industrial powers. Would such a geographical shift in these industries represent a revolutionary or evolutionary change?

Oil, gas and industrialisation

We do not expect our readers to have any pre-existing technical know-ledge about the chemistry of oil refining and petrochemical processes, though we have included an Appendix for those who want to have a clearer idea of what various products (such as naphtha, styrene, ethy-line or caprolactam) can actually be used for. It is important to make clear, however, just how important oil and gas are as the base for quite extensive industrialisation.

Refining is, quite naturally, the first industry which can be based on crude oil. Before World War II, in fact, it was quite usual to locate refineries in the oil producing countries and then to ship the resulting products out to consumers. There was a major shift to market-oriented refineries in the post-1945 era, as the industry continued to expand, products diversified and super-tankers evolved. A typical development in this era was the growth of the Rotterdam refining complex, which pre-empted a significant slice of refinery expansion planned in places such as Abadan in Iran, and Ras Tanura in Saudi Arabia.[1] What the oil producing states would now like to do is to reverse the logic of the post-1945 shift to ensure that they obtain a larger share of any future refining complexes. They feel that their hold on oil supplies gives them the right to expect such a shift in their favour.

Refineries are generally surrounded by chemical complexes which feed off certain by-products from the refining process — naphtha, gas oil and refinery gas being the main feedstocks involved. It is not, however, this petrochemicals-via-refining route which has captured the imagination of the oil producers. Rather, they are hoping to use their relatively abundant supplies of natural gas as the basis for the petrochemical complexes which they are determined to erect.

The point here is that 'gas liquids' such as ethane, propane and butane, which are generally produced in association with crude oil production, make an alternative source of feedstocks for the petrochemical industry — an alternative to the refinery by-products method mentioned above. For instance, the US petrochemical industry has been substantially built round that country's large (though now diminishing) reserves of natural gas. Within the Middle Eastern context, there has hitherto been virtually no use for these gases, which have usually been flared. As late as 1974, 67 per cent of the gas produced by the five leading Middle Eastern oil producers was thus wasted.[2] Taking into account the fact that Iran has extremely substantial reserves of 'non-associated' gas (i.e. gas found on its own, not produced as a by-product of oil production), one can see why the Middle Easterners want to build industries using gas. In particular, there is the argument (which we shall criticise in chapter 6) that, since this gas is currently being burned, it can be fed into petrochemical industries at next-to-no cost, thus making such industrialisation even more attractive.

If oil refining and petrochemical products are two closely-related industries based on the processing of oil and gas, there is a third type of industries which are being considered for location in the Middle East. These are energy-intensive ones, such as aluminium and steel production, for which, it is argued, the raw materials could be shipped into the region and then processed using the area's plentiful supplies of energy — in the same way as bauxite has been moved in the past to sources of cheap hydroelectric power for processing into aluminium. A further attraction of this third type of industrialisation is that Middle Eastern countries such as Saudi Arabia and Iran are just starting to assess what other minerals they possess. The Saudis, for instance, have minerals such as copper, iron, gold, phosphate, zinc, lead and some bauxite, and have been assured by one geologist that Saudi Arabia could become as important an exporter of minerals in the future as it is of oil today.[3] In these circumstances, basing mineral-processing industries now on

3

imported raw materials could be good preparation for a tomorrow when it might be possible to take simultaneous advantage of indigenous mineral and energy resources.

We will leave the economics of these various approaches to chapter 6. Here, though, we would stress that the Middle Easterners are motivated as much by political considerations as by strictly economic ones. For one thing, it is now a question of national pride that they consolidate the successes they have had in the oil-pricing field by encouraging the type of industrialisation which they believe is commensurate with their newly-won power in the world oil industry. Secondly, they genuinely tend to flinch from a future in which their prime natural assets (the oil and gas) are thoughtlessly burned in order to keep the citizens of the industrialised world living in the style to which they have become accustomed. Instead, there is a strand of thinking within the oil-producing world which agrees with the now exiled Shah of Iran that 'Oil is a noble product which must be put to noble uses'.[4] By this he meant that oil is too precious to be burned as energy; other sources are available for this, ranging from rivers and sea waves to wind, sun and uranium. Instead oil and gas should be transformed into more permanent resources, such as a range of petrochemical products, for which only hydrocarbon feedstocks can be used. Since we have become more fully aware of the finiteness of certain resources (oil in particular), this appeal to the 'nobility' of the hydrocarbons should not be too lightly discounted.

The 1973 watershed

The two countries we have studied — Iran and Saudi Arabia — make a nice contrast among the oil-producing would-be industrialisers. On the one hand, Saudi Arabia had virtually no industrial base by the early 1970s. Taking into account the great unreliability of statistics for this country, the figures indicate that under five per cent of the employed population was engaged in manufacturing activities in the mid-1960s.[5] In 1973, there were four refineries operative as well as a fertiliser plant, a small operation for producing iron and steel products for the building industry — and little else.[6] Obviously, Saudi oil income was rising in the early 1970s as prices moved upwards and oil exports increased. On the other hand, this underpopulated desert Kingdom had obviously no ambitions to become a world force in any industry other than in crude production. The events of 1973-74 were to change all that.

Iran was at the other extreme of the Middle Eastern oil producers. A population numbering 35 million was already starting to provide both a reservoir of skilled indigenous manpower, and a home market of sufficient size to encourage import-substituting investment. In addition, commercial quantities of oil had been discovered in Iran as early as 1908, some 30 years before similar discoveries in Saudi Arabia. Although this had inevitably allowed Iran to go further along the industrialisation path than the Saudis, there were few indications, even in the mid-1960s, that the Iranians might genuinely aspire to a major role in world industrial affairs. There was some development in the form of textile plants, a small steel mill, a moderately-sized, Soviet-built steel complex (which became operative in 1973), four chemical plants, fledgeling car and consumer durables industries, machine tool plants, and the inevitable refineries.[7]

Although Iranian industrial development was at a more advanced stage than that reached by the Saudis in the early 70s, there was nothing about these countries to suggest they were likely to become particularly important industrial powers by Third World standards. Iran might have had a largish labour force, but neither country had the kind of hard-working, disciplined, and adaptive labour force which was the major factor in the success of the South East Asian 'miracle' economies. Then again, although these two Middle Eastern nations had the hydrocarbons, they did not have the capital to back a major investment programme in refining and petrochemicals. This had to wait until the 1973-74 price explosions.

We are sure no reader needs reminding that the producer government 'take' per barrel of crude went up over five-fold from January 1973 to December 1974, and that, even with such price increases, the demand for oil was still buoyant enough in 1974 to allow the crude production in Saudi Arabia to increase by 50 per cent over 1972 figures. The combination of these two factors meant a totally unprecedented surge of income into the oil-producing economies. In the Saudi case, it meant that revenues went up from $2.7 billion in 1972, to $4.3 billion in 1973, to $27.8 billion in 1974.[8] In the Iranian case, these revenues rose from $2.5 billion in 1972-73 to $18 billion in 1974-75.[9]

Faced with this bonanza, leaders in both countries rapidly expanded the scope of their national plans, and started thinking of their countries as potential world industrial forces. In the case of the Shah of Iran, these dreams were expressed in his article of faith that Iran would be the fifth Great World Power within 20 years.[10]

The fact that events in Iran in late 1978 and early 1979 have finally put paid to such dreams should not blind us to the fact that in January 1979 the Shah left behind him an Iran which was about to see the completion of a range of large industrial projects authorised in the heady years of 1973 and 1974. Any new regime will still have the option of driving Iran forward to an industrial future if it so chooses.

This book, then, is about the reality of such dreams. Are Iran and

Saudi Arabia ever going to be able to take the necessary steps toward becoming industrial super-powers? . . . or is it inevitable that they must settle for a more limited role in one or two key industries? . . . or is even such a limited role unrealistically ambitious?

Notes

1   British Petroleum, 1977, p.246.
2   *Petroleum Economist*, July 1976, p.250.
3   *Middle East Economic Survey*, November 20 1978, p.ii.
4   Graham, 1978, p.20.
5   Sayigh, 1978a, p.140.
6   Sayigh, 1978a, pp 145, 149.
7   Amuzegar, 1977, pp 78-110; Graham, 1978, pp 43-49.
8   Sayigh, 1978, p.144.
9   Fesharaki, 1976, p.133.
10   Graham, 1978, p.17.

2 The Saudi projects

In the aftermath of the 1973-74 rise in the oil price, Saudi Arabia's determination to industrialise started to arouse international attention. This fascination stemmed partly from the incongruous popular conceptions of the country — how could the Lawrence of Arabia image be compatible with the undoubted economic power that Saudi Arabia now held? Many became riveted by the size of the financial surpluses Saudi Arabia was now starting to run, and there was general disbelief that industrialisation could ever be fast enough to absorb the oil revenues which came pouring in; after all, its population was tiny (was it five million people? The estimates varied a couple of million people on either side of this figure); and it had virtually no experience of industrialisation, if one ignored Aramco's refinery at Ras Tanura and some extremely small-scale entrepreneurship which Aramco had fostered in the Eastern Province.

Industry and the second Five-Year Plan

As the second Five-Year Plan was finalised during 1974, it became increasingly clear that Saudi Arabia was now earning an income from oil exports which it could not immediately hope to spend. On the other hand, the fact that exports rose from $2.7 billion in 1972 to $27.8 billion in 1974 meant that the planners were suddenly freed from all financial constraints. The result was a second Five-Year Plan for the years 1975/76 to 1979/80 which proposed public expenditures of $142 billion (in other words, over ten times as great as the planned expenditures of the first Plan).

Although the Plan gave a great deal of weight to infrastructural development and the development of educational facilities, the $15 billion intended for the setting up of hydrocarbon-based industries naturally caught the attention of foreign commentators. The key project was to be a giant gas-gathering and treatment system which was planned (exceptionally optimistically) to cost $4.7 billion. The resultant 1.6 million cubic feet of gas per day would be made available both for export and for use by a number of industrial projects located primarily in the traditional oil-producing area, the Eastern Province —

but including some to be located in the Western Province as well. There were to be five petrochemical complexes (four in the East and one in the West), each of which would produce 500,000 tons of ethylene a year. There would also be three export refineries (two in the East; one in the West; 250,000 b/d each); a 107,000 b/d lubricating oil refinery; two one-million tons/year fertiliser plants; one 210,000 tons/year aluminium plant; and one 3.5 million tons/year steel plant.[2]

Although respected international consultants, such as the Stanford Research Institute, advised on the formulation of the Plan, it was not a particularly coherent piece of work. The principle of developing energy-intensive industries based on Saudi Arabia's gas supplies was clear, but there was a certain arbitrariness about the number of projects decided upon. There was no clear attempt to come to terms with the cumulative demands these projects would make on the country's inadequate infrastructure. Nor was there sufficient consideration of whether the export-oriented projects would actually find international markets. In fact, this part of the Plan was as much a statement of the planners' general aspirations, as it was a coherent, step-by-step blueprint of how the country's industrialisation might proceed.

The Plan envisaged Petromin, the state oil agency, administering these ventures. It was becoming obvious, however, that some new body would have to be set up to look after the petrochemical and mineral processing projects. This was necessary partly because the over-centralised Petromin was unable to handle the sheer volume of potential foreign participants; by mid-1974, long before the second Plan was approved, there were already some 150 letters of intent awaiting action (and this was after a radical pruning of the number of would-be investors).

Then, as 1975 progressed, it became clear that the projects most directly concerned with oil and gas production were going to be more than enough to keep Petromin fully stretched. Petromin's critics, recalling the disastrous early history of the SAFCO turnkey fertiliser project, argued that the more purely industrial projects should be put in the hands of a new, more specialised agency. So, in October 1975, there was a general reorganisation of the country's central administration. The Central Planning Organisation was granted the status of a ministry, and a new Ministry of Industry and Electricity was created. In December, a Royal Commission for Jubail and Yanbu was formed, whose task it was to eliminate bureaucracy holding back the building of the gigantic port, road and other infrastructural development necessary for the two industrial zones at Jubail and Yanbu. Finally, in August the following year, the Saudi Basic Industries Corporation (SABIC) was created, under the auspices of the Ministry of Industry, with a capital of 10 billion Saudi Riyals ($2.8 billion). This state company was charged with undertaking the new industrial projects assigned to the Ministry of Industry by the second Plan — these were the ventures in the petrochemical, iron, steel and aluminium sectors, along with other activities beyond the capabilities of the private sector.

So, by late 1976, administrative responsibilities had been clarified. Petromin was left in charge of the oil and gas sectors and would be the Saudi partner of any foreign company becoming involved with refinery projects. The Royal Commission would primarily be in charge of providing the basic infrastructure at the two industrial ports around which the major industrial projects would be based. SABIC, reporting to the Minister of Industry, would be responsible for all the major projects, other than refineries, gas-gathering and oil production which were reserved for Petromin.

From then on, the only major source of organisational ambiguity stemmed from Saudi Arabia's curious unwillingness to move from 60 per cent ownership of Aramco to full nationalisation. As early as March 1976 the two sides had agreed on the main issues involved in a full Saudi takeover. By December, Sheikh Yamani was claiming that negotiations were at the strictly legal stage and that a final takeover would require only one small final meeting. In fact, at the moment of writing (January 1979), the deal has still not been finalised, so that Aramco remains a partnership in which the four American participants (Exxon, Texaco, Chevron and Mobil) still have a 40 per cent share between them. Despite this, Aramco has very much become a leading agent connected with domestic Saudi development. For instance, the company has been charged with the organisation and construction of the massive gas-gathering system as well as with expanding and integrating the electricity grid for the whole Eastern Province. The ambiguity of its role stems from the fact that the most logical development — the creation of a unified State Oil Company by the merger of Petromin and Aramco — obviously leaves many people uneasy. Some worries may stem purely from the consideration of what such a merger would do to the political influence of some personalities connected with Petromin. On the other hand, there are more pervasive worries as to whether the current Aramco partners would have any strong financial incentive to do their best for the Kingdom once Aramco is fully expropriated. In addition, there are Saudis who can see positive virtues in keeping policy formulation separate from policy implementation in the more complicated industrial sectors. There is no universal agreement that the current division between Petromin (policy formulation) and Aramco (the major operator on Petromin's behalf) is totally unreasonable. Hence, the Saudis may be satisfied with an expropriation of Aramco which establishes their national control over the oil sector, accompanied by Aramco's resurrection as a service company which would concentrate decreasingly on the international marketing of oil, and increasingly on project management within Saudi Arabia.

The gas-gathering scheme and East-West pipelines

The twin key components of the Saudi plan for industrial development have been the above-mentioned gas-gathering scheme to feed the proposed petrochemical plants, and two East-West pipelines (one for oil, one for gas) which would allow some of this industrialisation to take place in the Western Province. Thus two centres for heavy industry would be created, which is desirable from strategic and development points of view.

The gas-gathering scheme was originally budgeted to cost around $4 billion, and so was never expected to be cheap. However, the thinking behind this project was that the gas streams should be fractionated, with the more easily transportable liquids (propane, butane and natural gasoline) being exported. Saudi industrialisation would then be based on the remaining gases (ethane and methane) which could only be exported after undergoing the expensive liquefaction process, and which are anyway the basic feedstocks from which basic petrochemical 'building blocks' (such as ethylene and methanol) can be derived. It was thus hoped that the Liquefied Petroleum Gas (LPG) exports could be used to underwrite the costs of providing ethane and methane to the industrialisation programme.

The Ministry of Petroleum and Minerals put Aramco in charge of the project which was originally intended to be substantially completed by 1979. It soon became clear, however, that the initial cost estimates were over-optimistic and that the whole complex might cost over four times the $4 billion originally estimated. Part of this increase was caused by continually extending the scope of the project, e.g. an East-West pipeline was added. Another factor entered as the engineers got down to detailed costing of proposals which had not been fully thought out. Much of the additional cost was the result of trying to push through the construction of a genuinely very ambitious scheme at a time when the Saudi infrastructure was under extremely heavy strain (in the spring of 1976, ships had to wait up to six months before getting into Jeddah). Finally, the project was re-examined, and it became clear that it was not necessary to realise these plans as fast as was originally envisaged, at least in part, because the gas would not be needed for the industrial plants until well into the 1980s. So, it was decided that the scheme would be phased in more gradually, using one work force to build one 'module' after the other, rather than building all the modules at once as was originally intended.[3]

As mentioned earlier, the Saudi planners have also given the go-ahead for two East-West pipelines. It was thought undesirable to site all the new projects in one particular region and so cause an agglomeration of a highly-developed infrastructure, construction operations and population increase. Another reason, particularly for the oil pipeline, was to reduce Saudi dependence on the use of the Gulf and the Strait of Hormuz, the route through which all oil carriers must pass before reaching the open sea. The Strait is effectively controlled by Iran, and the Iranian crisis has reinforced Saudi determination to find alternative routes for her exports.[4]

Over the years there has been talk of running a pipeline to the Indian Ocean via some corridor through Oman, the People's Democratic Republic of Yemen (an extremely unattractive option) or Sharjah in the United Arab Emirates (UAE). Such a venture would reduce the chance of Saudi oil exports being terminated by some political crisis or accident affecting traffic of oil through the Strait. On the other hand, the increasing radicalism of the PDRY has rammed home to Saudi leaders how risky it would be to assign even part of their crude exports to a pipeline running through a country whose political sympathies may change. The history of the Trans-Arabian Pipeline (Tapline) has shown just how much such pipeline ventures are in danger of becoming targets for political ends. The proposed pipelines to the Western Province, then, have the advantage of increasing Saudi exporting options by giving access to the Red Sea, without leaving Saudi territory. They also shorten sea routes to the West by some 3,000 miles. Of course, any development on the Red Sea then becomes vulnerable to possible interference with transit rights through the Suez Canal and the SUMED pipeline, or through the Bab el Mandeb Strait leading to the Indian Ocean. But at least the Kingdom will have increased its ability to export by providing four different possible exits (if Tapline is included) for its crude oil and/or gas.

In any case, both the pipelines fall under Petromin's control. The crude pipeline will run 750 miles to the Yanbu industrial complex. It will be owned by Petromin and be financed from Saudi sources such as the Public Investment Fund. Mobil won the contract to manage the design and construction of the line, which is due to be completed in 1981, and to have an initial capacity of 1.85 million barrels a day. The parallel gas pipeline will have a capacity of 250,000 b/d of NGLs and is being constructed under the overall management of Aramco. Contracts to build the pipeline were awarded in autumn 1978 to a joint Argentinian and private Saudi company (Techint Saudi Arabia Ltd) for completion by January 1981. Some of its gas will be used to fuel the oil pipeline running alongside; its ethane will be used as feedstock by the Mobil-SABIC ethylene complex when that eventually becomes operative; the rest of its gas liquids will be exported.

The petrochemical ventures

The second Plan originally called for the construction of five very large petrochemical complexes. Each was to be capable of producing 500,000 tons/year of ethylene or its equivalent. Four were to be sited in the East; one in the West. One of the eastern ones was to be finished by the end of the Plan's five years (i.e. in autumn 1980); the remaining four were to be completed soon afterwards. In addition, two new ferti-liser plants were to be built with capacities of around one million tons/ year each.

The Saudis themselves, however, have always emphasised that the Plan's time elements were not as important as laying out a strategy of development for all to see. Thus it is hardly surprising that, by the time we finished this book (January 1979), it was clear that these goals were over-optimistic. The earliest anyone can conceive of one of the major complexes coming into operation is 1983, but most would cautiously add that 1985, or later, seems more realistic. In addition, although the planners soon settled on only four ethylene-based complexes, the potential of other projects was evaluated and some were added to the planners' checklists. By 1977 it had become accepted, for instance, that the Saudis would like to see at least one methanol-based complex built in addition to the ethylene plants.

Mobil would appear to be one of the two front-runners in the rather cautious race to start construction on one of the ethylene complexes. Its Yanbu project would produce 450,000 tons/year of ethylene, with varying amounts of Low Density Polyethylene (ldPE), Ethylene Glycol and High Density Polyethylene (hdPE).[5] Fuel and feedstock for this complex would come from the NGLs provided from the Eastern Province's oilfields via the second of the two pipelines. Although Mobil helped the Saudi government in choosing Yanbu as the major centre around which to base industrial development on the West Coast, it was not until the autumn of 1976 that the company signed an agreement with the Ministry of Industry and Electricity to make a $10 million feasibility study, with the intention of having the complex in operation in 1980 (a target date fixed in 1974). In early Autumn 1977, Bechtel was appointed as main contractor to conduct preliminary engineering studies and to develop cost estimates (in 1976, an overall investment of $800 million was envisaged). The feasibility study was completed in mid-1978 and was handed over to SABIC, which apparently used the World Bank mission in Riyadh to double-check the study's assump-tions. SABIC's assessments should be completed in early 1979, and,

12

assuming these will be positive, we should then see a final flurry of negotiations aimed at laying down the exact terms on which capital, gas and crude oil will be provided by the Saudis. 1983 is still the official target for this project to be completed (construction would have to start in 1980), but 1984 would now seem to be the very earliest that this could happen.

The second front-runner is the SABIC-Pecten joint venture planned for Jubail in the East. Pecten is the name used by non-US subsidiary companies of the Houston-based Shell Oil, which is, in turn, a 69 per cent owned affiliate of the Royal Dutch/Shell grouping. This venture is slightly ahead of the Mobil one at Yanbu, since Fluor was given a management contract in winter 1976-77 for some pre-engineering work. In February 1978, SABIC announced that the joint studies with Shell were completed, demonstrating that this venture was economically feasible. At the time of writing, though, Shell had still not decided to move on to the construction stage. In the meantime, this project has become somewhat more complex than the Mobil one. Originally conceived as producing 450,000 tons/year of ethylene along the same lines as the Mobil venture, the SABIC-Pecten project has been extended to produce 650,000 tons/year, of which 250,000 tons/year will go to a neighbouring Exxon ldPE plant. What this means is that Exxon has postponed its interest in building an ethylene plant of its own, in favour of providing some capital towards the SABIC-Pecten project (it is not taking an equity share), in return for which it will enter a contract to take part of the output for its ldPE operation.

The SABIC-Pecten project is thus quite complicated and is made more so by the fact that it is the US-based Shell which is involved. The motivation of this particular company will be examined in chapter 4, but it is still worth adding here that entitlements amounting to at least 250,000 b/d of crude are definitely part of the package which Shell is considering. It is also worth adding that there are strong signs, as we write, that Shell Oil is not going to be rushed into any hasty decision about starting construction on the project.

Dow Chemical, via its European management arm, Dow Chemical Europe, is the third potential partner of SABIC in an ethylene venture. This is now being planned and involves a project which would cost around $1 billion and would be producing ethylene, polyethylene and ethylene glycol. This project will be built at Jubail in the East. Should the SABIC-Pecten complex get to the construction stage, then the logistical difficulty of simultaneously building two such plants would probably mean that the Dow project would be delayed a year or two, thus pushing it towards the late 1980s.

Moreover, the fact that the first plant to be constructed will inevitably satisfy the markets at which subsequent projects will also aim, will give foreign partners lower in the investment queue some cause for concern. Dow sources argue that the existence of their company's world-wide marketing network for chemical products should reduce this problem of over-supply. This is, therefore, one good reason why the Saudis would prefer a large successful chemical company (such as Dow) rather than an oil company to participate in these ventures.

Mitsubishi is the potential partner in the fourth ethylene complex. The proposals to this one have had such a chequered career that they look even less likely to come to fruition than the Dow ones. Mitsubishi was discussing the possibility of entering such a venture as early as 1973, before the dramatic rise in oil prices. When originally conceived, it was hoped that the venture would cost around $346 million, but by mid-1976 the estimates had reached $1.7 billion and Mitsubishi was asking the Saudis for a three-year delay, a request which was taken as tantamount to backing out of the project completely. Mitsubishi's decision caused Saudi resentment against the Japanese in general, and when a semi-official Japanese business mission visited Saudi Arabia in early 1977, it was shaken by Saudi hostility which was then extremely strong (as one of the authors personally discovered during a field trip around that time). The result was that the Japanese government pushed Mitsubishi back into the fray and since then the company has been negotiating seemingly about two potential projects. The ethylene complex is still under discussion, with the Japanese authorities doing all they can to reduce Mitsubishi's exposure. Throughout 1977 and 1978, the Japanese side wrestled with how best to handle their end of the project. In June 1977 the Japanese government agreed in principle to take part in any eventual project. In July 1978, the Mitsubishi Group handed an in-house study of the project to SABIC. In January 1979, Saudi Petrochemicals Development Co. Ltd. was about to be formed with 54 Japanese companies — not just from the Mitsubishi family, but including petrochemical, oil refining, electricity and gas companies and banks. This consortium was to launch a full eighteen-month feasibility study with SABIC. Should this study show the overall feasibility of the project, then the Japanese government would participate through the Overseas Economic Co-operation Fund.

The impression we have gained is that the Saudis are quite interested in signing a major deal with Japan, if only to provide an alternative to becoming over-reliant on the Americans and Europeans. On the other hand, there is some impatience with the lengthy Japanese decision-making process. This seems to grate on Saudi officials who, while not always being speedy decision-makers themselves, appreciate being able to receive answers reasonably fast from potential partners. It is clear that Mitsubishi has decided to minimise its risks by bringing a good part of the Japanese company-government Establishment into any final

14

venture. And the Japanese government is being extremely cautious, refusing to make any final decision until it has seen the results of the current feasibility study.

The other Saudi petrochemical venture in which Mitsubishi is involved is one of the two possible methanol projects which are under consideration. In May 1977, SABIC signed an agreement with a consortium which included Mitsubishi, C. Itoh and W.R. Grace for a feasibility study involving a 600,000 tons/year methanol plant at Jubail. (Grace seems to have been included as compensation for the fact that SABIC had allocated a fertiliser venture, which interested this American company, to the Taiwanese.) In February 1978, another agreement was signed with the US companies Celanese and Texas Eastern for a similar-sized plant. These projects should be complementary, with one looking primarily to Japan and the other to the USA for markets.

These ethylene, methanol and (in Exxon's case) ldPE projects are the most important chemical ventures under consideration in Saudi Arabia. The two new fertiliser ventures which the second Plan envisaged have not attracted much interest, though in January 1978, the Taiwanese Minister of Economic Affairs reached an agreement in principle to set up a joint Saudi-Taiwanese fertiliser plant in the Eastern Province. Subsequent negotiations have taken place with the Taiwan fertiliser company. Somewhat earlier (around 1974-75) there was also some discussion with BP (British Petroleum) about building an artificial protein plant which would use this company's oil fermentation process. This was a technology, however, whose economics were particularly affected by the oil price rises of 1973-74. Moreover, the Saudis were not totally convinced that it was a clinically safe technology.

Refining ventures

The second Plan called for the building of three export refineries (two at Jubail, one at Yanbu), the expansion of domestic refineries at Riyadh and Jeddah, the expansion of the existing lube-blending plant at Jeddah and the construction of a lube oil refinery in the same town. Of these, the three export refineries may be fifty-fifty joint ventures between Petromin and foreign partners; the two domestic refineries would be owned entirely by Petromin; while Mobil would have 29 and 30 per cent respectively in the two lube-oil ventures.

Not only is it Mobil's ambition to be involved in managing the crude pipeline to Yanbu as well as in negotiating to build an ethylene cracker, but the company is also more heavily involved than its rivals in the refining sector. Mobil and Shell International are both proposing

15

250,000 b/d export refineries, while Chevron and Texaco are negotiating a joint venture with Petromin for a 120,000 b/d lube refinery. However, Mobil has already proved itself more ambitious than the others by being also involved in the two lube-oil ventures. Neither of these projects is particularly large, with the refinery being designed to produce only 3,000 b/d of products, enough to make Saudi Arabia self-sufficient in these oils, but in effect a small-scale exercise by world standards. What is striking, though, is that Mobil took a 29 per cent stake in the Petrolube (lube-blending) joint venture as early as 1972 and a 30 per cent stake in the Lubref lube-oil refinery in 1974. What is even more striking for the Saudi environment is that these joint ventures have actually been realised, with Mobil overseeing the construction of the refinery which came into operation in early 1978. This gives Mobil the operating experience which no other company of comparable size has had in Saudi Arabia. Certainly, Exxon, Texaco and Chevron have gained experience at one remove through their involvement in Aramco, but this is not quite the same thing as entering Saudi ventures directly, as Mobil has done. The other Aramco partners continue to negotiate with the Saudis, but only Mobil has moved from the negotiating to the operational stage.[6]

The three export refineries are in exactly the same kind of limbo as the ethylene complexes discussed above. All are at the stage of feasibility-cum-preliminary engineering studies, but none of the foreign partners has yet proved willing to commit themselves to actual construction. What the construction or non-construction of the refineries will do is to affect the amount of flexibility the planners will have with the second generation of chemical plants which will be built in the Kingdom. The existence of refinery products would give them a flexibility that a purely gas-based approach could not.

Other large-scale industrial ventures

The refining and petrochemical industries described above are hydrocarbon-processing ones, in which Saudi Arabia's oil and gas are converted into higher-value products. The planners did, however, see that this plentiful oil and gas could also be used to attract energy-intensive industries such as steel and aluminium, along the lines followed by countries with abundant supplies of hydroelectric power.

The second Plan specifically called for the building of a 3.5 million tons/year steel plant and of a major aluminium plant, both of which were to be located in the Eastern Province. The aluminium smelter never really attracted much interest, though there are reports that the US company, National Southwire, is looking into it. Saudi officials insist

16

that plans for such a smelter are still alive, but they are aware of the existence of a competing smelter in Bahrain and another one which will come into operation in the UAE in 1979. At the time of writing, the chances of a Saudi plant being completed during the 1980s seem remote.

The steel project, mooted even before the 1973 oil price rises, is still alive, even if it has been heavily downgraded in size. By mid-1976, negotiations were chiefly centred on a joint venture between SABIC (50 per cent) and a consortium, which would have included the US company Marcona (22 per cent) as well as Gillmore (US), Nippon Steel (Japan) and the German-Dutch company Estel. One possibility was that the joint venture would ship slurried iron ore in from Brazil (where Marcona have ore sites) which would be turned into sponge iron, and then either be exported or turned into steel in three small steel-making plants within Saudi Arabia. Logistically, this was perhaps the most ambitious industrial venture which the Saudis had to consider, and the Brazilian angle apparently owed a lot to the enthusiasm of Charles Robinson, the President of Marcona, who became Under Secretary for Economic Affairs in the State Department under Dr Kissinger.

It is to the credit of SABIC and its advisers that this proposal was allowed to wither, for it was abundantly clear that there was a world steel crisis of over-supply. A conscious decision was taken to scale Saudi steel ambitions down to a level which would meet the Kingdom's own needs, but which would not produce significant quantities for export. The resultant change in policy led the Saudis to look more closely at companies which might be willing to build a Direct Reduction (DR) unit of around 800,000 tons/year capacity (Direct Reduction is a technology which is ideally suited to LDCs, being a much smaller-scale technology than the traditional blast-furnace approach which only becomes competitive to DR when the plants run continuously at rates which far exceed the domestic needs of a country like Saudi Arabia). By early summer of 1977, the Saudis found their foreign partner in the German company Korf Stahl (which proved, in late 1978, to have a substantial Kuwaiti equity share).

The joint-venture approach

One noticeable characteristic of Saudi Arabia's export-oriented ventures is that the country's planners are insisting quite rigorously that foreign partners be brought in on a basis of up to fifty-fifty. This contrasts with countries such as Algeria and Libya which have had chemical plants built as turnkey projects, leaving their national companies to manage them when they come into operation.

17

The initial Saudi insistence on the joint-venture formula seems to have stemmed from their disastrous experience with the early operations of SAFCO, which taught them only too well the dangers inherent in the turnkey approach. So, when the lube-blending and lube-oil refining ventures were broached in the 1970s, Petromin was willing to accept Mobil as a junior partner, even though Petromin kept 100 per cent control of the expanded domestic refinery in Riyadh and will do the same for the expansion of domestic refining capacity in Yanbu. With the export refineries and petrochemical complexes, though, there has been a rigid insistence by the planners that Petromin or SABIC should enter into joint ventures with foreign companies.

In one sense, this is excellent discipline for the Saudis. Under the turnkey formula, it is only too easy for inexperienced officials to underestimate the difficulties in buying reliable plant, operating it efficiently and finding world markets for the products. By insisting that foreign partners have a financial and managerial share in the plant, the Saudis are attempting to write their own insurance policy. They hope the foreigners will have a powerful motive to ensure that any project in which they become involved is sound, and to dispose of the products within their international marketing network.

On the other hand, an over-rigid application of the joint-venture formula may restrict the Saudis' freedom of action, because the interests of the country and of the foreign partner will not necessarily always be identical. There would be little problem if the export projects were clearly going to be profitable, but, as we shall explain in chapter 6, this is unlikely to be the case for the first generation of Middle Eastern industrialisation. In these circumstances, there are problems. As we shall again argue later, the crucial importance of Saudi Arabia to the international oil industry will make companies embark on joint ventures there, even though these are somewhat less economically attractive than possible investments elsewhere in the non-OECD world. But there are limits to corporate purses. Once it is clear that a project will not give an adequate return on investment, the only way the Saudis can get the project moving is to increase subsidies of one sort or another until the return becomes adequate (two would-be partners have assured us that they are looking for a 15 per cent return on their Saudi investments). In a sense then, the joint venture formula makes the Saudis dependent on the strategies of foreign partners. However badly the national planners may want some of these ventures to go ahead, the profit and loss calculations of the corporations will be the decisive factor.

Saudi planners have argued with us that they have no intention of going ahead with unprofitable export ventures, so that there is no conflict between national goals and the commercial self-interest of foreign partners. They point with justifiable pride to the way in which the steel project has been scaled down as the commercial realities became apparent, as well as to the refusal to sanction the General Motors' assembly plant which would have needed permanent subsidies. Similarly, they point to the fact that they dropped the idea of producing protein from gas when it became clear that this process was still at an experimental stage, facing technical and legal difficulties in the West. They also put back their plans for an aluminium smelter once it had been realised how little room was left for it by the competing ventures in Bahrain and Dubai. On the other hand, such rigour is not found throughout the whole of the Saudi industrialisation process. The Saudi Industrial Development Fund, which concentrates on loans to the domestic sector, publicly accepts that it must back projects which may not qualify for commercial loans.[7] Even within the export-oriented sector, the insistence that only commercial ventures will proceed is belied not only by the fact that apparently foreign partners are being offered loans at well below world interest rates, but also by gas prices which may bear little relationship to the cost of gathering it, and by entitlements to crude oil over and above the quantity that foreign partners would be purchasing under normal commercial arrangements.

Saudi attitudes toward financing export ventures are complex, as befits a country whose major comparative advantage is the fact that it has vast financial surpluses, but which also works under the Islamic ban on charging interest.[8] For the major projects the basic formula has been that the foreign partner is expected to hold 50 per cent of the equity, but can approach the Public Investment Fund for a loan covering 60 per cent of this investment at an effective interest rate which should be between 3 and 6 per cent per annum. Thirty per cent of the foreigners' shares should come from their own resources, with the final 10 per cent coming from a commercial bank. Naturally, since negotiations on the major export ventures are not yet properly under way, it is too soon to say that this will be the final pattern of financial aid by the Saudis. It does, however, roughly agree with the arrangements made to finance the Petromin-Mobil lube-oil refinery.[9] Given the fact that this was a domestically-oriented project, one would expect partners in export projects to obtain marginally better terms.

If substantial financing at 3-6 per cent per annum can be seen as one way of 'sweetening' such deals for foreign partners, it appears that low-cost gas supplies will be needed as well. The foreign partners generally confirm that they will be negotiating to obtain their gas feedstocks at somewhere between 35 and 50 cents a million BTU. A few comments are to be made about this. Firstly, such a price range is well below the levels at which gas is due to be sold in western economies such as the United States, whose autumn 1978 Energy Plan envisages gas prices rising to around $4 per million BTU in 1985 (which is roughly when

19

the first Saudi project should come into operation). On the other hand, the Saudis and their foreign partners retort, the Kingdom's ethane has few uses within the Kingdom and can only be exported through the capital-devouring liquefaction process. The costs involved in processing and transporting this gas to export markets would be so high that the residual 'net-back' price to the Saudi exporter would be little different from the 35-50 cents a million BTU at which the authorities are offering it to industrial projects within the Kingdom. In a later chapter, we shall discuss whether a cheap gas policy in such circumstances counts as a subsidy, but it is abundantly clear that expected feedstock prices are low by world standards and that without some such 'sweetener' foreign partners will find it difficult, if not impossible, to proceed with these ventures.

Just as their cheap financing takes advantage of their abundance of petrodollars, the Saudis are capitalising on another of their fundamental advantages in the world economy — massive oil reserves — to offer potential partners the right to purchase extra quantities of crude. This factor, undoubtedly, explains much of the interest of the major oil companies to become involved in Saudi refining and petrochemical ventures. In the case of US Shell, for instance, it is understood that more than 250,000 b/d of crude are involved. It is not at all clear exactly on what terms this crude will eventually be supplied (it is unlikely to be offered at a discount), but this is exactly the kind of offer which, in a potentially oil-short world, will attract foreign partners to ventures which may only be marginally profitable. The fact that the Saudis are willing to offer such an inducement must indicate that there is still considerable uncertainty about these projects on the Saudi side.

The combined offers of these incentives suggest that these export ventures are of marginal attractiveness to foreign partners. However, further Saudi spending on the basic industrial infrastructure might also be considered as an incentive to foreigners. After all, the Kingdom is building Yanbu and Jubail with the sole intention of basing industrial enterprises there and, although the relevant projects will be charged for the use of services such as water and electricity, the export projects will not be requested to make any significant contribution to the overall initial cost of ports, roads, power stations, desalination units, wells, telecommunication systems, airport (in the case of Jubail only?), housing and educational facilities. But then this is only fair. The tradition of governments heavily under-writing the development of infrastructure for industry is well established around the world, and if the Saudis want to become an industrial force, an ambitious commitment to infrastructural development is acceptable. Certainly, it would be unusual and unfair to ask the first projects using such infrastructure to share the basic costs of providing it. No, it is the other forms of official aid to these export ventures that are likely to worry non-Saudis.

Indecision

Despite all the foregoing, it is the slowness with which all the major projects are creeping forward which is most noticeable, and there is a growing suspicion that some of the foreign partners would not worry too much should these ventures waste away. Since the autumn of 1976, when our study started, none of the foreign partners then considering the most important ventures has yet made any commitments to move on to the construction stage. Certainly, there was a burst of activity around late 1976 and early 1977 when a number of the potential partners turned letters of intent into formal agreements to commit themselves to major feasibility studies. By the spring and early summer of 1978, the foremost companies, Shell and Mobil, had completed these studies and had reached a position where hard decisions were needed from the Saudis on matters such as gas pricing, the conditions under which extra quantities of crude would be supplied, overall terms of financing and the terms of using facilities, such as electric power and water. On Saudi initiative, the companies' feasibility studies were handed over to the World Bank mission for further analysis. So the agreement between Saudis and foreign partners to proceed to the construction stage was once again put back from 1978 to 1979.

Explanations for these delays are difficult, since there is probably no administration in the world whose decision-making process is more obscure than that of the Saudis. Some western observers tend to blame the slowness with which Saudi officials make decisions. These observers point to cases such as the excessive time taken to move Aramco into 100 per cent Saudi ownership and argue that difficult decisions tend to be delayed in order not to antagonise any powerful vested interests. This is not a totally convincing explanation. Inter-bureaucratic rivalry, however, can probably explain some of the delays in the industrialisation process. For one thing, the gas-pricing and crude oil entitlement issues involve both Petromin and the Ministry of Industry, and the interests of these two will obviously be distinct. As the agency in charge of the production and distribution of oil and gas, Petromin has a vested interest in receiving a fair price for its products, while the Ministry of Industry and SABIC will want these provided on terms which are attractive to foreign partners. Should the export ventures be economically viable without subsidies, then there will be no clash of interests. However, as soon as subsidies do become necessary, Petromin will be asked to accept a price for its products which it may well find too low.

21

This is the type of clash which outside observers suggest leads to procrastination. The final decision on these issues is taken by the Supreme Council for Petroleum, which brings together Crown Prince Fahd, Foreign Minister Saud bin Faisal and the Ministers of Petroleum and Industry (among others). It was this supreme decision-making body which thrashed out the earlier big decisions, such as the need to stretch out the construction period of the gas-gathering system. As we write, there is no sign that it has yet come to any final decision on the gas-pricing and crude-entitlement issues which are so important for the viability of the major industrial ventures.

However, it would be unfair to put all the blame for the delays in Saudi Arabia's industrialisation plans on Saudi indecisiveness. After all, the period since 1973 has been one of the most turbulent in this century. Virtually every industry's projections of product markets in the 1980s have been consistently downgraded year by year since 1973. This has made planning a nightmare even for far more experienced decision-makers than the Saudis. For instance, in the autumn of 1976, the British government backed a report which projected the construction of four new ethylene crackers in Britain by 1985. In 1979 it was clear that only one such project — if that — could be operative by that date.[10] Certainly, it is not for two London-based authors to criticise Saudi planners for being unable so far to bring various foreign partners to the construction stage of petrochemical and refining ventures. The international economic situation has been deteriorating ever since the announcement of the second Plan. If anything, Saudi planners are to be congratulated on avoiding any over-enthusiastic commitment to projects for whose products there may be little demand in present world markets.

On balance, then, we would suggest that Saudi planners have been moving with justifiable caution, and there can be no doubt that their planning procedure is designed to reject uneconomic projects. In the words of Dr Ghazi al-Qusaibi, the Minister of Industry:

> . . . I do not believe any industrial projects anywhere in the world are so carefully and extensively studied as ours. We start with market surveys carried out by our experts and experts from the potential partner. Then we proceed to a detailed feasibility study in which we take part with the potential partner and many world consulting houses. These studies are then submitted to a full objective evaluation, for which we have chosen the World Bank as a neutral party with wide experience in evaluating large-scale projects. Then comes the hardest test of all, the decision of the Board of Saudi Arabian Basic Industries Corporation (SABIC), which includes five of the most prominent Saudi economists.[11]

There is no doubt that the key decision-makers within the Ministry of Industry and its agency, SABIC, are genuinely determined to block any unprofitable investments, but there is a certain ambiguity about what will be considered as profitable or unprofitable.

In the speech from which the above quote is taken, the Minister quite clearly admits that the foreign partners are being attracted by 'numerous generous incentives' — and this is at the heart of the problem that Saudi planners still have to face. All governments give various subsidies to industrialists, and every country has ventures which are 'profitable' only after heavy subsidies. In fact, if one measures the profitability of a venture solely by whether it shows a balance sheet profit or loss, virtually anything can be made to look 'profitable' by increasing the levels of incentives (or subsidies). However, government planners have to make a subjective judgement about the exact point at which the required level of subsidy gets out of hand and produces a project which is 'profitable' to the company concerned but 'unprofitable' in terms of the overall economy.

It is possible that there will be no such dilemma for the Saudis, as the foreign partners may be able to dispose of enough products for these export-ventures to be profitable with incentives that are not too far out of line by world standards. Trouble would arise if the World Bank advised that these industrial ventures require an exceptional level of Saudi aid. The strong Saudi belief is that the possession of ample supplies of crude and flared natural gas makes it a natural base for export refineries and petrochemical plants. But equally strong is the commitment of those close to the industrialisation process not to waste money on worthless projects. Thus it is possible that the Saudi leaders might be forced to choose between these two strictly-held beliefs. It would be an extremely bitter choice for them to make.

Notes

1   Non-specialist readers may find chapters 2 and 3 somewhat indigestible. They are, however, not essential for full comprehension of the policy-oriented chapters in the second half of this book.

2   Wells, 1976, p.38; *Guardian* (London), October 22 1976, p.18.

3   *Petroleum Intelligence Weekly*, September 20 1976, p.1; *Middle East Economic Survey* (supplement), June 13 1977.

4   See Turner and Bedore, 1978a for a discussion of the wider strategic issues.

5   See appendix for full details of such projects.

6   Tavoulareas, 1977.

7   SIDF, 1976, p.7.

8   Dividends are permitted which reflect the level of an operation's profitability (Sayigh 1978a, p.167).
9   *Middle East Economic Survey*, March 20 1978, p.2.
10   *Financial Times*, August 9 1978, p.13.
11   *Middle East Economic Survey* (supplement), May 8 1978, p.7.

3 The Iranian projects

All authors have nightmares that dramatic world events will render their book redundant in the long period between their starting to write and their seeing the finished volume in the bookshops. The fall of the Shah of Iran has posed just such a threat to us. When we started writing in August 1978, the Shah was pretty firmly in power, though popular discontent was obviously running high. As we wrote the initial draft, his position steadily deteriorated until he was forced to leave the country, a month after we finished it. January and February of 1979 were spent revising the draft against the background of the Ayatollah Khomeini's return and apparent establishment of his authority.

In practice, none of this has changed our arguments much. For instance, we were already discounting Iran's chances of being much more than a marginal exporter of petrochemical and oil products during the 1980s, and events have merely reinforced our initial conclusion. Also, even under the Shah's regime, there was growing questioning of the returns to be gained from capital-intensive industrialisation, and post-Shah regimes will merely push this questioning ahead rather faster.

However, a watershed has been reached, and we shall concentrate for much of this chapter on writing an epitaph on the Shah's industrial ambitions in the post-1973 era. Undoubtedly, the planning decisions of 1974 were coming to fruition at the time he left the country, with a series of major industrial plants just starting to come into operation. The chances are that his successors will see that most of the unfinished projects are completed, so we are here discussing the decisions which have determined the structure of the Iranian economy for the 1980s. Only towards the end of this chapter shall we discuss the chances of the Shah's successors developing alternative industrial strategies. We shall end this chapter with the perhaps cynical thought that there is an almost irresistible logic behind the Shah's thinking on industrial matters, and that only the most imaginative of his successors will break away from backing the kind of industries he supported.

Industry and the Fifth Plan

In contrast to the Saudi case, Iranian industrialisation has taken place on a broad front. The range of industries under development has always been wide even by comparison with Iran's neighbours in the region, reflecting Iran's greater population and relatively early experience of industrialisation. Where there has been an overlap in the two countries' approaches, is in their commitment to the hydrocarbon-processing sector and to relatively capital-intensive projects.

The oil price rises of late 1973 and early 1974 caught Iranian planners as much off-balance as their Saudi counterparts. The Fifth Five-Year Plan was formally unveiled in the Majlis (the Iranian parliament) in January 1973 and came into force in March of that year. The oil price rises meant, however, that oil income would obviously run far ahead of the amount budgeted. Thus, a full-scale revision of the Plan was necessary, and this was achieved by August 1974. Inevitably, this revision was a hurried, scrambled affair, which badly overstretched the capacity of the Plan and Budget Organisation (PBO). The revision of the Fifth Plan was carried through, however, and projected a total fixed capital investment of just under $70 billion, which was double the amount called for in the original Fifth Plan and about six and a half times larger than that outlined in the Fourth Plan.[1]

Like many such exercises, the rhetoric of the Fifth Plan did not always bear much relationship to what actually happened. As with the Saudi planning experience, the various ministries and agencies drew up their 'shopping lists' of projects they would like to initiate, now that all financial constraints seemed to have been swept away. The planners at the PBO had neither the time nor the authority to impose any order of priority, and so by drawing up the very ambitious revised Fifth Plan, they avoided the hard allocative decisions which they should (with hindsight) have been making.[2]

Accepting, therefore, that the stated goals of the Fifth Plan should be used cautiously, they did show a marked commitment to the industrial sector. Admittedly, defence was singled out as the sector with by far the largest proposed expenditure, but manufacturing closely followed housing as the sector with the third highest expenditure targets for the 1973-78 period (it would be in second place if investments in refining capacity were included under 'manufacturing' rather than 'oil').[3] Within this sector, particular attention was paid to petrochemicals (with a proposed 27 per cent annual growth rate), cement production, the expansion and diversification of the iron and steel industry, initial development of copper deposits at Sar Cheshmeh, import substitution within the car industry, expansion of the refining sector and the tripling of machine-tool manufacturing capacity.[4] There was also some attention given to the need to encourage a number of the larger of these units to establish themselves along the Gulf, where there would be easy access to international markets, as well as to essential

26

supplies such as power, water, gas and petroleum.

Refining

The most important role in this industrialisation process was to fall to the National Iranian Oil Company (NIOC) and its then subsidiary, the National Petrochemical Company (NPC). Until the latter was formed into a separate company in 1977, the NIOC was in charge of virtually all developments within the refining, petrochemical and natural gas sectors (though it should be noted that the NPC subsidiary under Mr Bagher Mostofi's leadership had a fair amount of autonomy even before the NIOC-NPC separation — as did the National Iranian Gas Company). Although this overall responsibility was to give the NIOC an apparently important role, the separation of responsibilities within the Iranian manufacturing sector had, by 1973, already gone much further than in Saudi Arabia. Unlike Petromin, which for a while was to be the sole agency administering Saudi Arabia's industrialisation process, the NIOC did not have responsibility for the development of the steel and copper sectors, which had separate agencies to handle them. On the other hand, as long as the NIOC had formal responsibility for most of the hydrocarbon sectors, it had an industrial clout which Petromin lacked, as it shared these responsibilities with the Saudi Basic Industries Corporation (SABIC).

As far as refining was concerned, NIOC entered the 1973/74 period with growing experience. Admittedly, the country's largest refinery at Abadan was only formally taken into NIOC management under the March 1973 agreement with the Consortium of foreign oil companies. At this time NIOC took over all the latter's operations, formally reducing the Consortium to the role of technical adviser, contractor of services and purchaser of crude oil. Under its pre-existing responsibility for domestic oil marketing, NIOC had already been gaining experience in refinery operations. It had, for instance, taken over the 5,000 b/d Kermanshah refinery after the 1954 Consortium agreement, and had raised its capacity to 15,000 b/d by 1971. In 1968, NIOC brought into operation the 85,000 b/d Teheran refinery, which also supplied the domestic market. Then, in 1973, a further 40,000 b/d refinery was made operative at Shiraz.[5]

However, none of these ventures had given NIOC any experience of exporting refined products. This is self-evident in the case of the three small domestically-oriented refineries. In the case of the Abadan refinery, the arrangement with the Consortium meant that it was the latter's members — not NIOC — which found foreign markets for the share of Abadan's production available for export. In practice this

27

worked badly, since NIOC had first call on Abadan's products for the domestic market. NIOC thus ran the refinery at a high level in order to produce the light products which the Iranian economy needed, leaving the Consortium members to dispose of the relatively unattractive flood of fuel oil which was produced at the same time. The Consortium members felt that they were being asked to subsidise NIOC's domestic sales, and that NIOC, by just marketing the easily disposable products, was avoiding having to face the economic realities of running an export-oriented refinery. At the end of 1977, then, the Consortium re-affirmed its earlier notice that it would cease to take products under the Processing Agreement (as it was entitled to do) and left NIOC with the task of simultaneously disposing of both the heavy and light ends of the barrel. This was the first time that NIOC was really faced with the problems of exporting refined oil products.[6]

When the Fifth Plan was drawn up, NIOC was not particularly concerned with developing such an export. This was hardly surprising because domestic Iranian demand for refined products was rising by well over ten per cent per annum in the early 1970s, thus necessitating a constant increase in the amount of refining capacity devoted to the domestic market alone.[7] Already, in 1974, domestic demand for products was running at around 310,000 b/d, and this meant that one third of Abadan's [then] output was needed to satisfy it.[8] Attention initially concentrated on expanding existing facilities and on building new capacity to meet domestic demand. Thus it was decided to expand the Abadan refinery to 600,000 b/d and this was completed in early 1978. The existing refinery at Teheran was expanded and was joined by a second one which was completed in March 1975; their joint capacity is now some 225,000 b/d. There were also plans for an 80,000 b/d plant at Tabriz, which came into operation in early 1978; for a 200,000 b/d refinery at Isfahan, which was due to be fully operational in the first quarter of 1979; and for a 130,000 b/d one near Mashad, which seems to have been dropped.[9] By early 1979, Iran's total refining capacity should have been about 1.2 million b/d, and, with domestic demand for oil products increasing between 15 and 18 per cent per annum,[10] there was a clear need for a further 100,000 b/d of domestically-oriented capacity every eighteen months or so, although the growth of product demand was slowing down even before the events of late 1978. By that time, the only relatively firm refining project scheduled to come into operation after 1979 was a joint venture between NIOC and Shell, i.e. a 200,000 tons/year lubricating oil refinery at Abadan, which was to have been completed in 1981 — though the initial bids to construct this plant were higher than expected, so as to cause some serious re-thinking about the project's economic viability.

The fact that so much of this new capacity was aimed at the domestic market should not leave the impression that NIOC was uninterested in promoting exports. It was interested — in two different ways. Firstly, it was involved in several attempts to get another export refinery built, in addition to Abadan. During the 1973-74 period, it considered such a scheme with Japanese, American and German partners but all discussions proved abortive. The negotiations for the Irano-German scheme went furthest in the period around 1974, with consideration being focused on a 500,000 b/d refinery based at Bushehr. This was dropped when it became clear that the European Community would not waive its external tariff on the relevant products. However, the Japanese version of this refinery refuses to die. After negotiations were put on ice in 1974, the two governments signed a memorandum of intent in November 1976 reviving the project and talking of a 1983 start-up.[11] There does not seem to have been a great deal of movement since 1976 but, on the other hand, Iran's refining capacity available for export could well have been fully absorbed by domestic demand by the 1981-83 period. The cross-over point depended on exactly when growth rates fell below the then current 15 per cent per annum, thus making a new 500,000 b/d export refinery attractive to the Iranians.

Over the years, though, NIOC has also been interested in a second form of outward-looking refining deals — the setting up of joint ventures overseas. The first of these, in which NIOC has a 13 per cent energy share came into operation in Madras, India, in 1967 and is currently capable of producing just under 50,000 b/d. A second jointly owned refinery (17½ per cent equity share) is located in Sasolberg in South Africa, with a capacity which has stood at 78,500 b/d since 1977. Construction on a third overseas joint venture (50 per cent share) started in 1978 near the Onsan industrial zone in South Korea. A $180 million venture, this will have a capacity of 60,000 b/d. Finally, Iran and Senegal agreed in 1976 to study the building of a refinery of about 25,000 b/d capacity; Iranian sources were still mentioning this project in 1978, but it seems unlikely to go ahead.[12] One further interesting project was considered for Belgium during the early 1970s. The idea for a purely state-owned oil refinery came up there during the late 1960s and, by 1970, had come to include NIOC. The project became heavily involved in domestic Belgian politics and a vacillating administration allowed a key deadline in January 1974 to pass without a decision, allowing the Iranians to pull out of the deal (presumably they were by then more interested in setting up the Irano-German export refinery within Iran than in committing themselves to a refining venture within Western Europe).[13]

Finally, the Iranian government was also interested for a while in various deals whereby the Iranians might buy an interest in western oil companies such as BP, (Burmah Oil's crash had left the British government with excess BP shares), Occidental, Ashland and the Italian state company, ENI. The first of these deals was blocked by the British government, which disposed of the shares in question on the London and New York stock markets. The Occidental deal came up suddenly in mid-1976 and would have involved NIOC investing $125 million in Occidental shares, thus making it the largest single investment in an American company by a Middle Eastern oil producer. However, all the evidence suggests that this initiative was sprung on NIOC by the Finance Ministry, and after a short, sharp investigation of the de-merits of the deal, the initiative was laid to rest.[14] The negotiations between NIOC and ENI have seemed to be rather more substantial, the idea being that NIOC should join as a partner in ENI's non-Italian refining and distribution activities, and reinvest fifty per cent of the profits within the Italian economy. However, Iranian enthusiasm cooled during 1977, as there was a growing awareness of the problems of investing in an economy from which oil majors such as Shell and BP had withdrawn for sound commercial reasons. As Dr Jamshid Amuzegar put it, very shortly before he became prime minister in August 1977: 'We want to avoid being partners in losing gas stations. We want the meat and the bones together, and not just the bones. Some of their refineries are no good. They want to keep the good ones.'[15] Similar considerations seem to have led to the withering away of the Ashland deal.

So, what conclusions can we draw of Iranian post-1973 refining policies? Firstly, NIOC was clearly having to devote a fair amount of attention to satisfying future domestic demand in the mid-1970s. It seemed possible that the substitution of natural gas for the heavier products would lead to a significant slowing down in demand in the early 1980s. To take full advantage of this, however, the Abadan refinery would still have needed considerable investment in secondary processing facilities if it were to produce the lighter products most in demand both domestically and in export markets. Assuming that domestic needs would take precedence over exports, Iranian export capacity was expected to reach a peak of around 500,000 b/d in early 1979; this would be eroded by some 100,000 b/d per annum in the early 1980s, if domestic demand were not significantly curbed. Unless the giant export venture with Japan does come off, we should be surprised if Iran ever runs an exportable product surplus much in excess of that predicted for 1979. Certainly, there is no evidence that the NIOC wanted, or was being allowed, to build a major export-oriented refinery on its own. The advantages of having a foreign partner to help find export markets seemed to be fairly well accepted. This could obviously change, should oil markets have tightened by the time that Iranian oil comes back on to world markets in significant quantities.

It is also clear that NIOC was thinking much more aggressively than

Saudi Arabia's Petromin about the value of joint-venture refineries located outside Iran as a way of guaranteeing crude sales. Obviously, the Indian, South African and South Korean ventures do not absorb particularly large quantities of Iranian crude, but there is a certain logic behind them, even if the choice of the actual foreign partners is idiosyncratic. Clearly, the Indian deal has to be seen in the light of a developing special arrangement between these two countries, which has found its expression in further ventures such as a fertiliser project and an iron-ore supply agreement.[16] The South African deal was an expression of Iran's interest in maintaining relations with arms-producing but diplomatically isolated countries (some would say 'international pariahs') with relatively high technology, such as South Africa and Israel. The Korean deal may be seen as a gesture of co-operation to a staunchly anti-communist power (just as the Saudis seem to be giving the Taiwanese some preferential treatment), but it also fits in with the Far Easterners' diversification strategy (there is some evidence that the Koreans are aiming to involve oil-producing states as partners in their next few refineries).

Such deals with non-OECD nations are relatively safe investments, since they will probably all be protected by strong quantitative barriers. As there was no guarantee that the Abadan refinery would have been the chosen supplier to these protected markets, such joint ventures are pretty much pure gain for NIOC. There was also the added attraction for the Iranian government of tying certain countries more tightly into commercial relationships, which would presumably help cement desired political relationships. In contrast, the apparent unwillingness of NIOC and its political masters to commit Iran to refining ventures within the OECD world, gives some indication of greater difficulties in finding an optimum refining strategy for the industrialised world. In chapter 6 we shall discuss some aspects connected with the location of refining plant, but, for the moment, we confine ourselves to noting that the tentative deals with Occidental, Ashland and ENI show that there is a great deal of difference between trying to buy oneself into markets which are over-endowed with refining capacity, and entering relatively well-protected markets in the non-OECD world. In the latter, local governments will be willing to help protect the Iranian investments; in the former, local governments are only too willing to help the Iranians make marginal or loss-making investments.

Petrochemicals

As with the refining sector, petrochemicals show how much more developed the Iranian economy is compared with the Saudi one. Once

31

again, though, the demands of the large domestic market were due to make it difficult for Iran to become a massive exporter of products during the 1980s, Iran's strong commitment to move into export markets notwithstanding. All the same, the largest export-oriented joint venture within the Middle East was actually under construction at Bandar Shahpur until the social unrest of late 1978 brought it to a temporary standstill.

Iran's involvement in the petrochemical industry started as early as 1963 with the construction of a fertiliser plant near Shiraz.[17] This is currently being expanded to produce 396,000 tons/year of ammonia and varying quantities of urea, nitric acid and ammonium nitrate. From the start, it was based on natural gas piped from the giant Gach Saran oil field.

Given that Iranian crude production was inevitably accompanied by considerable flaring of associated gas, interest in the country's petrochemical potential grew sufficiently to require the organisation of governmental institutional arrangements. The National Petrochemical Company (NPC) was created as an autonomous subsidiary of NIOC in 1965, with the responsibility of developing the industry, and for this purpose it was empowered to enter into joint-venture agreements with foreign concerns. In 1969, the Abadan Petrochemical Company was inaugurated with B.F. Goodrich taking a 26 per cent share. Amongst other products, it can now produce 60,000 tons/year of PVC. Further joint ventures followed with Amoco (sulphur and LPE) and the Cabot Corporation (carbon black). A largish fertiliser plant, the Shahpur Chemical Company, started in 1971 as a fifty-fifty venture with Allied Chemical, though Allied Chemical decided to sell its share to the NPC as part of a retrenchment policy. The Iran-Nippon Petrochemical Company (INPC) is another joint venture, entailing co-operation between NPC and the Japanese companies, Nissho-Iwai and Mitsubishi Chemical. It came into operation in 1976 and produces plasticisers. However, this project ran into financial trouble, with the Japanese partners refusing to contribute to an increase in the company's capital, apparently arguing that the plant's performance was unsatisfactory and uncompetitive and showing little hope for improvement. As a result, when the Iranians did raise the capital, the Japanese share in the venture fell from 50 to 30 per cent.[18] Iranian sources suggest that the Japanese companies may have had difficulties in raising extra money in Tokyo because of tight economic conditions within Japan.

The other major Japanese petrochemical venture in Iran, the Iran-Japan Petrochemical Company (IJPC), is by far the largest and most complex petrochemical venture actually under construction within the Middle East region. It is being built at the port of Bandar Shahpur and is a fifty-fifty joint venture between NPC and a group of Japanese companies from the Mitsui 'family' (Mitsui and Co., Mitsui Toatsu Manufacturing, Toyo Soda Manufacturing, Mitsui Petrochemical and Japan Synthetic Rubber). In early 1979 it was costed at at least $3.25 billion and it involved three core units (olefins, aromatics and chloralkali) which would produce an extensive range of products such as ethylene dichloride, caustic soda, ldPE, hdPE, polypropylene, synthetic rubber, butadiene, benzene and LPG. At some later stage, the complex was to produce styrene, cumene and the xylenes. The various parts of this complex should have become operative in 1980, some three-and-a-half to four years after serious work had started on the site.[19]

These are the bald facts, but the IJPC project needs to be treated at greater length, because it is the major project in the area and its fortunes must tell us something about the experiences likely to be faced by its imitators. The project was conceived way back in 1969, when a top level team from Mitsui & Co. visited Iran and, when shown the country's flared gas, became excited by the idea of joining Japanese technological virtuosity to Iranian raw materials. In October 1971, NPC and Mitsui signed a letter of intent to create the joint venture, IJPC, the equity and loan finance of which was to be shared equally by the two sides. Bandar Shahpur was selected as the site (the Shahpur Chemical Company was already there), ground-levelling work was started and, in the autumn of 1974, thirty Iranian trainees arrived in Tokyo.

There was then a financial crisis. Originally, the complex was estimated as costing between $900 million and $1 billion, and the Japanese were ready to finance the whole project. By 1974, in the aftermath of the oil crisis, it was clear that construction costs were going to be much higher than had been budgeted originally, probably as high as $1.8 billion. Some time was needed for the financial problems to be sorted out. As of late 1977, the financing was to be structured as follows: both NPC and the Japanese consortium were to put up 50 billion Yen as an equity investment (worth $170 million then, and $250 million in February 1979); the Iranians were to provide a further 200 billion Yen loan ($690 and $995 million on the respective dates); the Japanese partners would provide a further 125 billion Yen ($430 and $620 million); the Japanese government would provide a 60 billion yen loan direct to NPC ($205 or $300 million); the Japanese Export-Import Bank would provide 36.2 billion Yen by way of a suppliers' credit to IJPC ($125 or $180 million) and there was to be a further 28.8 billion Yen which would be extended by the Japanese to the Iranian government ($100 or $145 million). With the exception of the 125 billion Yen provided by the Japanese partners, all other Yen-financing was tied to the imports of Japanese goods and services. Most of these loans were at annual interest rates of between 6.7 and 8.3 per cent, with the exception of the inter-governmental loan which was at 4 per cent per annum.[20]

The bulk of this financial structure was put together in the course of 1976, allowing the basic site work at Bandar Shahpur (the building of things like jetties) to be re-started, and the first engineering contract was awarded in the autumn of that year. By mid-1978, 10,700 workers were engaged on the site (4,800 from Japan, South Korea, the Philippines, Malaysia, Hong Kong and India, with another 1,000 foreigners about to be brought in). During the peak construction period, the number employed was due to rise to some 11-12,000 workers but, once the complex was finished, the work-force was planned to settle at around 3,500-4,300 people; Japanese sources suggest that between 800 and 900 of these would be Japanese technical staff — though the goal remained to reduce the number of such (expensive) non-Iranians as fast as possible.[21]

As of mid-1978, Iranian sources were claiming that the project was within budget, and that the mild winter of 1977-78 had allowed construction to move ahead of schedule. Statements such as this begged a lot of questions. Obviously, the fact that the project costs were denominated in Yen, and that the bulk of the supplies and services were tied to Japanese sources meant that, in Dollar terms, the overall cost estimates were badly affected by the Yen's rapid rise during 1978. By June 1978, these estimates had risen to $2.7 billion, roughly three times what was originally envisaged. Furthermore, keeping it that low was only achieved by putting the original plans for the production of styrene monomer, cumene and the paraxylenes off to a later stage (thus cutting some 250-350,000 tons/year from the project).

However, by the autumn of 1978, it had become clear that it was no longer possible to keep costs stable in Yen terms, and IJPC raised its estimates from 550 to 650 billion Yen ($3.25 billion in February 1979 currencies). An Iranian source suggests that this escalation was caused by a slight expansion of the project (a VCM unit was re-included), the inclusion of a fair amount of training and infrastructure costs, and the higher-than-budgeted cost of Japanese personnel. By the time of the Shah's fall, only part of the extra financing had been agreed. Quite clearly, the Iranians were in no position to raise any of the extra money needed to finish the complex, but a consortium of banks led by the Japanese Export-Import Bank agreed to provide 38.5 billion Yen.

As we completed this book, the complex was 85-90 per cent finished, and construction had been halted (the major problems had come from customs delays and difficulties in finding local currency). The initial indications are that the Khomeini/Bazargan regime intend to press on with the project, but the Japanese authorities would clearly have to find the remaining 50-60 billion Yen necessary for completion. This will leave the Japanese very much more exposed to a very much more expensive project than originally conceived. As, according to a rule of thumb, every dollar spent on a basic project such as this needs 2 dollars spent on downstream processing plant to utilise its products, it is extremely difficult to see where such investments are going to come from in the immediate post-Shah period. The IJPC project is thus shaping up as a major financial disaster for both the Japanese and the Iranians.

We shall discuss the wider economics of such ventures in chapter 6, but there are a few final points about the IJPC complex which need to be made at this point. Firstly, although the Iranian debate about the proper pricing for gas was continuing, NPC was getting its gas feedstock supplies at approximately 2 cents a million BTU, which was noticeably lower than the Saudis hoped to be able to charge their petrochemical ventures. Secondly, both Iranian and Japanese sources claimed that between 50 and 70 per cent of the complex's products would be absorbed by the internal Iranian market — a goal which interested outsiders suspected would stretch Iranian and Japanese ingenuity. The problem was not of there not being sufficient domestic demand, but of attracting the necessary downstream investments to convert IJPC's intermediate products into marketable end-products. With adequate tariff protection by the Iranian authorities, a fair amount of small-scale downstream investment would indeed take place to convert products such as ldPE and hdPE into the plastic films, pipes, buckets and insulating material which are the types of products that a country at Iran's level of development finds easy to dispose of. There were, though, rather greater grounds for scepticism as to the larger-scale downstream investments needed. It was always assumed that the other Japanese venture (INPC) would absorb approximately 30,000 tons/year of IJPC's propylene, but the reluctance of these other Japanese companies to extend their involvement meant that the NPC would have to shoulder the whole burden of this downstream investment.

It was Mitsui and its partners which would have to handle most of these problems. They were to be responsible for international marketing, and so would have to find a home for the ethylene dichloride, benzene and caustic soda which were not expected to be immediately absorbed within Iran. But the Mitsui group was also expected to help in the development of domestic sales, and was trying hard to encourage investment in plants designed to turn intermediate products like the polyethylenes into finished plastics. They, therefore, launched a campaign to persuade plastic manufacturers from Japan, the US, Europe and South Korea[22] to invest in extensions of the Bandar Shahpur complex.

As most of such plants could be built relatively fast, it was of no great importance that, whilst the complex was nearing completion, the commitments to downstream plants expected to cluster around it were still not finalised. It was assumed that continued expansion of the Iranian economy meant that investment opportunities would abound, but that there could be a period of some years before all the downstream investments were placed. This suggested that Iran would need to find export markets for around 50 per cent of the products from 1980 to 1982, after which IJPC's products should be increasingly absorbed by local demand.[23] However, events since late 1978 suggest that, whatever Mitsui and partners do to get the IJPC complex finished, other potential downstream investors are now going to be extremely reluctant to make any hasty commitments. The petrochemicals picture was thus similar to the refining one, with domestic demand due to rise hard on the heels of increased productive capacity. NPC did have plans for further petrochemicals expansion (notably a 760,000 tons/year aromatics complex at Abadan), but a great deal was going to depend on whether NPC won its battles within the Iranian bureaucracy to gain access to the necessary finance needed to expand capacity sufficiently in order to remain a significant force in export markets.

Petrochemical policy: conclusions

At the time of the Shah's fall, IJPC was only just in the process of becoming a serious exporter. In fertilisers, the expansion of the Shahpur Chemical Company meant that there was considerable excess fertiliser capacity, and the National Petrochemical Company was faced with the prospect of exporting up to 700,000 tons/year of urea. Local demand was not expected to catch up with expanded productive capacity until the late 1980s. In other products, NPC had been concentrating on import-substitution until the IJPC project was created. Large as this project is, it would never have made the Iranians much more than marginal exporters, because of the rapid growth of Iranian domestic demand. This is in contrast to the Saudis who have the potential to become a lasting force on world markets with their export-oriented ventures.

Iranian policy towards foreign partners was relatively pragmatic. NPC was not frightened to go it alone when foreign partners proved unsatisfactory (as in the case of the Shahpur Chemical Company) and fully intended to go ahead with its own aromatics venture at Abadan, finance permitting. On the other hand, the earlier petrochemical projects were mostly joint ventures with foreigners, and it was always accepted that the Japanese should have a major share in the IJPC project. It was also accepted that foreign private investors could have a role in the downstream processing sector which would be needed to use the base petro-chemical products coming from ventures such as the IJPC one.[24]

As far as products policy was concerned, it was clear that the NPC (particularly in its IJPC venture with the Mitsui Group) was extremely ambitious in comparison with the Saudis. Most of the latter's projects are designed to produce a building block, such as ethylene, and three or four main intermediate products. The Iranians, however, went to the other extreme, aiming to produce, in the case of IJPC, at least ten products for which export or domestic markets would have to be found. The Iranians were thus following a relatively high-risk strategy. Petro-chemical plants being complicated affairs, the planners have only to miscalculate the demand for two or three of the end-products and the economics of the others are also affected (if one product cannot be sold or stored, the production of other associated products may have to be cut back; transporting products to overseas markets may be economic if parcel tankers (which carry a variety of chemical products in separate compartments) are fully loaded, but uneconomic if certain products cannot pay for their share of the shipping costs). Even if the events of late 1978 had not occurred, IJPC's planners were probably being too ambitious to establish such a complex project in Iran by the late 1970s.

Finally, the future of Iran's petrochemical industry was always going to be heavily influenced by the outcome of the debate about natural gas pricing. In the 1960s and early 1970s, no such debate existed. Planners knew that Iranian gas reserves were the second largest in the world and they could see the flared gas that accompanied oil production. It was only natural to believe that exporting gas just had to make a positive contribution to the national economy. So the 1966 deal to pipe gas to the Soviet Union (in exchange for finance for Iran's first steel mill, a machine-tool plant and the necessary gas pipeline) led in 1975 to the larger 'triangular' deal (IGAT 2), whereby Iran would supply gas to the Soviet Union, which, in turn, would send a proportionate amount of its own gas to various countries in East and West Europe. In the middle of these negotiations, in 1974, the National Iranian Gas Company (NIGC) entered the Kalingas joint venture with American, Japanese and Norwegian companies. The aim of this project was to liquefy gas from the offshore Pars field, which is reputedly the second largest gas field in the world.[25]

However, criticism of the gas-export programme was growing in intensity. Whether gas was exported by pipeline or through lique-faction, Iran's distance from markets meant it would be unable to charge anything near the price of those countries closer to end-markets (Algeria to the West; Indonesia to the East). Analysts started to argue that the value of Iran's gas would vary according to the use to which it was put, and that export via liquefaction looked like very bad value for money. In fact, the highest returns could seemingly be expected from re-injecting much of the gas into the aging Iranian oil fields, under the secondary recovery programme, thus prolonging their life, while still leaving the gas available for exploitation in future years.[26] At the same time, the Shah apparently convinced himself that gas prices were far too low. It logically followed for him that there would have to be an explosion of these prices during the 1980s, similar to the oil price explosion of the early 1970s. At that point, Iran, with its gas reserves greater than those of the other Middle Eastern OPEC nations put together, would be in a position to reap the economic rewards that would be her due. In a January 1977 interview, he put it this way: 'Gas sells too cheaply. Oil sells for four times as much, comparatively speaking. On top of that, the investment needed to export gas is huge, especially for methane tankers. So we will keep our gas either to use at home, or until it is more profitable to export.'[27]

The result was a change in Iranian policy, with a decision being announced that no more gas export deals would be signed, though the second, 'triangular' deal with Russia and the Kalingas LNG venture would still go ahead. Instead attention was turned to the gas re-injection programme and to the substitution of gas for oil in the domestic Iranian energy market (this latter programme could yet be important for the country's export potential in refined oil products, since rapidly increasing, domestic oil demand was one of the constraints we identified). There was, however, no public reappraisal of whether the Iranian petrochemical industry was likely to get a return on its gas feedstocks comparable with alternative possible uses. If it could only survive by paying 2 cents a million cubic feet per day, then it was clearly not even starting to cover the costs of gathering and transporting that gas to its petrochemical plants. At the time of the Shah's downfall, NIOC's position was that its pricing of gas supplied to the NPC depended on who was financing the gas-gathering and transmission operations. If NIOC was to provide the capital, then its price charged for gas would be based on a fair return on such capital investment — and this would be very much more than 2 cents per million cubic feet. One senses then that NPC's export plans were as vulnerable to dispassionate economic analysis as those of its gas counterpart, NIGC. The former agency was undoubtedly more secure than the latter within the Iranian political system, but just as the NIGC would have to make a very positive case before being permitted to enter any further export ventures, the NPC would likely have found itself in the same position when the IJPC joint venture came into operation, and attention turned to further expansion schemes for the mid to late 1980s.

Other large-scale industrial ventures

Even though it is now clear that the Shah's belief in Iran's capability of becoming the world's fifth industrial superpower by the year 2000 was wishful thinking, the breadth of Iranian industrialisation was indeed impressive. In the steel sector there was rapid progress, but, however unwilling some Iranian officials were to drop the target, the country would not have become an exporter of steel during the 1980s. Domestic steel consumption, which was around 2 million tons/year in 1973, could well have been running at between 12 and 18 million tons/year by 1983. Against this demand, the Iranian steel industry was going to have been hard pushed to have 9 million tons/year capacity installed by then, though the official target within that period was still put at 15 million tons. Clearly, any regime's planners will be more concerned with satisfying domestic markets rather than export ones.

A point worth making is that there had already been significant downstream investments within the steel sector, and that these had generally kept pace with the construction of indigenous basic steel-making capacity. Thus the Industrial and Mining Development Bank of Iran backed a privately-owned 65,000 tons/year rolling mill at Ahwaz in 1966, and, by 1973, this bank had backed two groups with a combined capacity of some 580,000 tons/year of products. In addition, NIOC established a 240,000 tons/year pipe mill to manufacture large-diameter pipes from imported plate.[28] Such investments clearly illustrate that Iranian industrialists were willing to step into the downstream sectors of such a basic industry as steel. This, therefore, suggests that we may have been too pessimistic about the willingness of pre-Khomeini local businessmen to enter into similar sectors of the petrochemical industry.

Iran's industrialisation policies

In a book of this length, it is not possible to give a detailed analysis of Iran's performance in all the other manufacturing sectors such as car and truck production, copper smelting, machine-tools manufacturing and, even, electronic components production (a wholly Iranian-owned electronics plant was opened by the Shah in Shiraz in late 1978). Suffice it to say that this industrialisation effort was relatively widely based, and Iran was starting to be represented in all those leading industrial sectors which development economists such as Rostow believe are the key to a country's achieving technological maturity.[29] On the other hand, much of this industrialisation had been state-induced and had been financed not with the internally generated profits of the relevant state corporations, but with the central exchequer's foreign exchange earnings from oil exports and external credits. What we were seeing, then, was an ambitious import substitution programme along lines pioneered by other leading Third World countries, the one difference being that, because of the oil and gas reserves, Iran would inevitably give a higher priority to oil refining and petrochemical industries than, say, a country like India or Brazil would have done. It was far from clear, though, that Iran was capable of moving on to the latest stage in the development of Third World strategy — the promotion of internationally competitive exports of manufactures. In contrast to the South Koreas, Brazils and Taiwans of the world, there was as yet no sign that Iran would become a significant exporter of steel, ships, textiles or cars in the next decade or so.

It would be wrong, though, to be over-critical of the Iranian industrialisation effort. Certainly, the planners allowed the economy to run away with them in the years immediately after 1974, with the result that bottle-necks (best exemplified by port delays and power blackouts) occurred throughout the economy, and inflation reached 36 per cent in mid-1977. On the other hand, they were not the only planners in the oil-producing world to run into such problems, and the ministerial shuffle which took place in August 1977 was a clear sign that they and the Shah knew that economic growth had to be slowed. Attention had to be paid to completing existing projects without authorising a fresh wave of projects for the mid to late 1980s. To some extent, this emphasis on more manageable growth rates was given additional weight by the stagnation of the country's oil revenues through 1977 and 1978 as export volumes and OPEC's market price for oil remained static.

At the same time, the Iranians developed one distinctive approach to the problem of raising economic efficiency to western standards — they took shares in a handful of European companies. Since 1974, they were trying to buy into a variety of companies, including Pan Am, British Petroleum, Siemens, ENI, Occidental, Grumman and British Leyland, but these deals fell through on deeper scrutiny or on resistance from the relevant parent governments. Fittingly, since Krupp was involved in a deal before World War II to provide a small steel mill to Iran, a deal with this German company is most advanced. In July 1974, Iran bought a 25.04 per cent share in the company's steel-making subsidiary, then in 1976 went further to take 25.01 per cent of the parent company (the 54th largest non-American company in 1976), which is a conglomerate involved in manufacturing ships, steel, special alloys, machinery, industrial plant, and electronics systems. In November 1976, Iran extended its involvement by buying into two Krupp subsidiaries in Brazil. In addition, the country took a one third share in Deutsche Babcock, a major constructor of industrial equipment,[30] a 10 per cent share in the French-led nuclear enrichment consortium Eurodif, and a 25 per cent share in Coredif (yet another French-led uranium enrichment consortium).[31]

Taking into account NIOC's three overseas joint-venture refineries and the fact that, in 1977, Ritaco became the first private Iranian company to take over a western industrial concern (Philco Italiana), it becomes clear that Iran was following a policy of foreign investment, rather ambitious by the standards of most other OPEC members (Libya has taken a stake in Fiat; Montedison has sold a share to Kuwaiti investors; private Saudi interests have been active in the US). What did the Shah hope to gain from all this?

Obviously, there were different motives for different kinds of investments. The uranium enrichment interest was connected with the Shah's ambition to switch as much as possible of the country's power generation to nuclear sources, as well as to his longer-term view that a country with the status he wished for Iran should have a wide variety of nuclear options. NIOC's overseas refineries were a way of expanding Iranian crude sales, while at the same time building good will in countries such as India and, more controversially, South Africa, which figured in the Shah's search for allies around the Indian Ocean. The two German investments, though, were clearly in a class of their own. Firstly, they were aided by the legacy of goodwill from Germany's pre-1939 interest in the Iranian economic and political scene. Then there was the fact that the German government has been relatively more relaxed than the British or Americans about the Iranians buying into key companies. Finally, there was the general belief that investing in western companies would tie them more closely to the fate of the Iranian economy, and thus provide a more trustworthy source of technical help than could be bought from companies whose commitment to Iran extends no further than their current contract. As the Shah put it in an interview in early 1977: 'They were not good investments money-wise because Krupp was losing money. Babcock was all right. But what is important are the side effects, to get involved in the technological know-how of big, world-famous firms like Krupp. And together with Krupp we can go to Brazil, together with Krupp we can go elsewhere. This all tremendously boosts Krupp's possibilities outside, and will also open the doors of my country to Krupp even more. We will continue this policy if we have the money.'[32]

So, Krupp was providing the lion's share of the plant for the Sar Cheshmeh copper refinery, and Iranians now sit on Krupp's supervisory board. But, although it is healthy that Iranians should gain experience of management outside their country, the desired stimulation would inevitably take time to work. In the meantime, the Iranian economy was dominated by capital-intensive projects which were not clearly viable by international standards.

The problem, therefore, remains for both the old and new regimes of how the country will fill the gap in export revenues as oil income declines. Crude sales were running at around $25 billion before the Shah fell, but there seems to be nothing on the horizon to generate equivalent amounts of foreign exchange. The National Iranian Gas Company hoped to be selling some $1.5 billion worth of gas by the mid-1980s. The petrochemical industry was due to be exporting products worth about $600 million, once the IJPC complex came into operation and, according to NPC sources, the Iranian industry might have increased exports to $4-5 billion by 1990.[33] For reasons discussed earlier in this chapter, however, it would always be difficult to increase this total greatly, because of the rapid projected growth of domestic Iranian demand and the vast amounts of capital that would be needed to bring new plants into operation. Otherwise, there was the chance that the Sar Cheshmeh copper refinery would export a third of its 168,000 ton output when it became operative in 1981. But that is about all that was on the horizon, and even under the Shah's regime, which was fully committed to an industrialisation policy, it would have taken a heroic effort to generate the kind of revenues which are needed.[34]

After the Shah

Even when writing before the fall of the Shah, we were relatively pessimistic about the potential of Iranian industrialisation. We were not deliberately setting out to be Jeremiahs, but we had the distinct feeling that, once we had discounted the influence of the oil sector, the Iranian economy just did not have the kind of dynamism that is found in the industrial sectors of other countries which are leading the Third World's drive to industrialisation. Our impressions seemed to agree with those of development economists such as Adelman and Morris[35] who, on evidence from the 1960s, suggest that Iran is a country in which development has only an intermediate potential. The type of highly sophisticated statistical analysis on which their judgement rests can be taken with a large pinch of salt, but it is generally accepted that Iran's commitment to rapid modernisation was distinctly patchy: an educational system which still had to be made more relevant to the country's development needs; a system of political representation which had failed to mobilise most of the well educated, on whom any modernisation drive must rest; an agricultural sector whose reform had turned sour; and a religious leadership which had (perhaps inevitably) been alienated in the modernisation drive.

42

Taking all these considerations into account, we judged that the overall pace of Iran's industrialisation would be determined as much by future levels of oil revenues as by any other factor. In particular, the central authorities would remain essential in deciding how much of these revenues would be ploughed back into the export sector, for without such financial encouragement Iranian industrialists were not yet dynamic enough to make the running in export markets by themselves. In theory, the rapidly expanding Iranian population should make the country a natural site for labour-intensive export industries, but one of the problems facing oil-rich economies is that these are exactly the industries which cannot be developed. Since oil and gas exports boost the value of the national currency, the increasing costs of the indigenous labour force price these industries out of potential markets. It is not just OPEC members who have this problem; various Dutch industries were priced out of export markets during the country's gas-export boom of the 1960s and early 1970s; there are pessimists who think that North Sea oil may speed the de-industrialisation of Britain.

The fall of the Shah has not changed these judgements, though it is too soon to tell exactly how the policies of the Khomeini/Bazargan administration will develop. What seems to be emerging from the Ayatollah's camp suggests that little serious thought has been given to industrial matters, beyond the feeling that industrialisation should be played down in favour of the agricultural sector, but the petrochemical sector should continue to be developed.

The fact that no coherent industrial strategy had emerged, as we were finishing this book, merely reinforces our belief that the relatively broad-based Iranian manufacturing economy is not well-placed to develop into a Japanese or Korean 'super-competitive' sector, which can sweep the world in chosen export sectors. This kind of success demands a total commitment to industrialisation within a relatively wide national elite. Since one force behind the overthrow of the Shah was a rejection of at least the excesses of rapid industrialisation, there is no sign that such a commitment will emerge in the Shah's aftermath.

The chances are that Iran's industrial sector will continue to grow, albeit sluggishly. Attention will have to be paid to repairing the economic damage caused in the last days of the Shah. There will be a crisis of confidence among the more entrepreneurial sectors of society. The state sector will suffer from financial restrictions until oil exports pick up sufficiently to restore Iran's financial position.

Are there any alternatives to the kind of heavy industrialisation backed by the Shah? It is possible that the Iranians could look South East to India where the Janata party is stressing the development of small-scale village industries as an alternative to highly centralised industrialisation. This could make sense to an Iran which has become aware of the damage done by the lack of attention paid to the agricultural sector. On the other hand, it is a policy which is difficult to administer, and would certainly have to be backed by a broad commitment to small-scale development. Where are the necessary visionaries among the post-Shah generation?

Since we do not yet expect this kind of development to emerge, we presume that post-Shah administrations will continue backing much the same range of industries as did the Shah, with less emphasis on nuclear power, electronics, and arms-related industries. If the reaction against western consumption patterns continues, then industries such as cars will be placed at a much lower level of priority. It strikes us that the post-Shah planners will inevitably come back to the question of how to make best use of Iran's return from its oil and gas reserves. All the old debates about the proper place of gas exports or the development of gas-based petrochemical industries will re-emerge.

If there is to be a break with the Shah's industrial policies, it will be to move to a more Iraqi-style, nationalistic approach. Foreign partners will be discouraged, and the role of the state will pervade even more thoroughly into the whole industrial sector. This would be a rejection of the more relaxed approach of the Saudis and the other Arab Gulf states. But the range of industries to be developed would be much the same in either case. Petrochemical and refining developments will continue to be well to the fore.

Notes

1   Amuzegar, 1977, pp 166-77; Looney, 1977a, pp 52-7; *Middle East Annual Review* 1976, pp 185-7; *Middle East Annual Review* 1977, pp 211-2.
2   Graham, 1978, pp 76-92; Looney, 1977a, pp 52-7.
3   *Middle East Annual Review*, 1976, p.185.
4   Amuzegar, 1977, pp 173-5.
5   Fesharaki, 1976, pp 210-3.
6   *Petroleum Intelligence Weekly*, August 2 1976, p.1; March 27 1978, pp 1-2.
7   Fesharaki, 1976, pp 246-7.
8   Fesharaki, 1976, p.262.
9   Fesharaki, 1976, p.213; *Iran Economic News*, March 1978, p.4.
10   *Iran Economic News*, March 1978, p.4.
11   *Middle East Economic Survey*, November 29 1976, p.9.
12   *Iran Economic News*, May 1978, p.4; February 1978, p.3.
13   Turner, 1978a, pp 193-4.

14   *Business Week*, January 24 1977; *Petroleum Intelligence Weekly*, August 28 1976, p.5.
15   *Middle East Economic Survey*, August 1 1977, p.1.
16   Amuzegar, 1977, pp 57, 91.
17   Amuzegar, 1977, pp 68-9.
18   Amuzegar, 1977, pp 68-9; *European Chemical News*, August 11 1978.
19   *Far Eastern Economic Review*, June 16 1978, p.60; *Japan Chemical Week*, August 31 1978, pp 1-12.
20   *Petroleum Intelligence Weekly*, January 19 1976, p.7; September 6 1976, p.7; supplemented by interviews in Tokyo and Teheran.
21   *Japan Chemical Week*, August 31 1978, p.7.
22   *Japan Chemical Week*, August 31 1978, p.5.
23   *Japan Chemical Week*, August 31 1978, p.5.
24   McLachlan, 1977, p.213.
25   Amuzegar, 1977, pp 70-3.
26   Fesharaki, 1975, pp 178-81; Stauffer, 1975.
27   *Business Week*, January 21 1977.
28   *Iran Economic News*, April 1978, pp 4-5.
29   Rostow, 1978, pp 500-8.
30   Fellowes, 1978, p.20; *Iran Economic News*, March 1978, p.4; *Middle East Economic Survey*, October 25 1976, p.2; July 31 1978, p.5.
31   Department of Energy (US), 1977, p.215.
32   *Japan Chemical Week*,   August 31 1978, p.6.
33   *Forbes*, July 10 1978, pp 71, 74.
34   *Forbes*, July 10 1978, pp 71, 74.
35   Adelman and Morris, 1967 and 1968; Looney, 1977b, pp 161-3.

4 The foreign partners

The period immediately after 1973 saw a massive upsurge of corporate interest in the Middle Eastern oil producers. Some of that enthusiasm has cooled as economic prospects appear less promising and as political problems seem more daunting. Despite this, a number of the world's largest multinationals are still committed to entering joint ventures in the area. What motivates these companies?

The first point to be made forcibly is that these joint ventures are actually exceptional. The vast majority of the multinationals is involved with the Middle East as exporters of products, plants and services — not as investors. This is partly because some countries such as Algeria and Iraq prefer to keep their industrial expansion under national control, and partly because many companies have an extreme reluctance to get involved with investments in the area. It can, then, be argued that the Shells, Mitsubishis, Mitsuis, Dows and Celaneses of the world should not be given too much attention because they are atypical of the corporate community. This list of potential investors does include, however, some of the largest companies of the world, and the countries in which they are considering investing are of growing importance. We therefore need to find out what makes these companies interested in investing in the Middle East tick — but also what makes a lot of other companies deliberately turn their backs on exactly the same investment opportunities.

The oil companies

The motives of the four Aramco partners need little further explanation. Having developed the Saudi oil industry from its infancy, they have been striving to minimise their losses as the Aramco partnership is taken into Saudi hands. Much of their apparent success towards this goal has been achieved by quiet negotiation and a minimum of bluster, with a certain amount of quiet diplomatic backing from the US authorities. As mentioned earlier, Mobil is the only one of the four partners which has been notably adventurous in developing a wider role within the Saudi economy. Its junior position within the Aramco partnership, combined with the personal enthusiasm of its president,

William P. Tavoulareas, explains why this company — rather than the other three — has blazed the way. The other partners have been more cautious. Exxon, after apparently being considered as a potential partner in an ethylene complex, has decided to limit itself for the moment to a polyethylene venture attached to the Shell project. Socal and Texaco are restricting themselves to negotiating a lubricating-oil-refining joint venture with Petromin. The impression in these latter cases is of companies wishing to make gestures towards Saudi aspirations; they do not want to be over-ambitious, but certainly see the need to court Saudi goodwill. What is noticeable, though, is that the Aramco companies have generally not made similar offers to Iran, although one of them did have quite a substantial Iranian project on the table for discussion at the time of the Shah's departure in early 1979. This is despite the fact that all four were also members of the Consortium of companies which still markets much of Iran's crude. It is almost as if the Aramco four decided that they could not afford to antagonise the Saudi Arabians by showing interest in the next largest oil-power in the region (although NIOC's generally negative attitude to the majors undoubtedly helped to keep their interest at a relatively low level). . . . And who is to fault them for this lack of enthusiasm? Whatever the prospects for gas exports, Iranian oil production is reaching its plateau, leaving the field free for Saudi production to surge even further ahead throughout the 1980s. The American companies know this and have made their arrangements accordingly.

The motive behind Shell's involvement in Saudi Arabia is similar to Mobil's. Shell International, however, took the Shell group of companies one step further than its American rival by also committing itself to invest in a lube-oil plant in Iran. The latter was not planned as an export venture, which suggests that Shell had decided on a relatively low-key investment to cement relations with OPEC's second most productive member. If one takes into account its initiatives elsewhere in the Gulf (such as — along with CFP — helping Abu Dhabi move into the LPG export trade), it is clear that this company is pursuing a noticeably active and innovatory role throughout the region. This is what one would expect from a company which has traditionally been relatively short of access to crude oil.

The relative failure of British Petroleum to become involved in Middle Eastern industrial ventures makes an interesting contrast. This company responded to the 1951-4 crisis by intensifying its search for oil elsewhere in the region, and at least partially compensated for its loss of the Abadan refinery by building another one in Aden. Apart from this and a 1966 minority share in a Kuwaiti fertiliser venture, the company was involved in no further industrial projects within the region, and events in the 1960s swung the company's attention away from the region toward the OECD world. By the end of the 1960s, it was making major discoveries of oil both in Alaska and the North Sea, and was breaking into the US market (in which it was weak) by its bid for Sohio. These developments meant that the company spent the early and mid-1970s consolidating its rapidly strengthening position within the OECD world, and paying less attention to the Middle East. For a short while around 1974, there was a chance that the company might become involved in Saudi Arabia through a venture based on its Industrial Protein technology, but this fell by the wayside on economic grounds; this was, however, an exceptional effort for BP within the Middle East. There are some slight signs that the company may be rethinking its strategy toward the area but, in the meantime, it leaves the impression of being a company which is convinced that it can survive with a good part of its future feedstocks being supplied from OECD sources. In addition, it is clearly diversifying into downstream chemical operations in America and West Europe, making it less rather than more likely that it will become involved with competing investments in the Middle East.

The same probably goes for Gulf Oil. It was the one other major oil company excluded from Saudi Arabia, and was always able to compensate through its 50 per cent stake in Kuwaiti oil production. Since 1975 when, finally, this holding was totally expropriated, the company has played an increasingly less important role in the Eastern Hemisphere in general — not just in the Middle East. For a while, it considered taking on one of the Saudi petrochemical ventures at Jubail, but eventually turned the idea down for budgetary reasons. This would seem to fit in with a general policy of retrenchment: in 1973, it largely pulled out of the West German market and in mid-1975 it regrouped its world-wide operations on a functional, rather than geographical, basis. This was generally interpreted as signalling that the company was becoming much more profit-conscious than it had been in the past.[1] We are left with the impression that the company is satisfied to keep its crude purchase agreement with Kuwait ticking over, but that it has no intention of trying to guarantee this, or any other Middle Eastern source of crude, by making relatively high-risk industrial investments in the region. Elsewhere, the company has its North Sea oil stake to give it a residual interest in West Europe. Otherwise, the emphasis is on the Western Hemisphere.

Not many other oil companies have become involved. The French company CFP has joined with Shell in Abu Dhabi to help in developing an LPG exporting plant. Otherwise, it has not seriously investigated investment opportunities within Saudi Arabia or Iran. The one French company of note which has got involved is the state-owned coal-to-chemicals company, Charbonnages de France, whose petrochemical subsidiary CDF-Chimie has a minority share in an ethylene complex in

Qatar. This has been a politically inspired venture, originally intended to provide ethylene feedstock to an associated plant in France, in which Qatar took its own minority stake. Unfortunately, it has proved impracticable to link the two plants in the way originally intended. CDF-Chimie is now in bad financial trouble and is hoping that the government in Qatar will increase its stake in the French venture.

Finally, we should also note the fact that the aggressively-managed, medium-sized Occidental was involved with the SAFCO fertiliser plant, which was one of Saudi Arabia's very first, faltering steps down the industrialisation path (apart from Aramco's efforts). This was not a particularly successful deal and Petromin's and Occidental's conflicting claims on each other were finally settled in 1977. However, despite the ultimate fate of the original 1964 deal (Occidental was in charge of construction and management), this was the kind of venture which fitted in with the maverick role that Occidental has played within the oil and chemical industries since the 1960s.

Occidental is one of the very few non-major oil company interlopers in the field of Middle Eastern industrialisation, despite the fact that in oil exploration and production, such 'independents' have been a feature of the region, at least since Aminoil and Getty entered the Neutral Zone between Saudi Arabia and Kuwait in 1948-49. By 1972, there were at least fifty non-major oil companies with exploration and development interests in the Middle East.[2] In industrial projects, however, such companies are almost totally absent. Excluding the five American majors and US Shell, among the next eleven largest US oil companies (Amerada, Atlantic Richfield, Cities Service, Continental, Getty, Marathon, Standard Oil of Indiana, Phillips, Standard (Ohio), Sun and Union),[3] we can only identify one (Standard of Indiana) as playing, or trying to play, any investment role in Saudi Arabian and Iranian industrialisation — and we cannot identify their involvement anywhere else within the Gulf states.

This signals a significant change in the competitive situation between the majors and their independent competitors. The increased competitiveness of the majors probably comes from the fact that they have moved more aggressively into the more complex downstream technologies such as petrochemicals. They have, therefore, more to offer than the 'independents', who have remained more dependent on simple oil exploration and production technologies.

At the same time, the Middle Easterners have significantly raised the ante required to stay within the regional economy. At the risk of some overstatement, oil exploration never genuinely stretched a medium-sized company. Sending a handful of employees to operate a drilling rig in the Middle East cost little in the 1960s, and, if oil were found, further investment was virtually risk-free. On the other hand, joining a lube-oil venture, even as a junior partner, is very much more deman-ding. The required initial capital is greater; plant construction in a LDC is a great deal more complicated than operating a drilling rig; pulling a rig out of a country is child's play compared with disengaging from an industrial joint venture which turns sour.

What is happening, then, is a sorting out of the men from the boys amongst companies which might be interested in the Middle East. Companies such as BP and Gulf have probably decided to keep out of the region's industrialisation for quite clear reasons of corporate strategy — and no-one can say they are wrong. Equally clearly, though, the entry fee required to win a position as a potential investor in the area has been significantly raised. Before 1973, there was room for companies wishing to drill a few speculative holes in territory not wanted by the majors. Today, the picture has changed. Companies must be willing to make a genuinely significant commitment of manpower and investment in a region which looks more and more politically un-stable. On the whole, then, only the largest companies, with most to lose, can afford to take the gamble.

The chemical companies

In contrast to the major oil companies, the major chemical companies have generally chosen not to become involved in Middle Eastern ventures. Some of them came to Iran before the 1973 price rises (Bayer, Du Pont, Cabot and Allied Chemical, which pulled out); Mitsui is actively involved in the IJPC scheme under construction in Iran; Dow, Mitsubishi Chemical and Celanese are negotiating with the Saudis over various schemes (W.R. Grace seems to have withdrawn from the Japanese methanol venture). In general, though, there is little evidence of any widespread positive interest in the Middle East as a site for a major round of chemical investments. Of the four leading US chemical companies, only Dow has chosen to try to launch a major project in Saudi Arabia; in early 1979, Union Carbide agreed to set up a small joint venture with private Saudi interests in the field of industrial gases;[4] Du Pont and Monsanto are still staying on the sidelines. Within Iran, Du Pont has a share in a synthetic fibres joint venture, with the other three chief companies showing little involvement. Amongst the leading West European companies there has been an almost total lack of interest. Bayer has been involved in three small-scale nylon or textile factories in Iran, but when asked by the Iranians to consider a 100,000 ton caprolactam plant, the company respectfully turned them down on the grounds that the project's return on investment would be far too low. Hoechst, another of the three leading German companies, apparently considered entering an aromatics venture, but decided not to become involved. Similarly ICI evaluated a turnkey fertiliser project in Saudi Arabia, in the period 1973-74, but turned it down when asked to take an equity share.

All this suggests that most of the non-oil chemical companies are refusing to be stampeded into Middle Eastern petrochemical ventures, whatever the competitive attractions of breaking into a feedstock-rich area which was previously dominated by the major oil companies (who have nearly all been expanding into base petrochemicals, thus moving in on the territory of the traditional chemical companies). Of the leading 35 American chemical companies,[5] two have Iranian shares, another invested in Iran but pulled out, and four others are negotiating with Saudi Arabia. Of the fifteen leading non-American chemical and pharmaceutical companies,[6] only Bayer had a direct stake in the region (and that is small), and only Mitsubishi Chemical is still negotiating to win itself a share in a new venture in the Gulf region. Montedison is taking a share in an Egyptian venture and sold part of its equity to Arab interests.

Unlike the non-major oil companies, whose lack of interest we have put down to lack of expertise and lack of resources, there is no doubt that the leading chemical companies would have been welcomed as investors if they had chosen such a role. However, with the exception of Dow, Du Pont, W.R. Grace and Mitsubishi, they have either not seriously looked at the region's major projects, or rejected those which were on offer to them.[7] This makes them rather different from the oil companies which have had many of the same doubts about the economics of the proposed joint ventures, but have soldiered on in the hope or expectation that an eventual bargain can be struck which will make such projects justifiable.

The difference in approaches towards the region follows from the fact that the companies in the oil and chemical industries (insofar as they can be distinguished) are following different strategies. The oil majors want to hold on to access to Middle Eastern crude for as long as they can. At the same time they are diversifying into downstream industries such as petrochemicals which are a logical extension of their refining expertise. Investing in base petrochemical ventures in the Middle East kills two birds with one stone; the Middle Easterners are kept happy and the oil companies consolidate their position in base petrochemicals. In these circumstances some of the doubts they inevitably have about investing in this region will be ignored, particularly if tied crude supplies are involved as well. The large, established chemical companies, on the other hand, have few historical ties with the Middle East and generally see no real gain from trying to win Middle Eastern goodwill for the sake of oil supplies. They have little first-hand knowledge of doing business with the region and may legitimately fear the long experience of the oil companies there. At the same time, the challenge from the oil companies' move into the base end of the chemical industry has been around for some time. Moreover, the American chemical companies seem to be following a strategy of reducing their involvement in what is now an over-crowded sector, in favour of concentrating on higher-value, more specialised chemicals. Therefore, to ask them to enter base chemical ventures in the Middle East is to ask them to become involved in a technological sector from which they have been slowly removing themselves. So, neither on historical, geographical nor technological grounds do the kind of ventures in which the oil majors are becoming involved make much sense to the average chemical company.

Despite this, some chemical companies are involved, so what singles them out? Mitsubishi can be disposed of swiftly since it gives every impression of being a somewhat reluctant potential investor in Saudi Arabia. Its original calculations suggested that an export-oriented ethylene complex in Saudi Arabia could not be profitable, and it decided to drop the idea. The only reason the company is now back in the arena, involved in two separate sets of negotiations, is that the Japanese government has strongly urged reconsideration and is going to provide a fair amount of extra financial aid in order to make the ventures more attractive. In the case of Bayer, its relatively limited involvement in the Iranian industry seems to be due to the special relationship which has existed between Germany and Iran from before the Second World War. Bayer presumably saw Iran as a relatively rich, fast-growing Third World economy with a more-than-average pro-German sentiment. Entering import-substituting joint ventures there would have made a great deal of sense.

Of the American companies, we know little about Celanese's motives but it is the world's largest producer of methanol and thus was a logical contender once the Saudis decided they wanted a methanol plant. This leaves Dow.

We are not sure if this is a compliment, but Dow is the chemical company which thinks most like a major oil company. It is a chemical company which has always thought in world-wide terms, having been the most successful US chemical company to enter Western Europe during the 1950s and 1960s, and one of the first into Latin America. Today, its new Yugoslav venture makes it the first US chemical company to invest in East Europe. Foreign business contributes some 45 per cent of Dow's revenues, which is more than in the case of Union Carbide, Du Pont or Monsanto.[8] Then again, it is far stronger in base chemicals than most of its competitors (in 1976, 60 per cent of its revenues came from these building blocks, compared with Du Pont's 19

52

per cent). This has inevitably given Dow relatively strong motives to try to develop new feedstock sources for the 1980s. The company has been moving back towards its sources of oil, most spectacularly through a 200,000 b/d crude-oil processing unit which it was building near Freeport, Texas in 1977.[9] Involvement in Saudi Arabia in order to obtain access to crude therefore makes sense. All the indications are that it is looking quite seriously towards Middle Eastern and Indian Ocean markets for the product exports of such plants and this tallies well with the company's strategy; Zoltan Merszei, then Dow's chairman, noted in an interview in 1977[10] that the company was faced with problems of world over-capacity in base chemicals, but this was still not preventing him from negotiating some half-a-dozen new ventures around the world. What he stressed, though, was that these must be in areas which will allow Dow to conquer 'new frontiers', by opening up new, promising, untapped markets.

The Europeans and Japanese

Superimposed on these industry differences, there are some geographical variations in motives as well. Compared with American companies, West European ones have, with the exception of Shell International, been remarkably uninterested in refining and petrochemical openings in the region (the picture is somewhat different when one looks at steel or car ventures where some European investment can be found). This is despite the relative geographical closeness of the Middle East to West Europe.

There is obviously no single explanation for European coolness, but one can point to some factors at work. The fact that BP has chosen to stay aloof from Middle Eastern industrialisation is probably related to its particular disillusionment with its treatment in Iran during the 1940s and early 1950s; after all, Shell International and the French chemical firm CDF-Chimie are both establishing a significant industrial stake within the region. The German chemical companies are more puzzling, since, during the 1970s, their sales have outstripped those of nearly all other chemical rivals. On the other hand, this fits into the conventional historical picture of West German industry; its foreign holdings have been expropriated in each of this century's two world wars, which has caused German companies to take a much more cautious approach to overseas investment than their British and American rivals.

The overseas investment location which has, during the 1970s, fascinated the West Germans is the United States and, to a lesser extent, Latin America. As the Dollar has fallen in relative terms throughout the decade, European chemical companies (many with a long history of involvement in the US)[11] have strengthened their positions in the Western Hemisphere. Partly, this investment has been triggered by relatively high US tariffs on chemicals and, since 1973, relatively low-cost US feedstocks. But most of the interest has been motivated by the realisation that the era of the 'American Challenge' is over and that relative exchange rates now mean that Europeans can find cheap buys in what is still the politically safe, leading economy of the world. Until this wave of investment slows down (and it was still riding high as we finished this book)[12], Europeans are unlikely to pay a great deal of attention to the Middle East.[13] The development of North Sea oil and gas means that there is somewhat less worry amongst European chemical producers about future supplies of feedstocks; this is in contrast with the situation in the US where the industry is having to come to terms with a lowering of domestic gas production, with a resultant greater emphasis on imported gas or alternative, non-gas feedstocks. All in all, then, one can understand why the West Europeans (additionally plagued by significant amounts of surplus capacity) have shown less enthusiasm for Middle Eastern ventures than their North American competitors. However commercially sound this may be, it does pose problems for West European political leaders. They would be happier if more of the EC's companies were investing in the Middle East, instead of remaining satisfied with trading at arm's length.

In the case of the Japanese, it is impossible to analyse the behaviour of their companies without also looking at the role of the Japanese government. Since we will devote chapter 9 to this wider analysis, we need not spend too much time on Japan at this point, but there are aspects of this investment which are well worth stressing.

Firstly, there are signs of the disintegration of the allegedly monolithic 'Japan Inc' — that Japanese example of an industrial and political elite so intertwined that it is virtually impossible to tell where Japanese corporate motives end and government goals begin. All the signs are that Mitsui and Mitsubishi made their way into the Middle East independently of any encouragement they may have received from the Japanese authorities. For one thing, petrochemical companies have been discriminated against within the Japanese economy because naphtha prices have been kept artificially high; official government decrees promoted this in order to keep kerosene prices down for the Japanese consumer. This faced Japanese-based chemical companies with relatively high feedstock prices by world standards and undoubtedly encouraged them to look outside Japan for investment opportunities. Secondly, the Mitsubishi family of companies is dominated in size by Mitsubishi Heavy Industries (the 24th largest non-American industrial company in 1977)[14] and it seems that Mitsubishi's original interest in Saudi Arabia came from this part of the trading company 'family'.

Once it became clear that some form of investment was called for, the rather smaller Mitsubishi Chemical (Number 85 in the non-American world) was called in to try to convert what was originally seen as a turn-key construction venture into a more long-lasting direct investment. In the Mitsui Group's case, a recent company history put the Iranian project specifically within a paragraph on plant exports, suggesting that there has been a similar mixing of goals.[15] Thirdly, one senses that there was a certain amount of defensive 'me-too-ism' involved in the Japanese chemical companies' investment strategies in the mid-1970s. Not only did one find both Mitsubishi and Mitsui investing directly in Iran and, in Mitsubishi's case, considering a Saudi share, but one also found Sumitomo Chemical negotiating hard to set up an ethylene joint venture in Singapore; the latter could well play havoc with the economies of the Mitsui and Mitsubishi ventures further West.

By most standards, these Japanese companies are taking (or considering taking) a big risk. Contrasted to American or European corporations, Japanese companies have not been particularly large overseas private investors — and where they have invested, it has generally been to develop various raw materials. In 1976, Mitsui was claiming to be Japan's largest overseas private investor, despite the fact that it only had $773 million committed in this way. So, to become enmeshed in a project like the one in Iran, whose costs have escalated to $3.4 billion, obviously always involved a major gamble — which the Mitsui Group seems to have lost.

There are signs, though, that Mitsubishi Chemical is acting very much like its competitors from elsewhere in the world. Its first reaction to the Saudi proposal was to decide that the whole thing was uneconomic and that it should be put into cold storage. In Iran, once it had decided that its share in the Iran-Nippon Petrochemical joint venture was not promising, the company refused to extend its involvement. However, its decision to extricate itself from the Saudi project did not hold once the Japanese government became aware of the damage such a withdrawal would do to wider Japanese interests in the Kingdom. Thus the company was forced back into negotiations — though with a considerable reduction of its share in the venture — as the Japanese government decided to take part and to encourage other Japanese commercial interests to become involved as well.

So, even if Mitsui and Mitsubishi have shown some independence from the ubiquitous MITI (the Japanese Ministry for International Trade and Industry), there is clear evidence from Saudi Arabia that companies can be pushed into renegotiations if the Japanese government decides such action is in the Japanese interest. And from Iran, where Mitsui has urgently called for financial help, as its initial calculations went awry, the lesson is that the Japanese government stands ready to bail its companies out of trouble, especially when major energy-supplying countries are involved.

This is certainly quite different from the European case, where no government forced ICI or BP to reconsider their refusals to invest in the region. Again, in the American case, there has been no suggestion that the US government might step into the Mobil or Exxon negotiations to offer low-interest government loans as a sweetener to the would-be US investors. This is not to say, however, that the US government would not be extremely uneasy if the American partners walked away from all the industrial joint ventures now under consideration. The danger of a resultant anti-American backlash would greatly worry Washington.

Conclusions

To sum up the arguments of this chapter, there are a number of factors at work. Firstly, within the oil industry, the opening up of Saudi Arabia to industrial ventures outside the Aramco framework has permitted a delayed reshuffling of positions within the remnants of the oligopoly which once dominated the oil industry. Shell and Mobil are now taking steps to improve their claims on future supplies of Saudi crude, mindful of the relative difficulties they had with crude supplies in the past.

At the same time, if the Shell and Mobil moves are those of oil industry outsiders (very relatively speaking) moving to improve their position on the industry insiders (the three biggest partners in Aramco), it is possible to argue that the oil companies in general are outsiders within the chemical industry and that their Middle Eastern moves are controlled gambles to strengthen their position as chemical companies. Events in Iran clearly show that Middle Eastern investments will remain risky for some years to come and this, undoubtedly, explains why the established chemical companies have generally proved very reluctant to become involved in any of the major projects on offer. On the other hand, oil companies with growing petrochemical interests, such as Shell, Mobil and Exxon, have been given the chance to capitalise on their Middle Eastern experience. Assuming that this region is going to become an increasingly important centre for petrochemical production, these companies' early involvement in the relevant projects should give them an important boost in their competition with the traditional chemical companies.

However, although it is superficially attractive to argue that it is 'outsider' companies which are most positively examining the new Middle Eastern investment opportunities, we should probably beware of putting too much weight on such 'insider-outsider' analyses.[16] After all, the number of major projects on which any analysis must rest can still be counted on the fingers of two hands. Most of the world's oil and chemical companies are still steering well clear of major investments in the region.

Clearly, most companies still have considerable doubts as to whether they can make any profitable investment within the Middle East at all, and would prefer to concentrate their managerial attention on other more obvious opportunities. Where companies have chosen to become involved, one senses that the specific goal of making an acceptable return on investments in the petrochemical and refining sectors was far from being the prime motive at the initial stages of their involvement. Thus, Shell, Mobil, Exxon, Socal, Texaco and, perhaps, Dow clearly entered into their Saudi negotiations with their eyes firmly on crude oil entitlements. The Japanese, far from discounting the oil issue, were initially also thinking of opening up the Middle Eastern market for Japanese processing plant. Dow's interest in the Middle East probably reflects a corporate strategy which put a relatively high premium on geographical diversification. This is not to say that any of these companies intend to subordinate short-run profitability to longer-run strategic considerations. It was likely these strategic factors which determined that they would look for investment opportunities within the Middle East, rather than in the many other parts of the world where profits can be made with less risks. So, many of the delays in Middle Eastern ventures reflect the fact that companies have had to search quite hard for projects which would actually give them an adequate return on their investments. Such delays also reflect the fact that the area is seen as a relatively risky one, and that there is little prior history of industrial investment in the region on which to draw.

We are still, therefore, in a period in which only a few, relatively bold companies are assessing the region's prospects in a serious way. If these pioneers are relatively unsuccessful with their first ventures, then other companies will remain uninterested. However, as soon as one or two companies show that major petrochemical or refining ventures within the Middle East can indeed be profitable, then there will be a sudden upsurge of interest in the region from the more cautious companies which are currently holding back. At the very least, these latecomers will start looking for moderately-sized investments which will give them a share while keeping their exposure reasonably limited. For instance, though ICI has rejected involvement with a major investment in the region, it was, in 1978, considering building at least one small plant to produce the catalytic materials which the abundance of petrochemical and refining ventures in the Middle East and North Africa will need.

It is clear for the moment, though, that the Middle East is no place for faint-hearted investors, and there is a distinct impression that corporate strategies have been polarising. A large number of medium-ranking companies which, during the 1960s, believed they had a Middle Eastern future, have now convinced themselves that manufacturing investment there is not worth the risk, and that business within the region should be kept to trade and non-investing relationships, such as various service contracts. Increasingly, then, there is less and less room in the Middle Eastern (perhaps OPEC) world for investments from companies such as Amoco (Standard Oil of Indiana), Cabot, Allied Chemical or B.F. Goodrich — four companies which invested in Iran before the 1973 watershed. If such companies are only offering fairly standard industrial technologies, their role will be taken over either by indigenous, private entrepreneurs or, more often, by state companies. The only companies which seem to have any hope of carving out a significant, semi-permanent role as investors in the region are a handful which are large and technologically sophisticated enough to provide access to world markets, or control technologies which indigenous competitors do not yet possess. Such sophisticated companies are still taking a risk in believing that all but the most ideologically biased nations will continue to do business with them on a long-term basis.

We are distinguishing two types of company here — the ones which intend to concentrate primarily on the OECD, and those which are sticking to a truly world-wide investment strategy (the core multi-nationals). But there is a third category which is just emerging in a small but noticeable way. These are companies which are starting to sell-out to the oil producing world. Some do so because they are, to all intents and purposes, bankrupt. So, if the oil producers can find a role for their plant, then at least something is salvaged. Others such as Fiat, Montedison, Korf and Krupp are companies which can find uses for Middle Eastern money, and if that eventually turns them into captives of the new investors, then that is a problem which can be faced in the future. In the meantime, there are commercial opportunities which become available to companies willing to go this road, and problems of future management control can be forgotten in the interests of short-term survival or profit.

Finally, the emerging national companies remain a brooding presence. A few, such as the National Iranian Oil Company, are making smallish, controllable overseas investments to guarantee markets and to win experience. Most are concentrating on mastering their own domestic challenges and are happiest with nationalistic solutions if they can make do without foreign partners. We are, however, still too close to the oil revolution of the early 1970s to form a firm idea of each national company's long-term potential. So far, there are few outstanding successes or failures to analyse. On the one hand, no Middle Eastern national company has proved as disastrously incompetent as Indonesia's Pertamina (which ran up $10 billion's worth of losses);

this reflects the fact that most state companies in the Middle East are quite tightly controlled by central authorities (though what will happen in Iran?). On the other hand, though the national oil companies of the largest oil producers, such as Saudi Arabia and Iran, must become significant agents on the world scene, none of the smaller ones is yet showing a level of performance which singles them out to play a regional role far larger than their original size suggests.

But then, as with our attempts to categorise different kinds of responses by OECD-based companies, we are really too close to the 1970-73 period which re-cast the region's competitive structure. One thing only can be predicted with confidence. Very few OECD-based companies will obtain a major investment share within the Middle East. Entering one of the joint ventures we have considered in this book should help win such a role — but does not guarantee it.

Notes

1   Turner, 1978, pp 209-10.
2   Jacoby, 1974, p.137.
3   Jacoby, 1974, p.148.
4   *Middle East Economic Survey*, January 15 1979, p.9.
5   As defined by *Business Week*, October 16 1978, pp 119-20.
6   As defined by *Fortune*, August 14 1978, pp 172-4.
7   The Mitsui Group is ignored here, since it is not in the top 15 non-American companies.
8   Morner, 1977, p.314.
9   Morner, 1977, p.318.
10   Morner, 1977, p.315.
11   Franko, 1976, pp 166-72.
12   *European Chemical News*, Chemscope, 'International Chemical Trade in North America', October 13 1978.
13   Both Professors Franko and Vernon think we are over-speculative here.
14   *Fortune*, August 14 1978, p.172.
15   Mitsui, 1977, p.294.
16   There is a long literature on the investment strategies of multi-national companies. See Buckley and Casson, 1976, pp 66-84; Vernon, 1974, for good introductions. This concluding discussion has particularly benefited from ideas put forward by Larry Franko in a personal communication.

5 Saudi and Iranian plans in a regional focus

It should be clear from the preceding chapters that neither Saudi Arabia nor Iran is going to become a massive exporter of products during the 1980s, so it is tempting to dismiss their plans as being of no real political interest. However, for a number of reasons this would be a mistake. Firstly, these two countries are not investing in a vacuum, as their ambitions are shared by most of the other OPEC members. Cumulatively, the investments of these oil producing states are showing signs of being ambitious enough to pose genuine policy problems for the industrialised world. Secondly, the success of the Saudi and Iranian plans will be affected by the speed with which other oil producers in the Middle East and North Africa develop competing ventures. It is not merely oil-producing countries that matter, since even non-oil-producing, manufacturing powers such as the East Europeans, Singapore, South Korea and Taiwan will be competing with the Saudis and Iranians in key markets. The danger for these last two is that they will find their ambitions thwarted by other Third World countries. Since both Iran and Saudi Arabia have such high hopes for their industrialisation strategies, it is probable that their disappointment would be correspondingly great, should their achievements — however limited in practice — be foiled by the industrialised world's unwillingness to accommodate their products alongside those of other countries already operating in world markets.

Because of all these factors, we seek in this chapter to put their plans into a wider, regional focus.

The Gulf and North Africa

There was nothing singular about the ambitions of Saudi Arabia and Iran in the months following the 1973-74 oil price rises. Virtually every other oil-producer round the Gulf and along the shores of North Africa announced plans for some sort of heavy industrialisation. For instance, as late as September 1976, an IDCAS/OAPEC study was still talking of fifteen ethylene projects in the Arab world which were either 'under construction' (four projects), at the 'advanced planning' stage (four) or 'under consideration' (seven). Added together, these would have given

60

an eventual 5 million tons/year of ethylene production, roughly equivalent to 40 per cent of EC productive capacity in 1976. Two years later, however, little remained of these Arab aspirations. Ethylene complexes listed as 'under consideration' in Abu Dhabi, Tunisia, Syria and Dubai have faded so far from view that they no longer merit any consideration. Of the four plants under 'advanced planning', one in Egypt has been modified so that it no longer has an ethylene-producing component, and another in Kuwait appears extremely marginal. Of the four projects actually listed as being under construction, one in Libya turned out to be a methanol project, with an ethylene venture no more than a remote possibility — and the Iraqi one proved to be a plant which was under serious consideration, but which had not as yet reached the construction stage. So, if we add in what we know of Iranian plans, the picture now looks something like table 5.1.

Table 5.1
Arab and Iranian Ethylene projects (January 1979)

Country	Location	In operation (t/y)	Under construction tons/year	Advanced planning (t/y)	Under consideration (t/y)
Algeria	Skikda 1	120,000	–	–	–
	Skikda 2	–	–	500,000	–
Iran	Bandar Shahpur	–	300,000	–	–
	Abadan	25,000	–	–	–
Iraq	Basrah	–	–	138,000	–
Kuwait	Shuaiba	–	–	–	300,000
Libya	Ras Lanuf	–	–	–	330,000
Qatar	Umm Said	–	280,000	–	–
Saudi Arabia	Jubail 1	–	–	650,000	–
	Jubail 2	–	–	–	200,000
	Jubail 3	–	–	300,000	–
	Yanbu	–	–	450,000	–
Total: 3,593,000		145,000	580,000	2,038,000	830,000

As the most speculative ventures have been analysed more critically, there has been a considerable drop in the number of projects 'under consideration'. On the other hand, the amount of capacity which is 'in operation', 'under construction', or at the 'advanced planning' stage has

61

only dropped some 12 per cent in the two years since September 1976, and, of this capacity which is more likely to become operative than not, the Saudis are hoping to produce around half.

Although the Saudi plans in the ethylene field are obviously highly ambitious by neighbouring standards, these other countries have been considerably more active on the wider industrialisation front than this narrow analysis of the ethylene sector would suggest. Saudi Arabia's potential impact in petrochemicals has to be put firmly into the context of the achievements of other Arab and Middle Eastern states.

In the Gulf, Bahrain inaugurated the Arab world's first aluminium smelter (ALBA) as early as 1971, a project which has since led to the creation of two or three aluminium-using plants. The UAE's Dubai has a similar aluminium smelter under construction. In the area of fertilisers, Iran, Kuwait and Qatar have had significant plants in operation since the early 1970s. In the autumn of 1977, OAPEC's Arab Shipbuilding and Repair Yard was opened in Bahrain; in 1978, while Saudi Arabia was inaugurating its lube-oil plant and the Iranians their copper smelter, fertiliser plant and extension to the Abadan refinery, Qatar opened a steel plant at Umm Said which is due to build up to a 400,000 tons/year capacity. By 1979, a further wave of projects should either be in operation or on the verge of completion: a steel venture in Iraq; aluminium projects in Iraq and Dubai; and more fertiliser plants in Qatar and Iran. By the end of 1979, the two major ethylene-based complexes in Qatar and Iran should both have become operative, but the opening date of the Iranian project is now very much in doubt.

The picture, then, is of quite considerable activity around the Gulf, in which Saudi Arabia and Iran are merely two of the agents. The Iranians were certainly growing into a major regional force across the industrial board. In the Saudi case, however, the further one gets away from the refining and petrochemicals area, the less of an industrial force the country appears to be. Other countries have entered the steel and aluminium sectors before it, and its fertiliser plant is nothing unusual for the area.

However, it is not only with the other Gulf states that Saudi Arabia and Iran must contend. Looking towards West European and North American markets, they have at least one very strong competitor — namely Algeria. This country does not have the kind of oil income which the two Middle Eastern ones have, but it has been pursuing a policy of developing heavy industry with a steadfastness which distinguishes it from Saudi Arabia and, to a lesser extent, from Iran. Despite the fact that its population and GDP per capita is roughly half that of Iran, it has had a steel complex at El Hadjar, producing 400,000 tons of rolled steel, since 1969; in 1970 and 1972 it brought into operation two fertiliser plants; opened a new refinery at Arzew in 1973; completed the first stage of an ethylene complex in 1978 (by 1980 it should be producing 500,000 tons/year); has four LNG 'lines' in operation, with another five either under construction or in the planning stage; finally it hopes to bring at least one refinery into operation (in 1979, Skikda, 300,000 b/d: a 150,000 b/d one at Bejaia now seems to have been dropped).[1] The Algerian model of development with its extremely heavy emphasis on industrialisation has impressed many commentators, and there is no doubt that Algeria's approach has been unique within the Arab world, although countries such as Iraq and Libya show signs of trying to imitate its example. In particular, Libya added to the North African industrialisation effort by bringing a 330,000 ton methanol plant into operation in late 1977 and, it is hoped, a 220,000 b/d refinery by the early 1980s.

Marketing implications

The most immediate importance of developments in North Africa is that they will pre-empt some Middle Eastern exports which might otherwise find their way to Europe. For one thing, both Algeria and Libya already have significant exporting ventures going, whereas the first of the new Saudi ventures is likely to be ready only in four or five years' time. In the case of the Iranian IJPC project, which should have an exportable surplus of products in the early 1980s, the North Africans will have the advantage of being very much closer to South European markets — a transportation saving which Iranian ethylene-based products would not be able to overcome. This will reinforce Iran's determination to look eastwards rather than westwards for markets.

Algeria has the extra advantage for its exports of products of being able to have free access to the European Community. This is the result of the Maghreb Agreement which was signed between the EC and the three Maghreb countries (Algeria, Morocco and Tunisia) in April 1976. There are safeguard clauses, which the EC can activate to control the amount of Algerian petrochemical and refined oil products, but the fact that Algeria has this tariff preference must give it a major edge over competitors from the Middle East which are subject to both significant transportation and tariff disadvantages.[2] A further consideration is that European reactions to Algerian exports will give an indication of the type of reception which will await the products from further East. As mentioned above, there is the safeguard clause which could allow the Europeans to retreat from their free access position, should Algerian exports prove troublesome to any industrial sector. The fact that the Algerians are so well advanced in the planning and construction of their export-oriented plants means, however, that European patience is going to be tested relatively early. We shall discuss how the Europeans might react in chapter 7, but, for the moment, we need only note that Middle Eastern plans have to be seen in the context of the plans of other countries or regions which will be established as suppliers of key markets before Middle Eastern exporters can become a significant force.

As far as Middle East ambitions to export to Japan and other Asian countries are concerned, an eye will have to be kept on developments in countries such as Singapore, Indonesia and South Korea. The indonesians, with their oil and shorter supply lines to Japan, might well have been important rivals, but the disastrous performance of their national oil company, Pertamina (which ran up losses of some $10 billion through unwise diversification) has meant that Indonesian plans remain relatively modest. On the other hand, two of the East Asian 'export platforms', South Korea and Taiwan, have their own ambitious petrochemical plans and are already major forces in the downstream plastics sector into which the Middle Eastern oil producers must eventually move. Both of these countries could well have their third ethylene complexes in operation before the first Saudi one emerges. The companies involved in the Far East projects include names such as Gulf, Mitsui and Dow, which have also been considering or are actually involved in Middle Eastern ventures. Even Singapore, which has not yet entered the petrochemical field in a significant way, negotiated in 1977 a fifty-fifty joint venture with Sumitomo and a number of smaller Japanese companies for the construction of an ethylene plant, which would inevitably compete with Middle Eastern ventures in Asian markets, should it ever be built.

As far as West European markets are concerned, the Middle Eastern planners must also take East European intentions into account, since these are even more likely to sour West Europe's response to chemical imports in the mid-1980s than those of the North African producers. The West European contracting industry was facing hard times in the early 1970s, and so became keen to sell plant to new customers such as the East Europeans, who were becoming particularly interested in building up their petrochemical industry at around the same time. Being short of convertible currencies, the East Europeans devised a sophisticated form of barter, known as Compensation Trading, to finance the construction of these plants. Under such an agreement, the plant constructors were to be paid back in products once the plants were actually operative. By the nature of these deals, there was a considerable delay between the signing of the contracts to build these plants and the date when products would start to flow in the reverse direction. So, for instance, between 1972 and 1975 a number of West

German (Salzgitter, Kloeckner), French (Litwin, Creusot-Loire), Italian (Montedison, Snamprogetti/Anic, Snia Viscosa) and American (Occidental) companies signed a series of such compensation deals, but the reverse flow of products would only start at different times between 1977 and 1981.[3]

It was inevitable that this system of petrochemical investment would cause problems. On the one hand, the state enterprises of East Europe (the East Europeans were partly seduced by buoyant pre-1973 estimates of growth rates) blithely assumed that West European markets would absorb any amount of products which might flow back under these compensation deals. On the other hand, western plant constructors were not ideally placed to monitor the cumulative impact of these deals, since they were generally not producers of chemicals themselves. The result was a scale of export-oriented investment in Eastern Europe which was not justified by the prognosis of western chemical markets in the latter part of the 1970s.

In world terms, the volumes of product involved are not particularly impressive (except in urea, methanol and ammonia). By 1985, East European sales of chemical products to West Europe will probably reach around $3.5 billion (1976 prices), of which about 40 per cent will take the form of imports from compensation deals. East Europe's total sales might thus represent the equivalent of one medium-sized petrochemical company.[4] However, although that may not sound like a great deal, we shall argue in chapter 7 that there is already enough controversy over this trade to possibly trigger off West European protectionist measures which might rebound on future Middle Eastern export ventures. Suffice it to say that, unlike many of the Middle Eastern ventures, these East European complexes are either in operation or under construction. Moreover, although there are some indications that parts of the Eastern bloc, such as Hungary, are becoming less enthusiastic about the compensation trading approach, there are enough petrochemical ventures to go ahead so that Middle Eastern producers will be competing with well-established East European producers from the very start. One final source of competition for the Middle Easterners is the US industry whose exports to Europe have been substantially boosted by the steady decline of the Dollar during the 1970s.

Lessons for Saudi Arabia and Iran

It should be clear by now that Middle Eastern petrochemical plans cannot be considered in isolation. Plants which by themselves seem unimportant take on a different status when their products are added to those from plants in the immediate region of the Gulf or from plants closer to end-markets. Of course, it may well be that plants based on Middle Eastern hydrocarbons do have an economic logic that is missing from those in oil-importing countries such as Singapore, South Korea or Taiwan. On the other hand, there is an underlying inertia in the international economy which means that investment and trading patterns respond relatively slowly to changes in comparative advantages between nations. Certainly, we would be surprised if the North African oil producers voluntarily gave way to allow exports from the Middle East to move into West European markets, just as the East Asian industrialising powers (such as South Korea) will prove extremely reluctant to make room for the Middle Easterners in Far Eastern markets. So, the first lesson from this chapter is that Saudi and Iranian planners must take into account the competition which is likely to develop even before their countries' projects become operative. They will not just be competing with producers in the OECD world.

Secondly, there is some evidence that the countries in the Middle East and North Africa which are pushing furthest ahead are the ones which have rejected the joint-venture approach. This is certainly true of Algeria, where Sonatrach has had its refining and petrochemical ventures constructed on a turnkey basis by foreign contractors. The Libyan National Oil Company has taken a similar approach, as has the Iraqi Industry Ministry within the fertiliser sector. At the same time, foreign partners have been given a role within other countries' projects such as the ALBA aluminium smelter in Bahrain, a similar smelter in Dubai, and the steel and ethylene complexes in Qatar. However, these are all projects in which the respective governments have made the running, with the possible exception of the ALBA smelter where foreign aluminium interests provided much of the initial enthusiasm, but gradually allowed the Bahrain government to take a larger and larger stake.[5]   In fact, the IJPC project in Iran seems to be virtually the only major petrochemical or refining complex to be under construction recently within the Middle East and North Africa, in which the foreign partner has a fifty per cent stake. The nearest similar case is the QAPCO ethylene complex in Qatar, in which CDF-Chimie has a 16 per cent stake (as a 'quid-pro-quo' Qatar is taking a 16 per cent interest in a CDF-Chimie complex in France). However, this is a stake which leaves the company very much less exposed than Mitsui is in Iran, or the various potential foreign partners would be in Saudi Arabia. This only goes to show how distinctive the Saudi industrialisation policy really is — and how much of a gamble the Mitsui Group took in going ahead in Iran.

This is not to say that the state-owned projects outside Saudi Arabia have been universally successful. The sophisticated Shuaiba refinery constructed by the Kuwait National Petroleum Company (100 per cent government-owned) in the late 1960s has had a history of losses, largely due to technical problems stemming from the company's decision to go for what was virtually prototype technology. The Libyan methanol plant which became operative in 1977 is expected to run below capacity for a couple of years until it has adequate storage facilities and the relevant port is dredged from its present eight metres depth to 15 metres.[6] Algeria's ethylene plant at Skikda was slow in being constructed. The related ldPE plant stood idle for some time, and then, when the ethylene plant was finally ready in 1978, developed technical hitches.[7] The Egyptians are reported to be unhappy with their steelworks at Helwan. Few outside observers are impressed with the efficiency with which the ALBA aluminium smelter has been run in Bahrain. It is probably unfair to add that Qatar's Umm Said NGL plant was destroyed by fire in April 1977.

Naturally, many of our Middle Eastern readers will resent our pointing to the alleged inefficiency shown in these cases. After all, plants are destroyed in other parts of the world. Nearly all plants experience teething problems when first commissioned. And what company can give an absolute guarantee about when any given plant will finally come into operation? We would defend ourselves by suggesting that there is nothing disgraceful in Middle Easterners failing to achieve the best western or Japanese standards in the first wave of industrialisation that the region has really known. It is inevitable that the shortage of supporting industries, for instance, will decrease efficiency, since plants either have to be over-designed (which raises costs) or else are badly inconvenienced by breakdowns which would be handled in longer-established industrial centres as a matter of routine.

For the record, readers of the initial draft of this chapter have suggested that the small refineries recently commissioned in countries such as Abu Dhabi, Iraq and Qatar have no known problems, and that a smallish Tunisian steelworks performs adequately. An Iranian reader suggests that the Shahpur Chemical Company's record in the fertiliser field has nothing to be ashamed of. On the other hand, most qualified observers of the Middle Eastern scene go along with our overall judgement that plants in the Gulf area are not generally run to the best standards of the industrialised world — exceptions are made for Aramco's Ras Tanura refinery, the Bahrain refinery and the less technically complex parts of Kuwait's refining industry.

There are mixed lessons from all this for Saudi Arabia and Iran, who both tend to stress the need for foreign partners in major ventures. Certainly, insofar as they are concerned with the overall efficiency of these ventures, their cautious approach should prevent the construction of any particularly disastrous projects. On the other hand, since they are competing with countries which choose to push ahead without foreign partners, they run the risk of finding markets pre-empted (although the foreign partners will be confident that they can reduce this risk through the full use of their pre-existing, international marketing network). It may be that the recent wave of investments or decisions to invest will be relatively less economic than those which the Saudis and Iranians are planning. However, as we shall argue in later chapters, once those competing plants are built, their products will presumably be priced at levels which will find them markets — whatever the underlying economics of their construction and operation. The dilemma for the Saudis, who are so much more dependent on exports than the Iranians, is that their determination to be as economically rational as possible will delay the construction of projects, thus allowing less rational investors to bring plants into operation which will blight the marketing chances of the eventual Saudi ones. Economic rationality thus may become its own worst enemy.

Conclusions

Whatever the relative efficiency of the competing ventures, some conclusions can be drawn. Firstly, there are a few signs of growth in intra-regional trade between the countries around the Gulf. QASCO, the Qatar steel project, made its first sales to Saudi Arabia and Kuwait but, since its ultimate capacity will be 400,000 tons per annum (half the planned size of the Saudi venture with Korf), it will be able to service only part of the market in the Gulf. Recently planned cement plants in Bahrain and Kuwait will have a significant Saudi stake, thus indicating that some of their products will find their way into the Saudi construction boom.

None of these intra-regional flows show signs yet of becoming particularly large by world standards, and (despite the cement cases mentioned above) one is struck by how little co-operative investment has yet taken place within the Middle East. The one striking example has been OAPEC's Arab Shipbuilding and Repair Yard in Bahrain, in which seven of OAPEC's members have taken a share. However, this did not stop Dubai from going ahead with a competing dry dock of its own. OAPEC has also sponsored the setting up of the Arab Maritime Petroleum Transport Company and the Arab Petroleum Services Company, but there has been no real progress outside the auspices of OAPEC. Kuwait had hoped that it could interest other Gulf states in taking a share in the olefins and aromatics complex it would like to build at Shuaiba, but has had no visible success. Otherwise, a Gulf Organisation for Industrial Consulting has been created with the aim of co-ordinating the plans of the Gulf states in the smaller industries, such as cement and glass. However, at the level which concerns us, the various national governments are going their own way. Certainly, they are aware of the plans of their neighbours and they will, on occasion, modify their investment plans as a result of this knowledge (as the Saudis did in the aluminium smelter field, when they took the Bahrain and Dubai projects into consideration). In general, though, national self-interest tends to come first.

This all bodes ill for any major upsurge in intra-regional trade within the Gulf area, so most of the projects analysed in this chapter will tend to look outwards. In the past, refined oil products from Ras Tanura, Bahrain and (of decreasing importance) Kuwait and Abadan have moved eastwards, with about 50 per cent of the total going to Japan, and the rest to other markets in the Far East: Australia, New Zealand, India and East Africa.[8] Obviously this trading pattern owes much to the historic investment patterns of the oil majors who chose to service Europe and Japan from refineries located close to end-markets, while leaving the more scattered, marginal markets east of Suez to be supplied from refineries in the Gulf. It is not clear, however, whether the market for chemical products will be governed by similar consider-ations. After all, the big change which has taken place in the world economy has been the break-up of the integrated power of the old oil majors. The new national companies which are seeking to dictate the location of the next generation of petrochemical and refining plants will try to reverse the trend whereby such plants have been placed ever closer to end-markets. The oil-producing countries will want to supply West European markets from the Gulf, but this runs counter to the trading patterns which have built up since World War II.

On the evidence of this chapter, it is the Algerians and Libyans in North Africa who are the first to develop the desired trading relation-ship with West Europe and, even, North America. They already have products on offer to potential customers in Europe, and in the case of Algerian gas, to the United States. Transport economics inevitably tie these North African states to West Europe, in a way that is not appli-cable to the Gulf states.

Finally, whatever the exact paths taken by the products of the Middle Eastern and North African oil producers, a picture is emerging of the potential impact these products might have on world markets. It is far from being an overwhelming one. To start with the refining case, in 1976, OPEC members in the Middle East and North Africa con-trolled just 4 per cent of world refining capacity outside the Centrally Planned Economies, of which Saudi Arabia and Iran each contributed one quarter. By 1980, Iran might have 1.4 per cent of non-communist capacity; in 1985, some 1.7 per cent; then, should the Iran-Japanese

Table 5.2
Estimated demand v. refining capacity
(million b/d)

	1976						1980			
	Refining capacity 100%(a)	Refining capacity 85/90%(b)	Actual through-put	Oil demand (c)	Surplus/(deficit) v.85/90%	Surplus/(deficit) Actual	Refining capacity 100%(a)	Refining capacity 85/90%(b)	Oil demand (c)	Surplus/(deficit)
USA	15.2	15.2	15.1	17.1	(1.9)	(2.0)	17.0	16.8	20.8	(4.0)
Canada	2.1	1.8	1.7	1.6	0.2	0.1	2.4	2.0	2.1	(0.1)
W Europe (d)	20.2	17.2	13.5	13.8	3.4	(0.3)	20.9	17.8	15.0	2.8
Japan	5.3	4.8	4.2	4.8	–	(0.6)	5.6	5.0	6.0	(1.0)
Australia/New Zealand	0.8	0.7	0.6	0.7	–	(0.1)	0.9	0.8	0.8	–
Total OECD (d)	43.6	39.7	35.1	38.0	1.7	(2.9)	46.8	42.4	44.7	(2.3)
OPEC	4.5	3.8	3.1(e)	1.9	1.9	1.2	5.7	4.9	3.0	1.9
(Middle East – 2.3)(f)							(2.9)			
(Saudi Arabia – 0.6)(f)							(0.6)			
(Iran – 0.8)(f)							(1.3)			
(North Africa – 0.2)(f)							(0.6)			
Other LDC	11.0	9.4	7.8(e)	6.6	2.8	1.2	13.4	11.4	8.0	3.4
Total LDC	15.5	13.2	10.9(e)	8.5	4.7	2.4	19.1	16.3	11.0	5.3
World (excluding CPE)	59.1	52.9	46.0	46.5	6.4	(0.5)	65.9	58.7	55.7	3.0

70

Table 5.2 (cont.)

	1985				1990			
	Refining capacity 100%(a)	Refining capacity 85/90%(b)	Oil demand (c)	Surplus/(deficit)	Refining capacity 100%(a)	Refining capacity 85/90%(b)	Oil demand (c)	Surplus/(deficit)
USA	18.0	17.7	21.6	(3.9)	18.0	17.7	21.6	(3.9)
Canada	2.4	2.0	2.4	(0.4)	2.4	2.0	2.2	(0.2)
W. Europe (d)	21.5	18.3	15.9	2.4	21.5	18.3	16.9	1.4
Japan	6.1	5.5	7.1	(1.6)	6.1	5.5	7.4	(1.9)
Australia/New Zealand	0.9	0.8	0.9	(0.1)	0.9	0.8	0.9	(0.1)
Total OECD (d)	48.9	44.3	47.9	(3.6)	48.9	44.3	49.0	(4.7)
OPEC (g)	7.0	5.9	4.5	1.4	7.0(g)	5.9	6.0	(0.1)
(Middle East – 3.8)(f)					(4.5-5.1)			
(Saudi Arabia – 1.2)(f)					(1.4)			
(Iran – 1.3)(f)					(1.6)			
(North Africa – 0.9)(f)					(0.9)			
Other LDC	14.3	12.1	8.7	3.4	14.3	12.1	9.0	3.1
Total LDC	21.3	18.0	13.2	4.8	21.3	18.0	15.0	3.0
World (excluding CPE)	70.2	62.3	61.1	1.2	70.2	62.3	64.0	(1.7)

NOTES

(a) Estimated capacity at beginning of year. Only firm projects included in 1980/1985 figures. 1990 figures deliberately kept as 1985.

(b) 90% utilisation of refining capacity is considered a realistic average for USA and Japan, and 85% for all other areas, based on past performance. In the USA, an extra 1.5 million b/d has been added to account for NGL plant output.

(c) Figures for Japan exclude 400,000 b/d crude oil for direct burning 1976-1990.

(d) Includes non-OECD Western European countries.

(e) Estimate Department of Energy(US).

(f) Estimate by Turner and Bedore.

(g) The inconsistencies between the estimates of the overall OPEC total and the various sub-totals for the Middle East and North Africa reflect slightly different assumptions by Turner and Bedore and the authors of the Department of Energy study.

LDC = Less Developed Countries;   CPE = Centrally Planned Economies

Source: Department of Energy (US), 1978a, with some Turner and Bedore estimates.

Table 5.3
Ethylene: global demand and capacity projections (m. ton/year)

		1976	1990
United States	Demand	10,200	23,600
	Capacity	13,160	
Other W. Hemispheres	Demand	1,160	5,300
	Capacity	1,550	
W. Europe	Demand	9,980	22,000
	Capacity	13,280	
E. Europe	Demand	2,400	8,000
	Capacity	2,710	
Japan	Demand	3,770	7,400
	Capacity	5,140	
Asia/Pacific	Demand	1,040	4,080
	Capacity	1,310	
Middle East/Africa	Demand	180	4,400*
	Capacity	240	
OPEC/Middle East	Capacity	(25)	(2,800)**
Saudi Arabia	Capacity	(−)	(1,500)**
Iran	Capacity	(25)	(200-600)**
OPEC/North Africa	Capacity	(−)	(600)**
TOTAL	Demand	28,640	74,800
	Capacity	37,390	

NOTES

*Demand represents disappearance of ethylene in production of derivatives.
**Estimates by Turner and Bedore.

Source: Peter Spitz and Lawrence Weiss, reported in European Chemical News, August 4 1978a, p.20, table 11(a), with some additions by Turner and Bedore.

export refinery get off the ground, around 2.4 per cent in 1990. The picture for the Saudis is similar: if all three of their export refineries became operative by 1990, they would have around 2.1 per cent of non-communist capacity. As far as the whole OPEC group in the Middle East and North Africa is concerned, their share of this capacity could probably rise to 5.8 per cent in 1980, 6.8 per cent in 1985 and about 9.5 per cent in 1990. We obtain a more impressive figure if we note that this group is capable of providing just under 20 per cent of the new refining capacity which the non-communist world is likely to build between 1976 and 1990. However, we would stress that these projections tend to assume that most of the plants currently under consideration will eventually come into operation between 1985 and 1990, or will be replaced by similar projects. Although recent events in Iran may make this latter assumption over-ambitious, we feel that these projections outline the maximum impact that Saudi Arabia and Iran, on the one hand, and the Middle Eastern and North African regions, on the other, can possibly make.

In the petrochemical sector, very much the same picture emerges. We have taken one reasonably optimistic forecast of ethylene demand from Chem Systems analysts[9] and have built on our own assumptions about the likelihood of Middle Eastern and North African projects actually being constructed. The result (summarised in table 5.3) is that the oil producers in these two regions are likely to increase their capacity from virtually nothing in 1976 to 3.5– 4 per cent of world demand by 1990. By that time, Saudi Arabia might very well be capable of supplying 2.0 per cent of world demand, with Iran providing a less impressive 0.4 per cent.

As the oil producers will point out, these are not particularly alarming figures. Even if some 10 per cent of the world refining and 4 per cent of ethylene capacity came to be based in the Middle East and North Africa, would we really have an international crisis on our hands? We could argue that only marginal changes are taking place in the structure of the world industry, yet we shall see in later chapters that there is real unease in the industrialised world about these changes. After all, the apparently small Middle Eastern share in 1990's capacity will represent a rather larger slice of world incremental investment over the coming decade. It would be unfair to ignore such concern on the grounds that the industrialised world's fears are not supported by the forecasts we have made. As long as such fears exist, they may well be translated into diplomatic action aimed against the industrialisation of the oil producers. Thus, what we shall do in the rest of this book is look at these fears in the light of the forecasts we have made.

Notes

1   Algerian Ministry of Industry, 1974, p.51; Department of Energy (US), 1978, tables 12a, b; Ghiles, 1977, pp 149-58; Sayigh, 1978a, p.546.

2   Tovias, 1977, p.11.

3   The Occidental deal is not strictly a plant-for-product, but a product-for-product deal.

4   *European Chemical News* (European Review Supplements), July 22 1977, pp 4-12; July 21 1978, pp 32-67.

5   *Middle East Annual Review*, 1977, p.243.

6   *European Chemical News*, April 21 1978, p.11.

7   *European Chemical News*, August 4 1978, p.10.

8   Department of Energy (US), 1978, p.227.

9   Peter Spitz and Lawrence Weiss, reported in *European Chemical News*, August 4 1978a, p.20.

6 The economic pros and cons

Most readers will have realised by now that we are not just raising economic issues. A number of the projects under discussion will go ahead whatever their economic merits. On the one hand, producer governments would have political difficulties in remaining mere exporters of crude oil. On the other, consumer governments and multi-national companies are looking to the day when preferential access to crude will become crucial; if long-run security of oil supplies can be bought by investing in marginally economic industrial ventures in oil-producing countries, then so be it. Those investments will be made.

However, the economics of such projects do still matter. For one thing, there are limits to the amount of money which governments and companies are willing to throw away on bad projects, even though, for governments, those limits may be pretty generous. For another, the ease with which the products from such ventures find future markets will very much depend on the underlying economics of the initial investments. It may well be that a country can buy its way into inter-national markets by cutting prices, but there will come a point at which affected interest groups in the consuming world will resist such incursions. They will claim that the new source of products is 'disruptive' and that these are being 'dumped' on to world markets at uneconomic prices. In the very real likelihood of there being resistance to products from the Middle East, the economics of that region's industrial ventures become quite important. If the bulk of these are really uneconomic projects which have been realised for non-economic reasons, then they will be shown little mercy by their competitors in the industrialised world. However, if Middle Eastern export-oriented ventures are economic, the issues become clearer. The protectionists will still be around, but it then becomes easier to argue within the industri-alised world that the Middle Easterners should be allowed a share of the world trade in manufactured products.

Relevant variables

On the surface, the issues appear to be simple. The flared gas which is currently wasted in the Middle East can be used as feedstock for industrial ventures at prices far below those of gas and alternative feedstocks in the industrialised world. In addition, some oil-producing countries have abundant capital with which to back such hydrocarbon-processing industries. These two factors should be enough to give oil-producing countries a competitive advantage over an industrialised world with increasingly less resources. Then again, there is the 'value-added' argument, that processing gas and oil leads to increased value, thus apparently bringing automatic benefits to the producing country. Here again, the issues look simple. A barrel of crude oil worth $12 can produce goods worth approximately $84 when turned into a common commodity plastic such as polypropylene and, if converted to products such as polyester film or agricultural chemicals,[1] the value is increased by fifty to one hundred times.

Once more, the arguments are seductive but will fail to convince hard-nosed, non-OPEC economists, who will want to know what scale of investment is needed to produce the higher valued chemical products. Will relatively high investment and transportation costs affect the cheapness of capital and feedstocks?

At the risk of over-simplifying, there are at least eight easily identifiable variables which will affect the economic viability of these capital-intensive Middle Eastern ventures. Only two of these variables (feedstock prices and capital availability) are unequivocally in favour of the oil-producing states, with one other (environmental issues) cutting both ways. Three factors (construction, fixed operating and transport costs) will probably always work against the Middle Easterners, and two others (markets and tariffs) currently work against them, but will probably even out more as the years go by.

Variables in favour

Feedstocks

In earlier chapters, we have already given some idea of the relatively low gas feedstock prices which various Middle Eastern countries have increasingly accepted as adequate for projects. Certainly, Iranian petrochemical projects have been receiving their gas at 2 cents a thousand cubic feet, although this could well be raised for more recent projects.[2] The Bahrain aluminium smelter, ALBA, allegedly receives its gas for 9 cents a million BTU (a million BTU is very marginally greater than a thousand cubic feet of gas).[3] Then again, it is generally accepted that the Saudi petrochemical projects will receive their feedstock at prices within the 35-50 cents a million BTU range (this is calorifically equivalent to a barrel of fuel oil sold at between $2.24 and $3.20).

Undoubtedly, these prices seem cheap when set against the fact that decontrolled, new natural gas should be selling in the US for $3.80 per million BTU in 1985. On the other hand, because of its high volume in relation to value, gas is extremely expensive to transport, requiring either lengthy pipelines or liquefaction. The result is that when one does 'net-back' calculations (i.e. subtract transport, insurance, marketing and tariff costs from the price realised for gas in big markets like the US or Japan), one comes up with figures within the region that the Saudis are considering.[4] Seemingly, when this 'transport' factor is allied to the fact that gas does not sell for as much as a calorific equivalent of oil anywhere in the world (this is changing[5]), the Middle Easterners are not putting an 'unfair' value on their gas if it is priced somewhere between 35 and 50 cents a million BTU. The challenge then is to take this gas and to convert it into products which are both more economical to transport and which ultimately fetch a higher price in the international market-place. The petrochemical industry which turns gas into higher-priced liquids and solids is an obvious starter.

There are, though, one or two slightly less obvious points to make. For one thing, even if 50 cents a million BTU is a competitive 'net-back' price for Middle Eastern gas, it is not clear that gas at such a price inevitably justifies the cost of collecting it. In the chapter on the Saudi projects, we have mentioned the giant gas-gathering scheme which aims to produce the more easily transportable liquefied petroleum gases (LPG) for export, ethane and methane being left for feedstock and other domestic uses. Industry sources assure us that the whole gas-gathering scheme should produce a 10-11 per cent per annum return on investment providing the LPGs really do find adequate export markets. If they do not find such markets (and competition from other Gulf producers already exists), then the economics of the whole scheme look more dubious.

A second consideration is that there are alternative uses to which gases can be put, and these may well give a higher return to the national economy. The mere fact that the 'net-back' value of gases is only about a quarter of the value of crude oil indicates very forcibly that one extremely profitable way of using gas is to substitute it for oil usage in the domestic economy. It may seem relatively unglamorous to free crude oil for exports by burning gas to generate electricity, fuel de-salination plants or power pipelines, but it is good development economics. Then, as we have mentioned in the Iranian chapter, some countries have the option of re-injecting the gas into aging oil fields to prolong their productive life (the Saudis use sea water for most of their injection purposes).

So, as far as gas-pricing is concerned, the picture seems reasonably clear. Ignoring the alternative uses for gas within the region, gas is a relatively low-value product when exported from the Middle East. There is, therefore, a strong initial case for overcoming the transportation difficulty by taking gas-processing industries to the gas supplies. This is, after all, what happened within the United States; the petrochemical industry has increasingly centred round the gas-producing states, which have been able to provide cheaper feedstocks than have been available elsewhere in the country.

What is less clear is how far a Middle Eastern chemicals producer could drop the price of gas feedstocks before it would lay itself open to charges of 'unfair' trading practices. Certainly, the OECD world has lived with differential feedstock prices in the past without making them a 'dumping' issue. US gas prices, for instance, have been low by European standards since the 1973-74 oil price rises. This has undoubtedly given the US petrochemical industry a competitive advantage over the European industry, but has not been used as a justification for putting up trade barriers against US products. What might raise eyebrows and, eventually, some form of protectionist measures within the OECD world, would be if gas feedstocks were offered to Middle Eastern petrochemical ventures at prices well below either the 'net-back' value of the gas in its exportable forms, or below the level which would give a positive return on the investment needed to gather the gas. This is why commentators from the industrialised world tend to be somewhat equivocal when they hear of projects running on gas priced at under 10 cents a million BTU. They feel that such pricing starts to be 'unfair', and will only be reassured where they see gas prices firmly related to alternative use values.

So far, this discussion has been about gas pricing, but the situation seems to be rather different as far as refineries are concerned. Here, there seems to be a clear understanding that no oil-producing government plans to make refineries profitable by feeding them crude oil at subsidised prices. In contrast with gas (whose true market value has been difficult to determine), no member of OPEC can forget for a moment the precise world price for crude oil. All producer governments are aware of pressures on them to cut this price by subtle manoeuvres, such as varying the length of time for which buyers are given credit. They will then continue to resist using crude prices to increase the viability of refining ventures. This is a matter of communal self-interest but such resistance is probably reinforced by the fact that they know quite a lot about refining technology and are confident that they can go it alone in refining if the international companies choose not to co-operate.

In short, then, it is the availability of cheap gas which is of prime importance to the future viability of petrochemical industries based in the Middle East. What is not yet clear is the extent to which the disadvantages of various locations outweigh this one very substantial, positive factor favouring the region. Although the rest of this chapter will suggest that the disadvantages will generally dominate, it is by no means impossible for some of the first, major gas-based projects to prove viable, given the twin advantages of cheap feedstocks and capital.

Cheap capital

The second major comparative advantage that capital-intensive projects may have in the Middle East is access to extremely cheap capital. In the Saudi case which we discussed earlier, the foreign partners will be able to raise 60 per cent of their share of the overall investment at 3-6 per cent per annum. This figure is well below the rates charged within international markets, falls considerably below the most competitive rates (7½ per cent per annum) which the OECD nations will allow each other to charge for export credits and, in view of the likely inflation rates, probably represents a negative interest in real terms.[6] This means that the foreign partners in a $1 billion Saudi venture will save somewhere around $8-16 million per annum in interest payments on their share of the investment. Given that they would be expecting to earn around $25 million a year in post-tax profits to give them an adequate 15 per cent per annum return on equity, the savings on interest could boost their return on equity by 5-10 per cent.

It is however, difficult to know exactly how weighty this cheap capital factor is, for Saudi Arabia is the only oil-producing country we know of which is giving such an open incentive. In addition, the Kingdom is one of the very few oil producers which is going to have the financial strength to continue offering such incentives in the future (Kuwait could obviously do so, but is not so much concerned with industrialising at all costs). So, although less prosperous governments may find themselves subsidising export ventures for purely short-term reasons, it is really only Saudi Arabia and some of the other Gulf States which are capable of considering substantial capital subsidies as a long-term strategy.

'Unfair' subsidies?

Undoubtedly, there is a school of thought in the West which argues that cheap gas and capital provide an unfair advantage to Middle Eastern-based plants. It is, therefore, important to identify what is 'fair' or 'unfair' about such practices.

Middle Easterners correctly argue that practically all developed countries encourage their own industries by devices such as investment grants, subsidised infrastructure, tax holidays or free depreciation. They also respond to attacks on their cheap capital policies, by pointing to European companies such as Montedison, CdF Chimie, British Steel and the various French steel companies which are only kept going by government money provided at zero or negative interest rates. They feel, therefore, that where one of their members such as Saudi Arabia has spare capital, there is nothing particularly wrong in lending it cheaply to potential foreign partners.

As far as the feedstock prices are concerned, they point to the fact that associated gas is flared at the wellhead in vast quantities, and they argue that collecting it and adding value to it can hardly, therefore, be counted as an unfair practice. Anyway, the Middle Easterners are well aware of Western examples, such as the way the US petrochemical industry benefits from domestic oil and gas prices which have been administratively kept below those found in competing regions such as West Europe. Then again, the Bahrain aluminium smelter can be considered as a direct parallel to the two smelters in the UK, which have been supplied with electrical power at heavily subsidised rates to permit them to compete with Norwegian plants based on hydroelectricity.

On the whole, the Middle Easterners' defence is convincing, but they still do have to be careful. The chief development they should watch is the growing determination of the United States and some of the other leading industrial powers to start reducing some of the worst non-tariff distortions in trade and investment. Hence, for instance, the OECD code on export credits, and the fact that a significant part of the GATT's Multilateral Trade Negotiations has centred on the development of a code on subsidies, aiming in particular at export subsidies.

The Saudis should be able to avoid most trouble by showing that it is not only exporters who have access to cheap loans. Again, they should be able to show that their gas is fed into domestically oriented plants at equivalently cheap rates. In neither case are exports being specifically singled out for special treatment. In the case of gas, though, they should obviously watch for the fact that, as the 'net-back' value of LNG rises (and it seems to be so doing), there could come a time when the price of ethane used as a petrochemical feedstock falls well behind its price in alternative usages. They could then come in for criticism from abroad. In the case of their US markets, any Middle Eastern government offering the kinds of incentives found in Saudi Arabia, may well fall foul of the US Trade Act which requires the American government to countervail against any government subsidy — whether directly on exports or on domestically-oriented production — which significantly affects sales to the US. No show of injury to US industry is necessary, and it strikes us that the Middle Easterners' subsidies are extremely visible, and therefore vulnerable, to attack through the provisions of this Trade Act. One commentator on the original draft of this book has suggested that the leading oil producers could subscribe to the subsidies code which emerges from Geneva, since it would force importing countries seeking to countervail against internal subsidies to prove that injury has been done before acting.

Market prospects: a bad time to invest?

As this chapter progresses, we shall see that there are a number of factors working against the economic viability of Middle Eastern export ventures, but that most of these will be of relatively minor importance as the years go by. There is, however, one overwhelming short-term factor which augurs ill for their profitability, and that is the extremely depressed market forecast which now extends well into the 1980s. It is as though the oil revolution, which has given the oil producers the money and confidence to seek entry into hydrocarbon-processing industries, has simultaneously so changed the economics of these industries that there is, paradoxically, minimal room for new entrants.

Discounting the oil price rises of the early 1970s, the chemical industry was already slowing down in relative terms. Its growth rates since World War II had been extremely high compared with all other major industries. In every five-year period since 1960, however, there had been a fall of at least 1 percentage point in the annual growth rate of overall chemical production in the OECD world — a clear sign that the industry was maturing. (See table 6.1).

Table 6.1
Chemical growth-rates in the OECD world

Years	Growth rates p.a.
1960-65	9.5%
1965-70	8.5%
1970-75	3.5%
(1970-73	7.5%)

Source: Burchell, 1977, p.7.

What has happened since 1973 is that world economic growth has been slowed down by the interaction of fears over inflation and the deflationary impact of oil price rises. At the same time, the fact that the average price of a bulk petrochemical such as benzene is now three times what it was in the early 1970s[7] means that the relationship of chemical demand to GNP growth has been entirely changed. Instead of being two times GNP growth, the chemical multiplier has now fallen to around 1.3-1.4.[8] The relative slowness with which many OECD-based companies realised that the chemical world had permanently changed resulted in the creation of chronic amounts of over-capacity which may well last, in some regions and for some products, throughout the whole of the 1980s. As far as Western Europe is concerned, Bayer Company's chairman has argued at an OPEC seminar that capacity either available or under construction will be enough to satisfy European demand to 1990 (see figure 6.1) for ethylene, both the polyethylenes, polypropylene and ethylene oxide; only in the case of benzene and vinyl chloride might there be room for some slight increase in capacity by 1990.[9] This will inevitably play havoc with the market prospects of the Middle Eastern projects which are under consideration.

It is only fair to point out that there are Middle Easterners who would dispute this pessimism. One Middle Eastern source has cast doubt on whether the chemical multiplier has really changed. In the case of ethylene, which has been relatively unaffected by the problems of the synthetic fibre sector and which is thus a good indicator of the general health of the chemicals industry, the correlation between ethylene production and the Index of Industrial Production (IIP) was maintained throughout 1975 and the partial recovery seen in 1976. There is also a feeling that the Germans are notoriously pessimistic, their gloom having been displayed and subsequently disproved once before in 1970-71. Again, the Middle Easterners argue, much of the supposed change in the correlation between petrochemical demand and GNP (or IIP) is a matter of industrial forecasting, rather than of strict analysis of what has happened since 1973. Certainly, the Middle Easterners are right to suggest that depressed market conditions, such as those we have recently experienced, inevitably trigger depressing forecasts which may well be scrapped as economic growth rates pick up again. We concede, for instance, that the Germans are starting to become more confident, though this merely means that they are now expecting chemical growth rates to run at around 4 per cent per annum. This is still well below the 7.5 per cent figures seen in the 1970-73 period.

Our Middle Eastern source has also argued that not all markets are as depressed as the West European one. The US market, for instance, should be in balance for most products by the mid-1980s, if not before (though the US is not the easiest market to tackle from the Middle East). Secondly, there are the LDCs, whose growth rates are far faster than those of the OECD world, thus promising small, but rapidly expanding markets, relative to which the Middle East is well located.

The feedstock advantages which the Middle Easterners have only

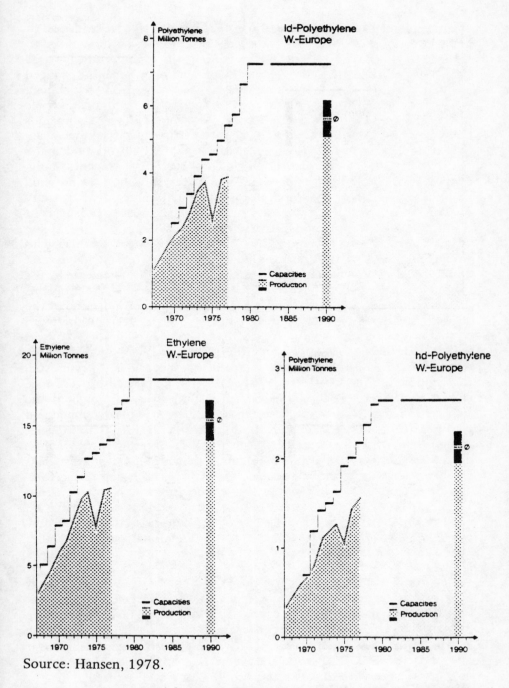

Source: Hansen, 1978.

Figure 6.1 Present and future petrochemical capacities in Western Europe

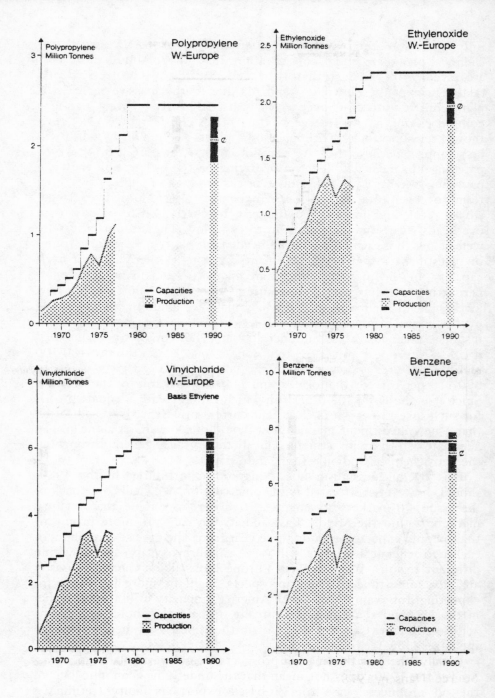

Figure 6.1 continued

Source: Hansen, 1978

fully come into their own when alternative locations for new petrochemical plants are under consideration. Instead the Middle Easterners
are faced with the fact that their new, world-scale projects will be
relatively expensive by past standards due to the massive increase of
plant construction costs over recent years. To justify building such new
complexes one has to foresee product prices considerably higher than
those prevailing today. Although some plants in the OECD world will
be scrapped, because they are now so old that they are just not worth
patching up, most will keep on operating on the assumption they can
pay their way as long as product prices are high enough in the short
term to cover total out-of-pocket expenses (wages, local taxes, feedstocks, etc), and in the medium term to cover a share of corporate
overheads with some contribution to cash flow. These 'floor' prices are
well below those which would be needed to justify a major new round
of investment in petrochemical plants. As long as there is major over-
capacity in the industry, prices are likely to remain as at present,
permitting existing plants to continue to operate, but making new
investment difficult to justify. A new plant for ammonia (which is one
of the more promising chemical sectors for gas-rich countries), for
instance, planned to become operative in 1980, could only be justified
if US and European prices rise to around $200-220 per ton or $180-200
per ton for urea. Spot prices in the autumn of 1978 were closer to
$90-110 per ton for the former, and $110-130 per ton for the latter. [10]
Since it is the last $30-40 per ton which would create adequate profits
for such investments, it is clear that current prices give little indication
that a new investment planned now would break even, let alone give an
adequate return on investment. This picture is fairly general throughout
the petrochemical and oil refining industries.

This overall pessimism about market opportunities in the 1980s
should, however, be treated with some caution. We shall come back to
the issue of markets in chapter 10, where we argue that regional
markets within the Middle East and its environs are more promising
than people expected two or three years ago. The precise economics of
each petrochemical product will vary, as will market prospects within
different regions. Whereas West Europe looks like a chemical disaster
area for some time to come, prospects might be more promising for
exporting, for example, to North America. Capacity utilisation is higher
in the US, and some companies really do have the choice of building
additional plants either at home or in the Middle East, benefiting from
the latter's low feedstock prices.

Finally, the fact that market prospects are not particularly encouraging for the 1980s does not mean that the underlying economic logic of
the oil producers' case for gas-based exports is faulty (refining is
another matter). Virtually anything which can be done to convert

ethane into chemicals will give lower-per-unit transport costs compared to liquefying that ethane for export. Thus, efficiently planned and operated ethane-based petrochemical industry should give a better financial return than the straight export of ethane, particularly since the price for petrochemicals is, in general, proportionally higher than that for gases, such as ethane, used as a source of energy. We would accept the argument that, in theory, gas-based petrochemical industries in the Middle East should improve a country's returns on its ethane (though we shall show how such further processing may lead to negative returns). On the other hand, we are not convinced that converting ethane to petrochemical products is the complete answer. For one thing, the volumes of chemicals required in world markets will not be sufficient to absorb a particularly large proportion of all the ethane available in the Middle East. Secondly, as long as there are no major developments in transportation technologies, using ethane within local economies will release more crude oil for export and thus almost inevitably give a country better economic returns than it would receive from creating a petrochemical industry.

High capital costs

One reason why the economics of the first generation of major plants in the Middle East remain problematical is that it is proportionally very expensive to build such plants in the region. We heard one potential foreign partner of the Saudis quite blithely admit that the 'investment premium' for building in Saudi Arabia is at least 100 per cent over the costs of locating a similar plant on the US Gulf Coast. We have also heard both expatriates and natives of Iran making similar claims about the costs of building refineries and petrochemical complexes in that country. One must, however, be somewhat cautious about analysing such arguments, for people are not always talking about the same things. Sometimes they may be comparing identical facilities in 1978 money. At other times, they may be comparing facilities required in different locations to produce the same annual quantity of product, or allowing for forecast differential inflation rates between the two countries, or even including infrastructure costs in the remote location. We believe it is necessary to break these variables down into their separate components.

Actually, the Middle East has some attractions for contractors. For one thing, the industry is probably now more used to problems of heat than to those of cold — bad weather and deep water causing problems in locations such as Alaska or the North Sea. Secondly, construction in the Middle East is possible all year round, which is not always true elsewhere (even though the holy month of Ramadan can cause problems in the Middle East). Then, again, one's labour force is generally well disciplined and pretty docile (though it will be interesting to see how Iranian labour unrest affects its industrial ambitions). Finally, it is genuinely possible to buy equipment and material in world markets, and one can play suppliers from Japan, Europe and North America off against each other more aggressively than if one is building in only one of these markets.

Despite this, we have heard no convincing argument that Middle Eastern plant construction costs can be less than 35 per cent above US Gulf Coast costs by the mid-1980s, and there are plenty of people who are very doubtful that this goal can be reached. The extra costs come from some necessary redesigning for Middle Eastern conditions, greater distances from suppliers, the lack of a pre-existing industrial infrastructure (e.g. hiring equipment is expensive; road and rail facilities may be primitive). Usually there are relatively high expatriate wage bills, although expensive managers can be balanced by relatively cheap unskilled imported workers, which is more true of Saudi Arabia than Iran, which has rather more local nationals to employ. There are straight managerial problems stemming from the fact that each project is like 'a mini-Kuwait' (in one of the earlier Saudi industrial ventures, eleven different nationalities were involved, including two South Africans, one Afrikaans and one English-speaking, who refused to talk to each other), and from the relative inefficiency of project management, since North American, West European and Japanese companies have considerable difficulty in persuading their best managers to work in the Middle East. One of the few hard studies[11] which have been done of such factors is drawing on Aramco's experience with large construction projects in Saudi Arabia. It argues that project costs there run some two-thirds above those of similar plants on the US Gulf Coast. We have also heard it forcibly argued by planners close to the Saudi authorities that the Aramco figures overstate the case, because Aramco has never had to be tough in controlling costs, and put a high 'contingency factor' into these calculations.

In any case, the coastal-based petrochemical and refining ventures which interest us are well placed to benefit from the use of modular prefabrication, by which large parts of the plants are actually constructed abroad in order to reduce the complexity of on-site construction, and of barge-mounted construction, whereby a trench is excavated by the side of the sea, and entire plants are floated in and then cemented into the desert. It is not yet realistic to think of barge-mounted construction for an ethylene complex, but modular construction has already been successfully used in the building of the Jeddah (Lubref) refinery in which Mobil has a share.[12] Interest is, however, growing in floating plants, along the lines of the two Japanese-built pulp and power plant platforms which have been floated across the world to the Amazon. The Iranians were seriously considering having part of the Kalingas project depend on a Norwegian-built floating LNG plant.

A second factor which will heavily influence overall construction costs is the length of time that construction actually takes. We have argued above that the Middle East is not an overwhelmingly difficult area in which to build, but the general impression left with us by people close to the various ventures is that they expect plant construction in the Middle East to take at least some 25-30 per cent longer than on the US Gulf Coast. Once again, this adds to the costs and is particularly important because any analysis of the viability of such projects is very sensitive to delays in financial returns (although, if the foreign partners receive loans at 3 per cent, and inflation runs at, for example, 7 per cent, delays may not bother them very much). It must be admitted, however, that the timely completion of large plants has not been a noticeable feat in developed countries either; Britain is perhaps the most notorious of several countries with poor industrial work records.

There is one further cost factor with which we have been unable to come to proper grips. This is in the area of corruption and legal payments to agents in the form of commissions and expediting payments. These are relatively hidden costs which are not peculiarly 'Middle Eastern', but we have heard one extremely distinguished US consultant arguing that the scale of rake-offs in the region is possibly the prime factor rendering these projects uncompetitive. This strikes us as very unlikely, but we really do not know the answer. Whatever the corruption angle (and one source assures us that the chemical sector is clean in Saudi Arabia), the foreign partners do not need to go through agents, but can deal directly with the government or enter into partnerships. In Iran, the National Petrochemical Company was under investigation for corrupt practices during the Shah's last months in Teheran, but then so was virtually every other ministry and government agency at that time. At one end of the spectrum, we have heard middle-ranking western businessmen suggesting that legal and illegal expediting payments may add 10-15 per cent to the costs of Iranian plant construction projects, and 20-25 per cent in the case of Saudi ones — but the charges have been extremely non-specific. At the other end, we have heard local officials denying that anything like this happens. We remain as confused on this issue at the end of our research as we were in the beginning.

All told then, the picture is one of quite high construction costs. Companies know very well that this is the most important single area over which they have more or less direct control. Interest rates are out of their hands but, once settled, can be taken for granted; market conditions in the 1980s can be predicted, but cannot be influenced by any one company. Construction, though, will generally be in the hands of the foreign partners and, if they allow construction costs to escalate or completion dates to slip, this will have a major impact on the ultimate profitability of the relevant project.

Operating costs and capacity utilisation

Once such plants are constructed, there are one or two other factors which will make day-to-day operations relatively expensive. Firstly, the proportion of expatriate workers will still be relatively high. The IJPC plant in Iran, for instance, will still need 10 per cent of its labour force to be Japanese. The Saudis are unlikely to be able to keep the proportions down to anywhere near that figure. Saudi sources have suggested to us that the capital-intensive plants being built will need at least 65 per cent expatriate labour, 15 per cent of that being of the expensive, 'Western' variety. Even Aramco, which has been in Saudi Arabia for well over 30 years, can only hope to eventually push the number of its Saudi employees (now slightly over 50 per cent) up to 75-80 per cent of the 29,000 work force. Obviously, it will be possible to replace many of the expensive 'Western' expatriates with cheaper, qualified ones from other countries such as Egypt, India and Pakistan. However, there are limits as to how fast this can be done. The more complex the plants under consideration, the more the experience of the labour force matters. A 25-year-old Middle Eastern PhD in petrochemical engineering may come much cheaper than a 45-year-old Texan, but the latter has grown up amidst refineries and chemical plants, while the 25-year-old has still to gain his practical experience. Obviously, this argument cannot be pushed too hard with simpler technologies, but the more complex the technology, the more difficult it will be to get rid of the 'Western' expatriates who are very expensive by US or some European standards (although not necessarily so by German or Scandinavian levels).

A rather more important factor is the exact level of capacity utilisation which will be achieved by Middle Eastern plants once they are in operation. It is generally assumed that they will tend to run at rates below those of equivalent plants in the OECD world. In the autumn of 1977, for instance, a task force working within the Euro-Arab Dialogue made the assumption that petrochemical production in Arab countries would be 75 per cent of the potential production rate, compared with 87.5 per cent for the OECD world.

This is, of course, a difficult case to sustain at a time when much of the world's refining and petrochemical industry is operating well below capacity; for instance, in 1977, OPEC's refining industry was running at 77 per cent of capacity,[13] which was better than the performance of parts of the OECD industry, notably in Rotterdam and Italy. There are, however, two parts to this argument. Firstly (and we shall come back to this), any plant which cannot find markets for the full range of its products will inevitably find that its economic viability will suffer — and the over-capacity plaguing much of the world's refining and petrochemical industries is of this lack-of-markets variety. There is a second type of capacity utilisation problem stemming from the fact that some plants suffer a relatively high proportion of technical problems requiring shut-downs, be it for routine maintenance or for emergencies. New plants everywhere have problems and the Middle Eastern evidence is incidental, rather than conclusive. One remembers Saudi Arabia's first venture into fertiliser production, SAFCO, which ran for the first years of its life at 30-40 per cent of its rated capacity, because of design inadequacies, but is now running effectively and is finding regional export markets. One thinks also of the destruction by fire of Qatar's NGL plant at Umm Said; the 1977 electricity supply disruption in Iran which led to industrial shut-downs and the worse troubles in late 1978 and early 1979; the Libyan methanol plant which cannot run at full capacity until its port is dredged and adequate storage facilities are added; or the Algerian ldPE plant which waited some 18 months for a related ethylene cracker to come into operation, only to have teething problems when the ethylene plant finally was ready.[14]

Clearly, many of these problems are temporary, and it is debatable whether they are any worse than similar ones suffered by European projects (Middle Easterners point to BP's Baglan Bay complex, the Petrochim olefins plant in Belgium and the Gulf cracker at Rotterdam as having had serious problems). Much of this is a matter of degree, but we are almost certain that it will be relatively harder to keep Middle Eastern plants running consistently close to optimum productive capacity than European ones. There is nothing disgraceful in this. It merely reflects that we are dealing with rapidly industrialising countries, with badly stretched infrastructures and a shortage of technically experienced workers. The Saudis believe they can get round such problems by entering into partnerships with leading western companies. In addition, some insurance against inadequate maintenance can be achieved by 'platinum-plating' the plants — i.e. building in a relatively high degree of redundancy so that a plant is never dependent, for example, on the functioning of a single compressor. On the other hand, the more that is spent on this, the more expensive construction costs will be, thus involving one of those difficult choices between spending more money at the construction stage or losing more money in high operating costs when operations begin.

Transportation costs

Because of the Middle East's location, well removed from key North American and Japanese markets, it is inevitable that transport costs will be important. Ever since the Second World War, the overwhelming consensus within the oil and chemical industries has been to locate refineries and petrochemical plants close to end-markets, and not close to sources of raw materials. Technology has been developed to permit this. What the Middle Easterners would like to do is to reverse the judgement of this consensus, but it is by no means clear that transportation economics will permit such a change. Certainly, in the case of refining, there is a strong economic case for continuing to export crude, rather than refined products, to end-markets. This will continue to be true until technology reverses the economics of the VLCC/ULCCs in favour of huge product tankers, and regular markets develop for large quantities of imports of individual products. It is only in the petrochemical industry that we feel the present transportation case is not critical.

Transport and refined oil

The case against Middle Eastern export refineries which look towards North America and Japan for their markets can be put simply: in an industry where a comfortable refiner's margin may be 35 cents a barrel, it is very difficult to see how the costs of shipping refined products over such distances will be less than the costs of shipping crude oil, which are now $1 a barrel. It is equally difficult to see how a Middle Eastern refinery could be built so much cheaper than an equivalent one in US or Japanese markets that this $1 per barrel handicap could be overcome. If Middle Eastern refineries are to be competitive, they will be so by supplying markets (i.e. in the immediate Middle Eastern and Indian Ocean region) where they have a transportation advantage over established OECD refineries; by feeding such refineries with crude at a price discount; or by taking advantage of tight oil markets to insist that consumers will be supplied with no oil at all, unless they take oil products as well as crude.

Our Middle Eastern readers will doubtless find this pessimistic, but the logic of this particular case seems watertight, at least until technology can be adapted to reverse the shipping economics spoken of earlier. Crude oil is relatively inert and can be refined in large volumes, thus making it suitable to be transported to refineries in the 300-400,000 ton super-tankers which are so much part of the world scene. Oil products are generally (but not universally) more volatile than crude (though this is not a major factor in raising their transport costs), and also need more complicated tankers which are designed to carry a range of products in separate tanks. Because of this need for product segregation, such vessels are, for any given size, more expensive than crude tankers with no such need. In addition, there are considerations which limit the size of product carriers, thus denying them the full benefit of the scale economies enjoyed by their competitors in crude oil. For one thing, there is a 'chicken or egg' situation regarding the lack of specialised terminals to receive and store oil products in large quantities. Secondly, the larger the product carrier, the more vulnerable it will be to the fickleness of the oil products market, which may reverse the relative profitability of the different products during the course of a three or four-week voyage.

For all these reasons, it seems unlikely that the transport differentials between crude and refined oil will be closed by the latter half of the 1980s. The most optimistic forecast we have seen is that the development of 120,000 ton VLPCs (Very Large Product Carriers) using the Suez Canal might reduce the price differential with crude oil transported in giant tankers (to the US East Coast via the Cape of Good Hope) to around 30 cents a barrel — but this is still high by refining standards.[15]

All told, then, the economics of Middle Eastern refining ventures are not very promising. The US market, for instance, will always be more profitably supplied by products from, for example, European refineries processing North Sea oil, or from Caribbean ones using Middle Eastern crude. Some of the transport disadvantages might be overcome by developing Very Large Product Carriers and the respective storage and handling facilities at both ends. Consideration might also be given to a concept formulated by P.H. Frankel and W.L. Newton: it is based on the idea of carrying out, at the traditional crude oil loading points, the processes of cracking, viscosity reduction and desulphurisation, making use of low-cost natural gas, and supplying to oil-importing countries a range of made-to-measure feedstocks. Such a procedure, far from increasing costs, might actually provide cost savings. The need for excessive investment in desulphurisation and conversion plants in receiving refineries and the expected difficulties in disposing of heavy crude would be obviated.

In general, though, Middle Eastern refineries will only become a worldwide force if they are subsidised, or if the oil market moves so strongly in favour of the oil producers that they can dictate the form in which the consuming world takes its oil.

The transport of petrochemicals

Transportation economics matter far less for gas-based petrochemical industries, for here the criterion is not crude oil transport costs, but the very much higher ones for exporting gas by pipeline or liquefaction. Virtually any processing of gas can bring transport costs per unit down below those for liquefied natural gas. Thus there is a fundamental difference between this and the refined oil case. With oil products, the best one can hope for from efficient technology is to bring transport costs down towards those of crude oil. With gas-based products, greater efficiency should merely increase the gains as transport of chemical products becomes relatively cheaper than that of LNG. However, it should be noted that gas transport costs would be reduced with the development of transportation systems that permitted LNG and the LPGs to be shipped as a single cargo.

At the moment, the industry works on the assumption that LNG costs some 6-8 times as much to transport as crude oil, while ammonia, LPG and cryogenic ethylene will only be some 3-4 times as expensive as crude. A further rule of thumb is that transporting intermediate chemical products from the Gulf to West Europe will be about half the cost of shipping them to North America or Japan (though this last point has been disputed by Saudi sources).

Because of the relative high value of chemical products compared with crude oil (benzene is currently selling at a price-per-ton which is three times that for crude oil), transportation costs are unlikely to be a make-or-break factor for Middle Eastern ventures. US Shell, for instance, is apparently quite happy about the prospect of using a new generation of larger carriers to ship styrene from its Saudi ventures back to the United States. It should be noted, however, that regular shipments of chemical products over this sort of distance are still very rare. Some quantities of products such as benzene, styrene, butadiene, ammonia and the xylenes are regularly shipped across the Atlantic. Within Europe, ICI sometimes ships the more complicated ethylene (it needs refrigeration) across the North Sea to its plant in the Netherlands. There is also a limited number of regular 'parcel' runs from Europe and North America to South Africa, and from practically anywhere to Japan.

This is a picture of a trading structure which is still relatively underdeveloped, and this must pose constraints for would-be exporters from the Middle East or North Africa. For one thing, creating a trade in chemical and refined oil products will call for quite substantive downstream investment in specialised import terminals, product storage facilities and pipelines. Doubtless this infrastructure will develop, but it will be a slow process and, until it takes place, the Middle Eastern exporters will lack a lot of the commercial flexibility they have in the crude oil trade. The Saudis claim that the products they are planning are already traded on a large scale, and that for most of the liquid products export/import terminals are well established in both Europe and the USA. Secondly, chemicals are unlike oil and gas which can always find markets providing their prices are competitive with those of other fuels. The more one moves into the chemical products area, the more non-price factors, such as quality, availability of technical services and reliability of supplies, determine whether the products sell. In particular, OECD-based chemical producers have traditionally taken their supplies of basic feedstocks under rigid, long-term supply agreements, and the Middle Easterners are going to have to prove their reliability before established chemical companies will use them as major suppliers. We have been left by European companies with the impression that, when the first major Middle Eastern petrochemical products become available, they will consider taking about 10 per cent of their feedstocks from these new suppliers, but will only expand this proportion if the Middle Easterners prove reliable.

Tariffs

Tariffs imposed on Middle Eastern chemical products are not as important as some of the other variables we have been considering (such as interest rates or overall market conditions), but variations will still produce up to a 5 per cent fluctuation in the results of Return on Investment calculations. However, tariff issues are extremely complex, made even more so by the fact that chemical tariffs are at the heart of the final stages of the GATT Multilateral Trade Negotiations, and have not been resolved as we finish this book. US tariffs on refined oil products range from ½ to 6 per cent, whereas for petrochemical products, those which fall under the notorious American Selling Price system, can have effective rates of 15-20 per cent. In the case of refined oil product imports into the EC, rates are either 3½ or 6 per cent, and most petrochemical products qualify for tariffs also around the 6 per cent mark. However, there are various non-tariff fees in the EC, such as border taxes varying from country to country within the EC, which can make markets there as costly to penetrate as the US one. The Japanese tariffs on products such as ethylene, propylene and vinyl chloride are around 8 per cent — again before any reductions are agreed on in the GATT negotiations.

It looks as though the reduced tariffs on petrochemical and refined products will settle at levels which will be enough to swing the ultimate viability of a project by some two or three percentage points in Return on Investment calculations.[16] However, in the case of the EC, there is the fact that the North Africans will not only generally benefit from having relatively short transport links with the EC markets, but will also (if present agreements remain liberal) be able to send their products tariff-free. Their Middle Eastern competitors are thus doubly handicapped. The difference in the overall rates of return may be quite small, but in projects as finely balanced as these are likely to be, the fall may be just enough to deter decision-makers from going ahead.

Finally, even if tariffs are not a make-or-break factor, they pose one particular problem. Most of the other variables we have discussed in this chapter can either be tied down in advance under the terms of the eventual joint-venture agreements, or can be foreseen since they are primarily controlled by market forces. In the case of tariffs, decision-makers may have to give the go-ahead for Middle Eastern projects without any firm guarantees as to what will happen to relevant tariffs in the years to come. It is tempting to assume that these barriers will inevitably fall, but this is by no means assured — just as there is no guarantee that vested OECD interests might not put up non-tariff trade barriers against Middle Eastern products, as they have against textiles, shoes and steel products from other Third World countries. Of course, Saudi Arabia's oil production should give it massive leverage over would-be protectionists, but in the arcane world of trade diplomacy, forces favouring the *status quo* normally have the whip-hand over those wanting further liberalisation.

Planning delays and environmentalist issues

It would be unfair to say that the Middle Eastern countries want to become 'dirt havens', i.e. countries which are willing to accept polluting plants. Saudi standards are generally based on those applying in the US, while the Shah brought in regulations to protect historic cities from too much industrialisation. On the other hand, the steady tightening of environmental controls on the oil and chemical industries within the OECD world has increased the attraction for companies of investing outside the OECD. Since the passing of the 1969 National Environmental Policy Act in the United States, there has been considerable lengthening in the time needed to obtain approval for any major industrial venture. These new US policies have led to numerous protests from industry, such as the one in 1977 when Dow Chemical dropped proposals for a new petrochemical complex near San Francisco, arguing that it had spent 2½ years and $4 million to obtain only 4 out of the 65 permits needed before construction could begin (we have heard doubts expressed about the extent to which changed market forecasts may have influenced this decision). Within West Europe, it is becoming more and more difficult to build industrial plants along the Rhine and, although a Mediterranean Pact to control pollution of this enclosed sea

95

has not yet emerged, it is clear that controls will have to come. Again, although EC attempts to develop a common environmental policy are stalled (Britain argues that standards for an exposed coastline like its Atlantic and North Sea ones do not have to be so restrictive as those needed for a non-tidal sea such as the Mediterranean), controls will inevitably be tightened.

As Du Pont President, Dr Edward Kane, has noted, any company investing on the basis of weak environmental laws is short-sighted, because the cost is merely delayed a couple of years.[17] On the other hand, relatively sparsely-populated countries such as Saudi Arabia and Iran may be able to take a slightly more relaxed view on aerial pollution — though the states bordering the Arabian/Persian Gulf are fully aware that this is another of the world's more enclosed stretches of water which must be positively protected from environmental deterioration. Even if Middle Eastern governments are fully aware of all the environmental issues, they are at least able to override any local environmental lobbies which, in the United States or Western Europe, are often powerful enough to consign planned projects to the dustbin, despite the wishes of the central government.

On the other hand, decision-making on industrial matters is now a slow business all around the world. Certainly, Middle Eastern bureaucracies are not known for their swiftness and, although deteriorating world market prospects explain a great deal, none of the cases which have concerned us in this study convinces us that this basic situation has changed. Therefore, although we sense that companies will get a much more understanding hearing on environmental issues in the Middle East than the West, we feel that companies would be foolish to cut spending on 'normal' pollution control. They would simply risk future bitter attacks from local policy-makers as the latter become more sensitive to these issues. Even if decisions can be taken more swiftly because of a lesser degree of current concern about such issues, general bureaucratic decision-making will remain a slow process. Thus the companies are not likely to save much money on plant design, nor much time at the planning stage.

Relative importance of differing variables

Hitherto we have avoided becoming bogged down in a statistical analysis of the various forces at play, for the simple reason that every product and market is different. It is quite possible that there are some commercially viable options open to the Middle Easterners, even if their immediate, overall prospects in product markets are far from encouraging. In order to get a clearer impression of the relative importance of the variables we have discussed in this chapter, however, we have tested the impact of various assumptions on two fictitious, gas-based ethylene crackers — one based on the US Gulf Coast, the other on the Persian/Arabian Gulf — and two, similarly located, methanol projects.

In searching for a legitimate way to analyse the issues, we decided to concentrate on a US-Saudi comparison. Partly, this is because we believe the use of foreign partners should mean that the costs of the Saudi projects will be as close to US Gulf Coast levels as is possible in the Middle East. Secondly, SABIC was kind enough to generate some comparative cost estimates for us, based on one basic assumption of our own — that the first round of such projects will cost some 50 per cent more than equivalent plants in the US. Their costings seem reasonable to London-based observers and, since we do not think any other Middle Eastern country is likely to out-perform the Saudis, we feel we are analysing the very strongest case that the Middle Easterners can make for their becoming fully competitive in world markets.

We need to make a few further points. For one thing, we shall be discussing the viability of these projects from two viewpoints: firstly, we shall look at the comparative economics of the projects as a whole to sort out whether Middle Eastern projects can be competitive; secondly, we look at the specific interests of the foreign partners, who have to make their own individual assessments of whether the terms offered give them an adequate return on equity for them to go ahead. For another thing, we have converted all figures into constant 1978 dollars which may cause some slight confusion. For instance, although we expect US petrochemical plants to be receiving their ethane feedstocks at around $3.80 per million BTU in the early 1980s, we have deflated that to $3.0 for the purposes of these calculations. The use of constant dollars means that we assume the foreign partners to be seeking a real rate of return on equity of 7-10 per cent per annum (in current terms, they are seeking 15 per cent post-tax, on the assumption that inflation remains around 8 per cent per annum). We also assume that the Saudis may implicitly be willing to accept no real returns on the first generation of plants, since in lending the foreign partners capital at 3-6 per cent, they are, in real terms, giving the money away in order to get these ventures built. It has also been felt useful to compare a wholly-owned US operation with a joint venture in the Middle East, to bring out the implications of the latter's gearing.

Finally, although SABIC provided the raw figures on which to base our comparisons, these are highly simplified cases, and it was we who dictated the assumption that there would be a 1.5 location factor for the Saudi projects. We have slightly modified some of the SABIC assumptions. We would stress that we alone are responsible for what we have done with the raw data; that the conclusions are ours alone; and that these cases should be used as illustrative examples, not as definitive judgements about the profitability of any specific project in real life.

The methanol projects

It is generally accepted that methanol manufacture is likely to show the maximum advantage to the Middle East, because it involves a relatively simple process, thus keeping unit capital costs down and giving maximum weight to the region's ability to capitalise on cheap feedstocks (in this case, methane). Although there are some worries about markets (it will prove a useful additive to gasoline if costs can be kept down), it is cheap to transport, using conventional non-cryogenic ships.

Under the simplified assumptions behind table 6.2B, the Middle Easterners can clearly justify a 'net-back' price for methanol around 40 per cent of that needed by a competitor seeking a 10 per cent real return from an American investment. This is an enormous difference and, given the relative cheapness of transporting methanol, the Saudis should have little difficulty with breaking into methanol markets all over the world.

The ethylene projects

Analysis of the ethylene projects gives very much the same picture. Once again, the Middle Easterners could probably accept a transfer price for ethylene as low as 40 per cent of that needed by competing US plants. What is more, should the Saudis manage to raise their prices above this level, their plants could become extremely profitable. Ethylene priced at $350 per tonne would give an American venture a 10 per cent real rate of return, but could give a Saudi one almost 20 per cent.

Many non-Saudis will be unhappy with these figures, arguing that they rest on very radical assumptions. For instance, the provision of cheap gas feedstocks to the Saudi projects is absolutely essential to their profitability; if ever this gas was charged at likely US rates, the Saudi Return on Investment would plummet to below 4 per cent per annum. Again, when arguing that the Saudis could accept transfer prices some 60 per cent below American ones, we assume that the Saudis would be willing to accept a nil rate of return in real terms (i.e. 5-8 per cent in nominal terms). However, if they should ever adopt profitability goals comparative to those of US competitors (10 per cent in real terms), they would have to keep transfer prices for the Saudi products within 30 per cent of American ones, thus leaving themselves with much less freedom to overcome their comparative disadvantages (transportation costs, tariffs, etc). In both the gas and capital cases, it thus appears that Saudi Arabia's apparently overwhelming competitive advantage stems from their accepting relatively low returns on their investments.

Then again, the above analysis is based on the static analysis of a single year's cost and profit situation. This gives no consideration to the time cost of money, thus weighting the calculations in the Saudis' favour, since one of our beliefs about the first major round of Middle Eastern plants is that they will be relatively costly and time-consuming to build. This means that Middle Eastern profits should be discounted properly to take into account that, initially, much more capital is involved than in the North American projects. In our chosen ethylene cases, the Middle Eastern profitability figures have to be reduced by at least 4 percentage points to reflect this time-cost-of-money factor. So, assuming the prices needed to give an American plant the desired 10 per cent Internal Rate of Return (IRR), the Middle Eastern plant generating the same transfer prices would be getting nearer a 15 per cent IRR than the 20 per cent Return on Investment indicated by the more static analysis of average costs and returns in a single year.

Further, unless Middle Eastern plants manage to tap some immensely profitable regional market, this 15 per cent Internal Rate of Return looks like the absolute maximum that any such ethylene complex could conceivably earn. All the odds are that they will earn considerably less, because there are a whole series of factors which will raise both their construction and operating costs, while reducing the transfer prices they can generate to levels well below those achievable in the US. In fact, one only has to postulate two simultaneous occurrences — e.g. if capital costs turn out to be double, and realised transfer prices run a quarter below those of American plants — and the profitability of the Middle Eastern plants would be virtually wiped out. Here is a checklist of the relative impact that a number of occurrences could have on the Middle Eastern IRR figures:

Charging likely US gas prices for feedstocks: any conceivable Middle Eastern profit is wiped out.

Realised transfer prices a quarter below US levels: IRR reduced some 7.5 percentage points.

Capital costs twice the American ones: 6 percentage points reduction.

Capital costs 75 per cent above American ones: 3.5 points.

Construction takes five years instead of the four years assumed for the Middle East: 3 points.

99

Middle Eastern inflation rates run 10 per cent above US ones during construction: 3 points.

Transfer prices 10 per cent below US levels: 2.5 points.

10 per cent fall in capacity utilisation rates: 2.5 points.

Feedstock prices double to 80 cents/million BTU: 2 points.

Middle Eastern inflation rates run 5 per cent above US ones during construction: 1.5 points.

The outcome of this is that Middle Eastern ventures are clearly very sensitive to their capital-intensity, to feedstock prices as well as to the exact prices they can realise in world markets. On the first issue it is absolutely clear that the cheap pricing of capital is essential if the first generation of Middle Eastern plants is to have the slightest chance of being competitive. Again, they are sensitive to inflation and delays in construction schedules. There is absolutely nothing that a company can do about the former factor, and no company involved in construction within the Middle East can be confident of controlling all the factors which may cause a plant to be completed a year or so late. On realisable prices, the Middle Easterners are, once more, not completely in control of their destiny. Shipping costs will vary considerably over the years but will tend to be relatively costly as products become proportionally more expensive than crude oil. There are individual tariff barriers which mean they will have to completely forego some markets, and the likely future of certain chemical tariffs may be the key to whether various projects will go ahead or not. Finally, if these projects are properly discounted over the length of their operational lives, there is no room for extensive price-cutting in order to penetrate depressed world markets. Each 10 per cent cut in prices below targeted levels will knock some 2½ per cent off these projects' returns — and very few of them will have margins wide enough to accept this as a long-term strategy.

Variable costs

Cheap feedstocks are a particularly important variable, although the difference between the 2 cents a million BTU being used for Iranian petrochemical ventures and the 35-50 cents being considered by the Saudis is only about 1.5 per cent on a project's Internal Rate of Return. On the other hand, we can see that cheap feedstocks could become extremely important once such projects are built. Throughout this book, we are arguing that there are non-economic reasons why more of these Middle Eastern projects will go ahead than are justified by strict economic analysis. OECD refiners and petrochemical producers who

100

accept this are then faced with the gloomy prospect that, once these projects are built, there will be a strong temptation to write off the initial investment and switch to marginal pricing. At this point, the Middle Easterners will have a strong competitive advantage for, depending on one's exact assumptions about non-feedstock operating costs, there is a real chance that there will be Middle Eastern projects with marginal costs of around $70 per ton, at a time when OECD competitors may have marginal costs of around $230 per ton. The latter companies, which will be working under rather more rigorous financial disciplines, will thus be extremely vulnerable to Middle Easterners who invest too optimistically within the next few years and then decide that plants must be kept operating at all costs. Should the Middle Easterners follow this strategy — however inadvertently — they must prepare themselves for likely protectionist action on the part of aggrieved competitors within the industrialised world.

The foreign partners

We should not forget that there are two different decision-makers who will decide whether the Saudi projects go ahead or not — as well as the Saudis themselves there are the foreign partners. Now, quite clearly, although the Saudis can consider investing in projects which barely cover their investment in real terms, the foreign partners must inevitably be looking for a real pre-tax return on equity of around 10 per cent, and the trick for the Saudis is to structure these projects' finances so that the foreign partners are motivated to go ahead, even if the return on the projects' overall investment remains low.

From the situation outlined in tables 6.2A and 6.2B it looks as though the Saudis should have achieved this feat. If these projects were ever to find nearby regional markets permitting the charging of ethylene prices equivalent to those needed to give an American investor his 10 per cent Return on Equity, the foreign partner in Saudi Arabia could be getting a ROE of approaching 50 per cent. Even if we make the more realistic assumption, that the partner will be happy getting 75 per cent of US prices, its ROE will still run over 20 per cent per annum. If one then adds oil entitlements into the equation, the foreign partners could do quite well out of such deals.

On the other hand, all the potential profit-reducing risks discussed earlier will affect the foreign partner as well as the Saudis, and one can identify a situation in which the realisable price for ethylene ranges between about $150 and $200 a tonne, thus making the projects unattractive to the partners, but conceivably still attractive to the Saudi authorities. In these circumstances, the Saudis might still be tempted to

Table 6.2A
Hypothetical Middle East projects compared with US Gulf

A Ethylene: 450,000 tonnes/yr from ethane (1978 prices)

Feedstock and fuel: 1.33 tonnes ethane/tonne ethylene at:
  Middle East: 40 cents/million BTU; $19.7/tonne.
  United States: $3.0/million BTU; $148/tonne.

Middle East project 1/3 Equity, 2/3 Loan; US project all Equity.

Middle East cases (a) analysis of case giving foreign partner a 10 per cent Return on Equity; (b) case giving Middle Eastern authorities 5 per cent Return on Investment; (c) case allowing Middle Eastern authorities to break even on their investment (all in real terms).

US $ million		(a)	M.E. (b)	(c)	US Gulf
Plant capital:	battery limits	250			180
	offsites	200			120
	Total	450			300
Preoperating costs		30			10
Working capital		10			20
Total investment		490			330
of which:	Equity	165			330
	Loan	325			—
Annual cost:	feedstock and fuel	12	12	12	90
	utilities	4	4	4	2
Other Plant costs		16	16	16	13
Interest at 5 per cent		16	—	—	—
Total cash costs		48	32	32	105
Depreciation (15 years)		32	32	32	21
10 per cent Return on Equity (pre-tax)		17	—	—	33
Desired Return on Investment		—	25	0	—
Total cost plus Return:	$m	97	89	64	159
	$/tonne	216	198	142	353

Table 6.2B

B Methanol: 2,000 tons/day (600,000 tonnes/year) from methane (1978 prices)

Feedstock and fuel: 35 million BTU/tonne at:
　　Middle East: 40 cents/million BTU.
　　United States: $3.0/million BTU.

Middle East project 1/3 Equity, 2/3 Loan; US project all Equity.

Middle East cases (a) 10 per cent ROE for foreign investor; (b) 5 per cent ROI for Middle Eastern authorities; (c) Middle Eastern authorities break even (all in real terms).

US $ million		(a)	M.E. (b)	(c)	US Gulf
Plant capital:	battery limit	120			90
	offsites	75			40
	Total	195			130
Preoperating costs		25			10
Working capital		10			20
Total investment		230			160
of which:	Equity	77			160
	Loan	153			—
Annual cost:	feedstock and fuel	8	8	8	63
	utilities	3	3	3	2
Other Plant costs		13	13	13	8
Interest at 5 per cent		8	—	—	—
Total cash costs		32	24	24	73
Depreciation (15 years)		14	14	14	9
10 per cent R.O.E. (pre-tax)		8	—	—	16
Desired Return on Investment		—	12	0	—
Total cost plus Return:	$m	54	50	38	98
	$/tonne	90	83	63	163

go on alone with the relevant projects.

Development

We have concentrated throughout this chapter on analysing whether Middle Eastern export-oriented ventures are likely to be economically 'viable' under varying conditions. A few final comments need to be made.

Firstly, we are fully aware of the argument that strict insistence on economic viability is but a way of trying to persuade Third World countries, such as the oil producers, that they are unable to establish any industries at all. We sympathise with this argument and we shall argue in a concluding chapter that the oil producers have a case for calling on the OECD world to give sympathetic treatment to a first round of 'infant' export industries in the refining and petrochemical sectors. However, we would be doing everyone a disservice if we glossed over the fact that these industries will need special treatment at the investment stage if they are to come close to being widely competitive with the OECD world. There is probably going to be a limit to the amount of imports various OECD countries will be willing to accept from projects set up in this way. The Middle Easterners will be deceiving themselves if they do not realise that the arguments used in this chapter will be used against them in the mid-1980s (if not earlier) as their product flows build up. 'Developmental' appeals may have a limited success. In general, though, they will have to defend the economic viability of their export-oriented ventures against much less sympathetic protagonists than us.

Secondly, the sheer capital-intensity of most of the proposed petrochemical projects starts to outweigh the apparent advantage the Middle Easterners have with their cheap gas. The result is that such a capital-intensive strategy looks less and less attractive to those thinking about the oil producers' wider development. In the likely absence of any significant economic returns from the first generation of export-oriented ventures, there is a strong case for choosing the far greater short-run returns of substituting gas for crude oil in their own domestic markets, thus increasing the exportable surplus of crude. In the more populous states of the area, job creation throughout the economy may need to be given greater priority than capital-intensive ventures that have relatively weak links with the rest of the economy and a moderately high need for expatriate workers.

Thirdly, there are those in the oil-producing world (particularly in Algeria and Iraq) who would argue that it is precisely because they are trying to maximise the 'developmental' impact of these high-technology ventures, that they will not be bound by the kind of 'First World' economic analysis found in this chapter. Certainly they want to find world markets for some of their products, but they would not put this so high on their list of priorities that they would bring in foreign partners to form export-oriented joint ventures. We have heard leading Iraqis argue at the OPEC Conference on Downstream Investment in October 1978, that joint ventures with foreigners slow down the learning process of indigenous managers and policy-makers — that short-term economic 'rationality' may lead to prolonged dependency on foreigners.

All we would reply to these observations is that we know that 'development' and the hard-nosed economic analysis in this chapter do not always go hand in hand. However, there are some final points which must be made. Firstly, whatever comparative advantage the oil producers may have from owning substantial oil and gas reserves, these are not yet enough to permit these countries to graduate into the same 'league' as petrochemical manufacturers and refined oil producers in OECD countries. As long as construction costs in the Middle East are significantly higher than those in the industrialised world, the oil producers will have to compensate by feeding in capital and gas feedstocks at levels which will reflect less and less their true costs.

Secondly, the industrialised world would be foolish to assume that Middle Eastern downstream investments are doomed to be uncompetitive with its own. The best-planned Saudi ventures, for instance, look as though they will be extremely competitive in Middle Eastern and Indian Ocean markets, as long as the Saudis accept low costs for key inputs. In fact, if they keep construction costs under control, they should prove competitive in limited product ranges within the West European, Japanese and American markets.

However, the main point of controversy between the two sides remains whether Middle Eastern pricing policies for gas and capital genuinely reflect costs. It is around this debate that all discussions about the competitiveness of the Middle Eastern plants must revolve.

Notes

1   *European Chemical News*, July 7 1978, p.6; July 21 1978, p.24.
2   Iranian sources.
3   *Middle East Annual Review, 1978*, p.163.
4   We have not done this calculation ourselves, but most people connected with the Saudi projects confirm a 'net-back' figure within this region. However, we have had one commentator who argues that this figure is much too low. Assuming that LNG can be substituted for fuel

oil you can get an equation like this:

Japanese fuel oil/crude:	$2.40 equivalent per million BTU.
LNG Regasification and terminal costs:	$0.35
LNG Shipping:	$0.47
Liquefaction:	$0.53
'Net-back' value ($2.40 -0.35 -0.47 -0.53):	$1.05

5   For instance, no.6 oil from Rotterdam was selling for $2.20 per million BTU in late 1978. At the same time, the UK was paying $2.30 for gas from the Norwegian sector, and LNG was landing at Wilhelmshaven at $2.45. Some would now argue that LNG should be priced in relation to naphtha, not fuel oil, reflecting the general convenience of LNG.

6   Cooper, 1978, p.109.

7   Hansen, 1978, table 15.

8   Eurofinance Study, cited *European Chemical News*, July 14 1978, p.34.

9   Hansen, 1978, pp 75-6.

10   Spitz, 1978, p.30.

11   Wallace, 1976.

12   *European Chemical News*, Survey, 'Storage and distribution', May 20 1978, pp 16-8.

13   OPEC, 1978, p.13.

14   *European Chemical News*, August 4 1978, p.10.

15   Department of Energy (US), 1978a, pp 92, 99, 108, 121.

16   As of October 1978, some effective US tariffs included ones around 21 per cent for Ethylene Dichloride, 15 per cent for VCM, 14 per cent for both High and Low Density Polyethylene, and 13 per cent for Ethylene Oxide. Calculated from *European Chemical News*, Chemscope, October 13 1978, p.62.

17   *Financial Times*, January 27 1977.

7 The issues for West Europe

If there is one market in the world to which Middle Eastern products must win access, it is the West European one. Cumulatively, Western Europe makes up the world's largest concentration of the chemical industry. Italian ports are some 30 per cent closer to the top of the Arabian/Persian Gulf than is a Japanese one like Yokohama — and 45 per cent closer than the East Coast of the US.[1] At the same time, European import policies have traditionally been rather liberal in contrast to the more obscure and mercantilist approach of the Japanese. If the Middle Easterners are not able to penetrate West European markets, they will have even greater difficulties elsewhere in the OECD world.

At the same time, though, the omens are not good. Quasi-protectionist attitudes and policies are found in Europe on a scale perhaps not attained since the 1930s. There are voices which are already warning of the coming industrial challenge from the Middle Eastern oil producers. There is absolutely no guarantee that these new industrial countries will be given free access to West European markets.

Structural problems

Why this defensiveness on the part of the Europeans? The heart of the problem stems from severe over-capacity in the West European refining and petrochemical industries, particularly since 1973 (see tables 7.1, 7.2 and 7.3). Oil demand responded to events rather faster than base chemicals, but it is very plain that the years 1973-75 marked a major watershed for both these industries in West Europe.

Refining

Events in the refining industry are quite easy to describe. Up to 1973, demand was growing at 8 per cent per annum. It then fell and, by 1977, had still not regained 1973 levels. By mid-1978, a Shell source was suggesting that growth in EC oil demand was more likely to range from 1 per cent per annum to a 'rather bullish 2.5 per cent' up to 1985.[2] This break with historic trends obviously affected refiners throughout West Europe, but two centres were hit particularly badly. The first was

Table 7.1
EC refining capacity and utilisation ratios
(capacity in million tons/year)

	1963-73	1974	1975	1976	1977	1978
Refining capacity	Varied	795	838	856	835	843
Utilisation ratio	85%	72%	58%	62%	63%	65%

Source: Petroleum Economist, 1978, pp 118, 295, 377.

Table 7.2
Effective EC ethylene capacity and utilisation ratios
(capacity in million tons/year)

	1969-73	1974	1975	1976	1977	1978
Ethylene capacity	Varied	11.1	11.8	12.1	12.5	12.6
Utilisation ratios	88%	88%	62%	79%	74%	79%

Source: CEFIC 1976b, table I; CEFIC 1977b, table B1: European Chemical News, March 5 1979, p.22.

Table 7.3
Effective EC benzene capacity and utilisation ratios
(capacity in million tons/year)

	1969-73	1974	1975	1976	1977	1978
Benzene capacity	Varied	5.4	5.5	5.8	6.0	6.1
Utilisation ratios	76%	77%	53%	68%	68%	72%

Source: CEFIC 1976a, table I; CEFIC, 1977a, table B1: European Chemical News, February 24 1978, p.6; March 5 1979, p.22.

108

the refining complex in Belgium and the Netherlands (particularly around Rotterdam); the second was the concentration of refineries in Italy — particularly in Sicily and Sardinia. In 1975, the former centre was running at 55 per cent of capacity and the Italian refineries at 47 per cent (against an EC average of 58 per cent).

It was no accident that Benelux and Italy should have been hit proportionally hard. These are the two main 'cargo markets' in Europe — that is, refining centres which pick up the marginal demand when any other national refining industry is unable to meet the demands of its local market. The Benelux complex, very much centred around Rotterdam and Antwerp, is generally controlled by the major integrated oil companies. The smaller Italian refining sector is a rather different affair; about half of its capacity is in the hands of independent Italian companies, and nearly another 20 per cent is controlled by ENI.[3] We need not be too concerned about why the Italian refining industry has historically developed this way, but it is important to note just how badly it has been hit by the slow-down in European demand. The joint development of North Sea oil to the North and OPEC refining capacity to the South and East are also leaving the Italian refining industry particularly exposed. Thus it is not surprising to find Italian voices among the strongest calling for some kind of centrally-orchestrated solution to the difficulties facing the European refining industry.

Petrochemicals

Demand for petrochemicals in West Europe was growing even faster than that for refined products in the years up to 1973 but, as with the oil sector, the years since then have produced a completely new situation. In the case of ethylene, West European demand growth dropped from around 15 per cent per annum up to 1973, to around zero in 1978.[4]

The EC ethylene sector responded extremely slowly to this changed environment and continued with a heavy investment programme at a time when an investment moratorium would have been more appropriate. Admittedly, the overall chemical sector within the EC responded to the new situation by keeping its annual investments (in real terms) well below the levels seen in the peak years of 1970 and 1971.[5] However, as late as 1978, ethylene capacity was still being added at an annual rate of 5.3 per cent — a rate of increase which will probably continue at least until 1982, as plants already under construction come into operation. The European Council of Chemical Manufacturers' Federations (known by its French initials, CEFIC) estimates that the EC will have some 16.9 million tons/year effective ethylene capacity in

1981, against a demand of 12.6 million. This will only permit a capacity utilisation rate of about 75 per cent, which remains well below that which was achieved in the early 1970s.[6]

Despite such figures (which show that over-capacity in the European refining and petrochemical industries is likely to last well into the 1980s), it is precisely in the refining and petrochemicals sectors that the Middle Eastern industrialising powers are going to compete. Inevitably, this is breeding a certain amount of schizophrenia within European circles. On the one hand, there are numerous politicians and a certain number of industrialists who want good relations with the oil producers, both for strategic and commercial reasons. Many of these argue that, whatever short-term damage Middle Eastern imports may cause in some narrow industrial sectors, it will be more than compensated for by West European exports in other sectors. On the other hand there are the companies which will be directly affected by increased competition from Middle Eastern and North African states. These tend to argue that such imports should be kept out until the West European industries have regained some form of structural stability. These industrialists have gained some important support both in national governments and in Brussels, where most of the key decisions affecting trade and industrial policies are made. The result is a debate within Western Europe which will decide whether the marketing goals of the Middle Easterners are in fact viable.

The Euro-Arab Dialogue

The most interesting attempt to seek some common ground is being made within the framework of the Euro-Arab Dialogue (or, from the Arab point of view, the Arab-European Dialogue). This initially stemmed from the panicky OPEC embargo-laden days of late 1973 and early 1974 when the EC members were divided on how to approach the changed circumstances after the Ramadan/Yom Kippur War. The Arab League countries wanted some form of dialogue, but the Americans under Dr Kissinger were hostile to any purely European-Arab relationship. There was a general feeling within EC circles, however, that agreeing to enter into such a dialogue would help to safeguard the Europeans from the anger the Arabs felt over American policies towards Israel, and might act as a moderating force on Arab militancy.[7]

By the beginning of 1977, however, the Dialogue was in trouble. There were proposals for the creation of a number of joint working commissions (on industrialisation, infrastructure, agriculture, financial co-operation, trade, co-operation in cultural and scientific areas, and political matters). The Arabs kept trying to make the Dialogue far more

110

political than the European side was willing to contemplate by, firstly, insisting that a Palestinian delegation be recognised, then, when that was side-stepped, by pressing for a meeting of foreign ministers with the aim of having a Euro-Arab summit of the relevant heads of government. This would inevitably have raised all those political questions which the Europeans did not want to face, but a rejection was difficult because Arab expectations were not being satisfied at either the political or commercial level.

The search was then on for areas in which some form of positive co-operation could be agreed. Petrochemicals and refining seemed to fill the bill — although fifteen other Dialogue projects had been approved by the end of 1978. Thus the Expert Group on Oil Refining and Petro-chemicals was set up within the framework of the Dialogue. The European membership of this group consists of national delegations including, in a number of cases, industrialists as well as officials. In June 1977, the two sides exchanged position papers on present and planned refining capacity, as well as evaluations of demand over the next ten years. The Arab League members said their members intended to build 3.8 million b/d capacity by 1985, bringing total Arab capacity up from 3.5 per cent of anticipated world production to 8 per cent. (They simultaneously presented a table of present, planned and proposed re-fining capacity which suggested that at least 4.8 million b/d capacity was on their drawing boards — which would give them an even greater share of world production).[8] Although there was some initial discussion on whether some form of complementary investment patterns could be worked out, it was abundantly clear that the quality of the projections on both sides of the table were far from satisfactory. Thus the Group's first priority was to reconcile the two demand and production projections.

For the meeting in October 1977, the Group discussed two analyses, one on the refining situation up to 1985, and the other on the petro-chemical one up to 1987, which relied heavily on forecasts prepared by the European chemical trade association, CEFIC. These mutually agreed reports came to conclusions which generally offered little en-couragement to the Arab side. On refining, it was agreed that there was not much prospect for significant export of Arab finished products before 1982, with the Europeans arguing that this would equally be true for the period up to and after 1985. There was only a glimmer of hope for the Arabs in the statement that the changing pattern of EC demand for petroleum products would probably show a growing need for light, low sulphur products and that further studies were needed to assess the appropriate adjustments required in world refining capacity.

On the petrochemical side, too, the Arabs were disillusioned. It was first of all argued that there was going to be no easy formula of complementary investment; for example, the Arabs would produce chemical 'building blocks' such as ethylene and propylene, leaving the Europeans to produce the derivative products. The cost of producing and transporting the building blocks or their intermediate products would rule out this solution. On the other hand, it was argued that some 25-35 new plants for petrochemical derivatives (in addition to plants already under construction) would be required by 1987 to satisfy growth in West European demand. Moreover, some 10-13 new benzene plants were likely to be required.

As it happened, CEFIC began to severely cut back its own petrochemical projections within five months of the Expert Group's October meeting. Estimates of demand in the early 1980s went down by some 16 per cent in the case of ethylene and some 27 per cent in the case of benzene.[9] This would obviously affect the number of plants for derivatives which would be needed. The European side pointed out that the Arabs might consider other areas of the world, such as Latin America, South Asia and Eastern Europe, which would also be developing into important consumers of petrochemicals, thus perhaps reducing the importance of West Europe to Arab plans.

Obviously this was all rather depressing for the Arab delegation. It put in a semi-dissenting report of its own, suggesting that demand growth figures seemed rather low and that it felt the Europeans were deliberately underestimating the number of plants that might be closed. The Arab side therefore made the most of whatever modest market openings were indicated. In refining, the Arabs argued, they should be treated on a Most Favoured Nation basis and should be granted tariff-free access to EC markets for their refined products. In addition, the Europeans should accept that refineries closed in West Europe should be replaced by capacity in the Arab world. Similarly, on the petrochemical side, the Arab world should be given encouragement to build up capacity for products such as methanol, styrene, cumene and ethylene oxide, areas where some market gaps seemed likely to exist.

During 1978, little happened to get this part of the Dialogue moving much further. A specialised group for fertilisers met in Cairo in March and went through much the same kind of statistical exercise, though it was noticeable that it broke its forecasts down in much greater geographical detail than the earlier studies had done. For instance, it became clear where East Europe or South East Asia fitted into the production scene of the early 1980s. What is more, both the European and Arab sides started to explore their respective conceptions of what a complementary investment pattern might look like for the two groups. Otherwise, the Expert Group on Refining and Petrochemicals seems to be settling down as a body for co-ordinating the two sides' estimates of future demand and production of various products. At the

112

same time it is also examining areas in which the two sides might be able to co-operate — whether it be in the form of the Europeans helping with technical training, of looking at the future of markets for natural gas and LPG, or of jointly studying market opportunities in the Third World. What does not seem any closer is some worldwide deal between the EC and the Arab League (or its member states) which will give all Arab countries free market access to Western Europe which they dearly want, in return for some understanding about different areas in which the two sides might invest.

So, has the whole exercise been a complete waste of time?

The Dialogue assessed

The Dialogue has obviously been symbolic of the enhanced importance of the Arab world. The cynic can, however, argue that the Europeans went into this Dialogue to constrain the damage. When it was first mooted in 1973-74, the oil producers were at their most militant, with the Arab members in the lead due to their anger over the Palestinian issue. Talking to the Arabs cost nothing except the time of a certain number of officials, and if it helped to bring about relatively stable oil prices and 'responsible' Arab positions regarding Israel, then it would be worthwhile in European eyes. Despite certain post-Camp David tensions in the Arab world, most would accept that Arab positions on oil and Israel have been rather less negative than one could have hoped for in late 1973. The symbolic aspects of the Dialogue have undoubtedly played some (smallish?) part in encouraging this moderation.

The cynic might then go on to say that the Refining and Petrochemical sub-group has been an equally useful group. It is pretty clear that it has played an educative role, because as late as 1977, the Arab delegations often had little idea of the amount of overlap in Arab plans, nor did they realise just how much estimates of potential growth in world markets had changed for the worse. The fact that the two sides now seem to mutually agree about subjecting each others' estimates of productive capacity and demand to constructive criticism, is again a definite bonus for the Europeans, since it reduces the risk that too many Arab plants are built. It is obviously impossible to prove that this part of the Dialogue has led to the tightening up of Arab planning which is mentioned in chapter 5. Each postponed Arab plant can be seen as removing some potential pressure from the European industry — and from those Arab projects which will still go ahead.

At the same time, preparing for this part of the dialogue proved a useful exercise for the Europeans. In neither the refining nor petrochemical sectors was statistical analysis on a European-wide scale particularly well-developed (true also of other sensitive industries). It was thus pure gain that EC and national officials had to sit down with industry representatives to analyse figures together. CEFIC, the petrochemical association, certainly responded by re-thinking the way in which it collected its data, thus improving their reliability. On the other hand, it can be argued that the fact that CEFIC changed its methodology in time for its December 1977 forecasts might not be as innocent as all that. After all, its data have come to be used heavily within the Dialogue, and the resultant, significant lowering of its estimates of demand for the early 1980s might at least be partially aimed at persuading non-Europeans to look elsewhere for markets. Whatever the accuracy of these suspicions (and CEFIC's explanations for the methodological change do not totally convince us)[10] improved communication between European industry and Brussels was desirable, given the degree of over-capacity within the refining and petrochemical sectors. The Dialogue has thus acted as a catalyst in developing European thinking about the issues at stake — particularly regarding the wisdom of making trading concessions to third parties, without considering the full implications.

What have the Arabs gained?

There are those on the Arab side who have argued that all the Dialogue has offered is a certain amount of market analysis which could have been bought from consultancies. This is somewhat unfair. For one thing, consultants' projections reflect the time at which they are written, and policy-makers can be led astray when these forecasts are overtaken by significant changes in the economic expectations which underpin them (one thinks here of the way in which Arab officials clung to the estimates embodied in Chem Systems' 1974-75 study for IDCAS/UNIDO, long after the world economy's failure to regain past growth-rates had made it clear that these forecasts needed to be amended downwards quite seriously). In contrast, the projections generated by the Dialogue's sub-group have been subjected to continuous critical assessment and have been modified accordingly. If the Dialogue continues, this process will develop, providing both Europeans and Arabs with reliable background information against which to assess investment intentions or, even, the forecasts of independent consultants.

Otherwise, it is not so clear what the Arab side has gained from all this. It may be true that the continuing cancellation, postponement and rationalisation of previously announced new European productive capacity have, to some degree, been influenced by Middle East investment intentions and/or the knowledge of other European competitors'

114

intentions gained via CEFIC's somewhat improved statistical information service — a fairly direct result of the Dialogue. However, the Arabs have not convinced the West Europeans that there is room for some general strategy of complementary investments, whereby certain sectors of these industries should be reserved for the Arabs to specialise in. The closest they came to this was when the Italian delegation suggested that the Arabs might be encouraged to use their cash to buy up the surplus capacity in the European refining and petrochemical industry in return for a European guarantee to continue to take Arab oil and natural gas. (This is not likely to prove attractive to oil-producing states which want to develop processing industries on their own soil, rather than help the Europeans rationalise their own industry.) Otherwise, there are European suggestions that the Arabs might specialise in desulphurisation (which needs a lot of hydrogen, and is therefore suited to countries with abundant natural gas), or that they might concentrate on producing 'reconstituted' crude, specifically tailored to meet the requirements of downstream refineries.

In general, though, the question of complementary investment has been resolved into a number of less sensitive and, for the Arabs, less important areas in which the two sides might co-operate. Joint studies of third markets, possible joint ventures in providing supporting services and spare parts, and assistance in improving the running of plants are the sort of things that the industrialising world ought to be offering to the oil producers as a matter of course.

However, what is referred to less and less is the question of market access. What can the Algerians, Libyans or Saudis expect as their various plants come into operation and they look towards West Europe for their markets? The Algerians have duty-free access into the EC for their products, but they cannot be really sure that the EC will not invoke the safeguard clause and apply restrictions. Arab countries outside the Maghreb and Mashreq agreements are even less clear where they stand. All the Dialogue seems to have done so far is re-convince the European side that there is no justification for imports from Arab sources until well into the mid-1980s — if at all. What the Dialogue has not done is to probe this assumption more deeply. For instance, supposing the Arabs are right in their assertion that at least some of their refining and petrochemical plants are fully competitive due to the comparative advantage of being located close to cheap supplies of gas, European statistics about production-capacity ratios within West Europe may not be relevant at all. Surely, the Europeans should accept that inefficient plants be scrapped and replaced by efficient plants, wherever they might be located? Just what are the ground rules under which the new Middle Eastern and North African plants should be operated?

115

In practice, these are exactly the questions the West Europeans do not want to answer, and it is their skill in delicately steering the debate away from them which has made the Euro-Arab Dialogue work primarily in Europe's favour. For one thing, whatever the official liberal position of the EC, there are strong interventionist voices within it. Even if it were true that the new Arab and Iranian capacity was fully competitive, there would still be powerful voices arguing that the European industries should be protected, come what may. There is also a second set of reasons why the EC has evaded these issues; these stem from the fact that most on the European side probably believe that the new Middle East plants are not going to be internationally competitive and that they will only be able to make inroads into European markets through heavy government subsidies and by what is, in effect, dumping. These are big, troublesome issues, best handled by a different forum, geared to discuss commercial issues, rather than by the Dialogue's refining and petrochemical group, which is designed to concentrate on industrial co-operation issues.

In the second half of this chapter we explain some of the other reasons why the Euro-Arab Dialogue may be a blind-alley in the search for an equitable distribution of industry between the oil-producing states and West Europe. In particular, we point to some of the international obligations which stop the EC from making any preferential deal with the Arabs (or the Iranians). We also, more pessimistically, analyse some of the protectionist forces at work within the EC which might make a liberal deal with the oil producers impossible, even if some of the other difficulties could be resolved.

Constraints on the Europeans

The first problem for the Arabs (and for the Iranians, who are not part of the Euro-Arab Dialogue) is that they are seeking a special trading arrangement, which is something the Europeans are probably not in a position to offer. The EC went through a sharp diplomatic exchange with the US during 1972-73 when the Community devised a policy which would have offered any interested country bordering the Mediterranean (Jordan was also included) a non-reciprocal phasing-out of tariff barriers on industrial products and an improvement in the treatment of their agricultural produce. This is precisely the kind of geographically preferential trade deal[11] which GATT discourages, and the US was unhappy with what it saw as an attempt to turn the Mediterranean into a European lake.

The EC Commission, therefore, took the formal step in April 1973 of having its Commissioner in charge of External Relations, Sir

Christopher Soames, clearly state that this would be a once-for-all initiative restricted to states bordering the Mediterranean (plus Jordan) and specifically requesting to be included in any such agreement. [12] This outline of the policy initiative was partly made as a result of US pressure, but also because of an internal logic which will make the EC very reluctant to go back on its commitments. The EC Nine know that the concessions they are offering the Mediterranean nations are inevitably causing jealousy among countries further afield. The Iranians, for instance, are uneasy about the apparent favouritism shown to the Arab world through the creation of the Euro-Arab Dialogue; they cannot see why the EC should be unwilling to be as generous to them as to Turkey. Yet, if an exception were made for Iran, how would the Europeans be able to resist demands for similar treatment from the other Middle Eastern oil producers? . . . and if the latter are shown favouritism, what about Indonesia, Venezuela and other countries? The situation would degenerate into a diplomatic quagmire, and more enemies would be made. In contrast, the current situation in which most of the Mediterranean coastal states have some form of trade agreement with the EC is just manageable, even if it does offend GATT principles. Thus, there are strong reasons why the Europeans will be wary of allowing the Euro-Arab Dialogue to become too involved in trade politics. Offers of technical assistance or of creating joint ventures in the Arab world are relatively safe for the Europeans. Commitments to guarantee market access to Arab products are more risky.

So, the EC and the Arab world are left in an awkward situation whereby some of the Arab countries enjoy preferential trading arrangements with the EC (particularly Algeria through the Maghreb agreement), while most of the Middle Eastern ones do not. In theory, this need not make much difference. Countries such as Saudi Arabia and Iran (along with all OPEC members) are beneficiaries of the EC's Generalised Scheme of Preferences (GSP), and are thus technically able to export some of their manufactured products to the EC at nil tariffs. On the other hand, the benefit of GSP schemes is limited. The lists of products which are exempt from tariffs are unilaterally drawn up annually by the importing group (in this case the EC). Ceilings are then set for the volume of each product which will be given tariff-free access. No one exporting country can get tariff-free access for a product, once the volume of its sales exceeds one fifth of the overall tariff-free quota set for that product (further exports are not blocked; they just qualify for normal tariffs). Similarly, once the overall annual tariff-free quota for a product is reached by the cumulative sales of the participating LDCs, then all further imports of that product, for that particular year, will be subject to the tariffs which were waived under the GSP scheme.

The Middle Easterners should worry about two aspects of GSP

schemes. Firstly, there is a possibility that the West Europeans might exclude countries like Saudi Arabia from their GSP scheme, on the grounds that the Saudis have become too successful as exporters.

More likely, though, is the possibility that the overall tariff-free quotas for the key refining and petrochemical products will be set so low, that a one-fifth maximum share will be virtually worthless to the Middle Easterners. After all, during the summer of 1978, the tariff-free quotas which the EC set for imports of gasoline, gas oil and fuel oil were reached by August. Since the Europeans have shown no enthusiasm for increasing the overall quota for oil products from the 1976 level of 2.5 million tons (50,000 b/d), this does not bode well for the 620,000 b/d of export-oriented refining capacity which is at the advanced-planning stage in Saudi Arabia. Again, the EC once offered free access to imports of fertilisers from the Third World, but withdrew the offer as soon as these imports became significant.[13]

Quite understandably, then, relying on a GSP tariff framework will prove insufferable for countries such as Saudi Arabia and Iran. Their Algerian rivals know that they are better placed under the Maghreb agreement, as the EC will have to go through the diplomatically embarrassing process of invoking safeguard clauses if it ever does decide to rescind the free-access conditions for refined oil or petrochemical products. On the other hand, the Saudis and Iranians know that they are totally at the mercy of the annual whims of the EC Commission, and they will be particularly aware that the process of drawing up annual lists of products covered by the GSP scheme is an open invitation to affected industrialists to ensure that the most sensitive products are exposed to the minimum of tariff-free competition. Finally, the Saudis must realise that, when they themselves become significant exporters of petrochemical products, voices will be raised asking if Saudi Arabia has not 'graduated' from the LDC ranks. When you are financially strong enough to be on the Executive Board of the International Monetary Fund (as the Saudis are), you can hardly be regarded as a Developing Country in need of preferential trading arrangements. On the other hand, Saudi Arabia has oil that Europe needs, and the Kingdom will presumably tend to use her great bargaining power to persuade the EC to be generous on the question of tariffs. But that is a topic for discussion in chapter 10.

Other claimants

Within the EC

One major constraint on EC freedom to strike a special deal with the Arabs and Iranians is the fact that the Middle Easterners and North Africans are not the only countries trying to develop petrochemical and refining industries.

Within the EC itself, for example, are a number of oil and gas producers. The Dutch probably do not want any special tariff protection since the Rotterdam refining complex has spawned its fair share of petrochemical plants. British interests, however, are somewhat similar to those of the Saudis or Iranians; they also have a sizeable oil-producing sector and are under strong, domestic, political pressures to use this situation to become a more powerful force within the world petrochemical and refining industries. Just as the Saudi projects are disappearing further into the future due to disappointing market forecasts, so has the (always faint) possibility of four new British ethylene crackers by the mid-1980s fallen apart. Hopes that around two thirds of Britain's North Sea oil would be refined on British soil have also been quietly dropped, as it became clear that investing in new refineries would give strongly negative returns. The fact, however, that the British are having to shelve projects today does not mean that they will not reappear as claimants, when market conditions do permit the building of a new generation of such plants. Countries such as Saudi Arabia and Iran may have a moral claim to obtaining a fair share of such new capacity, but the British are arguing within EC councils that a number of objective factors (ownership of hydrocarbons reserves, relative industrial underdevelopment compared with the Germans, cheap labour, etc) make it only fair that they improve their own position in hydrocarbon-based industries. This does not mean, however, that a strict economist will find the British arguments any more convincing than those of the Middle Easterners. Construction costs are not that moderate in Britain either, and the fact that Britain is an island adds to transport costs.

The expanded EC

The countries which probably have the next strongest political claim on EC generosity are Portugal, Greece and Spain, which have applied to become full member states of the European Community. Greek petrochemical plans are still relatively underdeveloped and Spanish expansion plans leave little or no room for significant exports. On the other hand, Portuguese industrialists have managed to steer their extremely ambitious petrochemical plans almost intact through the political upheaval which followed the 1974 revolution. When the Oporto aromatics and the Sines olefins complexes come into operation in the early 1980s, they will have a significant amount of surplus capacity available for export. In late 1977, the *European Chemical News* was estimating that Portugal would average some 30 per cent over-capacity in petrochemicals and intermediates through 1990, although the exact proportion would vary from product to product.[14] Portuguese planners do not sound overwhelmingly confident of knowing where their export markets are going to be, but they will inevitably look towards the EC, and thus be one of the claimants on West European markets with which the Middle Easterners will have to contend. Once again, one would expect the EC to be under strong pressure to show favouritism to a country which should, by then, be a member.

EFTA

Again, (though this is more problematic) we would not expect the EC to give better treatment to the Middle Easterners than to those other West European countries (mainly the members of the European Free Trade Association (EFTA)), which have had various forms of free trade agreements with the EC since the early 1970s. Sweden, Norway and Austria all have major olefins projects either under construction or in the planning stage. In particular, the Norwegians have capitalised on their North Sea hydrocarbons wealth to develop a billion dollar petrochemicals complex at Bamble in southern Norway. Coming into operation between 1977 and 1979, its timing was unfortunate and the plants are now expected to run at a loss well into the 1980s, but this will not stop plans for a second such complex, based on gas from the Statfjord Field.[15] Middle Eastern readers will once again feel unsympathetic to the suggestion that unprofitable operations in Norway should be given preferential treatment over their own projects, but it is a political fact of West European life that the Scandinavians, Swiss and Austrians are regarded as being part of the same political culture. In particular, there are strong, pragmatic, strategic arguments for being tolerant of the Norwegians, whose oil production policies are important to any West European effort to reduce dependency on OPEC oil. Norway's initial policies towards the development of its offshore resources have been quite restrictive. It therefore makes sense that the Norwegians be given every encouragement to relax their exploration and depletion policies — and giving preference to Middle Eastern petrochemicals over Norwegian ones is clearly not one of the best ways of getting the latter to become more reasonable.

The situation regarding East European products is much more complex. In chapter 5, we have already given some attention to this region's potential, arguing that there has been a rapid build-up of products available for export. The fact that much of the potential trade results from so-called compensation deals is making West European reactions particularly tentative. Major refining and petrochemical companies have enough problems with their own over-capacity to feel much sympathy for companies which have constructed competing plants in Eastern Europe and will eventually receive payment in products.

On one level, then, established West European companies have been trying to discourage compensation deals. There is some pressure on Brussels to set up a scheme for compulsory registration of chemical buy-back deals with Eastern Europe in order to improve the industry's statistical information. This might be enough to discourage some of these deals, once it becomes clear that they are cumulatively building up a potential glut of products for the future. The West Germans (15 per cent of whose trade with East Europe is now in the form of barter or compensation deals) are starting to insist that the Soviet Union should provide at least part of the compensatory payments for plant construction in the form of raw materials such as crude oil, rather than petrochemicals.[16] The West European industry is also turning to the more complex business of launching anti-dumping actions against East European petrochemical producers. There are difficulties in this approach, since products flowing under barter and compensation deals, and products being sold in job lots by middlemen (another common way in which East European products reach Western markets) are very hard to handle under conventional anti-dumping techniques. At the same time, however, the Western industry is angry enough about the Easterners' use of multiple exchange rates, the artificial allotment of fixed costs between exports and sales to protected home markets, and downright subsidies, in order to try anti-dumping procedures. One such attempt to stem Romanian exports of fertilisers was blunted when the Romanians agreed in January 1977 to limit such sales to the EC. Thus the Commission's ability to prove an anti-dumping case against Eastern Europe remained untested.

In June 1978, there was a new attempt to bring an action against the Eastern bloc, this time in the field of styrene-butadiene rubber (SBR — the most important form of synthetic rubber). The complaint was made to the EC Commission, and originally named six East European countries, including the Soviet Union. The charge alleges that the Easterners have used disruptive pricing, leading to a major loss of earnings and markets by the West European industry. The complaint is widely seen as a test-case of the EC's willingness to protect its industry against unfair competition. In the meantime, the industry association, CEFIC, has been drawing up lists of other sensitive areas where large-scale exports by East Europeans may undermine Western markets.

Implications for the Middle East

All this has implications for the Middle Easterners. In particular, it is very clear that if the West European industries are successful in mobilising the EC Commission to harry, on their behalf, the allegedly unfair practices of the East Europeans, then Middle Eastern products could also have a rough ride when in their turn, they seek to enter West Europe's markets. This is because the latter's industrialists will see many points of similarity between the would-be exporters of the Eastern Bloc and those of the Middle East. To western eyes, both these sets of potential exporters are fundamentally 'state traders';[17] that is, countries in which the state takes an extremely active role in planning exports and in creating the possibility of such trade by heavy manipulation of currency rates, direct and indirect subsidies, taxation policies, etc. (It is debatable whether current West European practices are really any more virtuous.) As a result, any moves to improve the 'transparency' and noted fairness of Eastern Bloc economic decision-making may eventually be used against the Middle Easterners. Certainly, any register of compensation deals with Eastern Europe will almost inevitably be extended to cover the terms of turnkey projects in the Middle East and North Africa that have a barter element. Such a register might even be expanded in scope to take into account any export volume-guarantees which western partners may give for their joint ventures in countries like Saudi Arabia. It makes a great deal of difference to West Europe if, for example, Shell or Mobil are obliged by the Saudis to sell, at all costs, a given amount of the products from their joint ventures, instead of having the freedom to cut back output in line with changing conditions in export markets. Any minimal export provisions would heavily increase the chance of quantities of 'distressed' products seeking a home in West European markets.

Again, it could be tempting for the EC Commission to develop some form of 'trigger' price against imports from Eastern Europe. This might involve some calculation of the operating costs of efficient plants within Europe, and would prevent new exporters from obtaining a share in the market by cutting prices well below European, economically viable rates. The Middle Easterners, then, would inevitably be subjected to the same scheme. We should note, in all fairness, that one EC official we have talked to resolutely denies that trigger prices would ever be used within the chemicals industry.

The growth of organised trade

It is by no means certain that the West Europeans will inevitably slide into the trade protectionist camp as far as East European and Middle Eastern products are concerned. For one thing, the West Europeans have a healthy, overall trade surplus with East Europe. Moreover, there are interests of *Realpolitik*. After all, détente has been heavily tied up with trade politics, and severe restrictions of East European exports might well have ripple effects on wider strategic issues. In particular, it could be awkward to become involved in a series of major trading disputes with the Soviet Union, a superpower one does not antagonise lightly. At the same time, the Saudis, through their hold on oil, will be at least equally difficult trading partners to resist. A further consideration is the spread of environmental restrictions which are making it more difficult, expensive and time-consuming to build chemical plants in much of Western Europe — in places such as along the Rhine, at Rotterdam and, increasingly, around the Mediterranean. This should make the West Europeans somewhat more enthusiastic about seeing new chemical investment taking place in areas like the Middle East (though it should be noted that countries with Atlantic coastlines such as Britain, Spain, Portugal, France and Norway will be reluctant to lose much investment because of such environmental worries). Finally, over the years, the West Europeans have expanded their trade concessions to various LDCs, either through the quite extensive Lomé Agreement (which involves many of the EC's ex-colonies), or through the even wider GSP scheme. The oil producers can hope to argue that they are still developing countries and that, therefore, they deserve a more sympathetic consideration than the rather more developed East Europeans. On the other hand, the Lomé deal is for ex-colonies only and, although the oil producers number countries which were part of various European countries' informal empires (Iran is one), the Middle Easterners fall into no convenient category of deserving countries, in an era in which further preferential trade deals will be difficult.

Anti-liberal trade forces have come very close to the surface in Western Europe in the years since 1973, however, and there is now a better than fair chance that they may be calling the tune in the mid-1980s — just when the Middle Easterners really want to enter world markets with hydrocarbon-based products. These forces are not necessarily crudely protectionist but have found expression in some pseudo-sophisticated forms, such as the call of M. Barre, the French prime minister, for 'organised free trade'.[18] Although it antedates M. Barre's call, the Multi-Fibre Arrangement (MFA) is currently the most elegant expression of such organisation; it sets the export growth rates of various textile products supplied by the Arrangement's LDC members to the industrialised world. We shall come back to the MFA in the final chapter, when we discuss various ways in which the industrialised world and the oil producers might come to terms over the latter's refining and petrochemical plans. For the moment, we only need mention the considerable hardening of the West European position when the MFA was last renegotiated in the winter of 1977-78. During these negotiations, the French and British insisted that the EC take a very hard line in negotiations, and the EC ended up as the most restrictive negotiator of the industrialised world. Again, when one looks at various *ad hoc* import bans and quotas in industries such as steel, shipbuilding and shoes, it is clear that industrialists who think themselves threatened by significant quantities of imports have proved pretty effective in getting the EC Commission to act on their behalf.

Certainly — and this affects the Middle Easterners — Western Europe's refining and chemical industries have not remained unaffected by developments in other industries. For instance, the synthetic fibre manufacturers convinced the Industry Directorate of the EC that a 'crisis' cartel should be formed, which would also involve parallel action by producers in neighbouring non-EC countries (such as Spain and Austria). The cartel was to lay down targets for reducing plant capacity through to 1981, as well as to set production quotas for the corporate signatories. It had a chequered career in 1978. It was twice rejected by the EC Commission as breaching the Community's rules on competition. In January 1979, there was still hope that a compromise could be reached in which the industrialists would drop their plans for market sharing, while keeping to the proposals for mutual cut-backs of excess productive capacity.

This train of events showed that the interventionists and non-interventionists in the EC Commission are quite finely balanced. But the fact that the Industry Directorate was willing to back a cartel for synthetic fibres encouraged parts of the European refining sector to call for EC action in order to reduce over-capacity in this sector as well. There were also loud calls for the creation of a similar cartel in the plastics industry — a demand which Vicomte Davignon of the Industry Directorate claimed he would fight.

Very little of all this deals directly with the potential industrial challenge of the Middle Eastern oil producers. Most of the intra-EC calls for 'crisis' cartels stem from the chronic over-capacity caused by the slowdown in European growth from 1974. It is a highly significant fact, however, that West European industrialists have received so much support from Brussels for solutions which run counter to the internal competition philosophy on which the European Economic Community was created (steel and agriculture excepted). The EC and its national governments will inevitably become involved, as troubled parts of the refining and petrochemical industries are rationalised. The Italians will be particularly affected with their export-refinery sector becoming redundant, as the refining industry polarises around the North Sea and the Middle Eastern and North African oil producers. The Italians have brought much trouble on their own heads by seriously over-investing in chemical capacity at a time when markets declined, and by failing to rationalise in time. In this particular national case, the political consequences of the necessary closures (predominantly in the relatively deprived southern regions) are so serious that EC aid in some form is almost inevitable. In addition to the Italians there are the French with their *dirigiste* tradition, who also have important, vulnerable institutions, such as their 'national champion' oil companies, Elf-Aquitaine and Compagnie Française des Pétroles (CFP). CFP has over-extended itself in the most affected parts of the chemicals sector, feels disadvantaged with regard to its crude supplies for its refineries, and is financially weaker than the giant international oil companies, which can afford to keep under-utilised capacity going longer than CFP (and other medium-ranking refining and chemical companies) can.

Protectionist alliances within the EC are too complex to sum up in one easy description. The British, for instance, joined the French in their insistence on hardening the EC position in the renegotiation of the Multi-Fibre Arrangement; and again teamed up with the French on the need for crisis measures to protect the EC steel industry from the consequences of its over-capacity. But in other industries, such as refining and petrochemicals, where the British corporate sector is relatively dynamic, they have been rather less enthusiastic about the need for crisis cartels. The German oil company Veba joined with ENI, CFP, Elf-Aquitaine and Petrofina to demand that the EC take action over problems facing Europe's refining industry. However, the official position of the West German government has been pretty consistently against any such action which might smell of market regulation. In general, though, it is possible to put the West Germans and Dutch at the liberal end of the spectrum, with the Italians and French at the other. The British have been equivocal, moving in a restrictionist direction in response to pleas from their textile sector, but remaining liberal on issues connected with the rationalisation of the petrochemical and refining sectors.

We feel that resistance to non-European industrial challenges partially stems from the fragmentation of the West European competitive structure. This still contains a lot of companies with most of their operations within a single country. When faced with increased competition, these companies are unable to respond like their more 'multinational' competitors by spreading plant rationalisation across several countries. Tied to one country (indeed, often specifically seen as national 'champions'), any cuts in their activities inevitably provoke relatively nationalistic reactions. And yet, the economic slowdown since 1973, combined with increased competition from peripheral state-led economies, has shown how vulnerable one-country companies are. It has become ever clearer that corporate survival in the 1980s will primarily go to technically progressive companies which are not just tied to the fortunes of a single, national market. Increasingly, the national companies are being left stranded and have responded by demanding European-wide 'structural' solutions, which will allegedly allow them to adapt to the new environment, without being driven out of business. So, in the refining sectors, it has been the companies which put too much reliance on their positions as national champions (i.e. Veba, CFP, Elf Aquitaine, Petrofina and ENI) which have been most vociferous in asking Brussels to limit the effects of international competition. Similarly, it is not accidental that a crisis cartel has come close to formation in the synethic fibres industry, where troubled national producers, such as the Montedison Group and other Italian manufacturers, are proportionally far more important than their opposite numbers in base petrochemicals, where multinationals such as the oil and chemical majors dominate the scene.

Conclusions

Finally, what are the implications of all this for the Middle Eastern producers? Firstly, they will inevitably be affected by Western Europe's growing concern with regulating imports from its 'state-trading' neighbours. It is extremely doubtful that the Middle Easterners will be able to avoid any backlash caused by East European imports. Secondly, the amount of over-capacity within Western Europe is such that any rationalisation process will be a long, rather than short, process, and will be politically controversial (in September 1978, 5,000 strikers closed down five refineries in Belgium, as a protest against Occidental closing its money-losing refinery in Antwerp). The controversy will guarantee that Middle Eastern imports will be given hostile scrutiny by trade unionists and by companies forced to scrap predominantly fairly modern plant.

Fundamentally, though, the distinctive tone of West European responses to the Middle Easterners will be set by the countries of Southern Europe (such as the French, Italians, Greeks and Spaniards). This is because logistics dictate that shipping products to Northern Europe through the Straits of Gibraltar will add at least half as much again to shipping times from the Middle East to Italy; and the further North such products go, the greater the transportation disadvantages com-

126

pared with products based on North Sea feedstocks.

So, how might the Southern Europeans be reacting in the 1980s to the challenge from the Middle East? Under most circumstances, one would expect the Italians to be wary since it is this economy, above all, which has most over-extended itself in the relevant industries. The rationalisation of the industrial structure of Southern Italy is probably the most explosive task facing industrial policy-makers anywhere in Europe, and this must inevitably push Italian governments toward protectionist positions. The French have already taken a similar stance regarding the two main industries concerned and, by the 1980s, they may well be having to respond to new industrial competition from Spain and Portugal which will, if all things go smoothly, be within the EC by that time. The Spanish have run an economy which, by tradition, has been heavily protected by tariffs; they will also be having problems of adjusting to their new role as a member of the European Community.

On the other hand, just as relative proximity makes the South Europeans particularly exposed to Middle Eastern products, it also may make them more psychologically attuned to North African and Middle Eastern needs and will give them relatively strong trade links with these regions. The French have rather strained ties with Algeria dating back to the days of French rule, but of all Western countries, they have, since Algerian independence, probably followed the most consistently pro-Arab policy. The Italians have close ties with the Libyans and have been doing well in Middle Eastern markets with industrial goods. They have not only allowed the Libyans to buy into Fiat, but seem happy enough that Kuwaiti and, possibly, Saudi interests decided in the autumn of 1978 to buy into the extremely troubled chemical company, Montedison. So, it could be that we are about to see Arab interests purchasing a market share within Europe by buying into South European companies. Certainly, there is a lot of spare refining and petrochemical capacity around Italy waiting to be picked up for knock-down prices. The indications are that the Italians would increasingly be glad to consider such deals.

But then the purpose behind Middle Eastern strategies is to increase the amount of economic activity on their own soil, not to buy up spare capacity elsewhere in the world. One could, therefore, expect any accommodation between South European and Middle Eastern industrialists to be a relatively fragile seedling, needing careful nurturing by the governments at both ends of the transaction. If this is true, then the Middle Eastern refiners and petrochemical producers are left with the fact that their products are likely to meet some middle-ranking resistance as they build up in volume. It seems inconceivable to us that they will be shut out of Europe altogether, particularly considering the

127

strength of the Saudi bargaining position if they choose to use it. On the other hand, it seems improbable that much of this flow will be allowed into Europe tariff-free. Much more likely is a trade regime which will involve sporadic anti-dumping exercises and perhaps some form of trigger-pricing mechanism. We could then eventually see various orderly marketing agreements being set up between the EC and individual Middle Eastern exporters. The Euro-Arab Dialogue could play a role in seeing that none of this gets too much out of hand.

But whatever the exact trading relationship that will emerge, we are sure of one thing — Adam Smith would not approve.

Notes

1   This assumes the Suez Canal can be used. British Petroleum, 1977, p.578.
2   *Petroleum Intelligence Weekly*, July 29 1978, p.1.
3   Department of Energy (US), 1978, pp 167-9; 207-9.
4   *Petroleum Intelligence Weekly*, June 26 1978, p.12.
5   Communication from the Chemical Industries Association, London, November 1978.
6   *European Chemical News*, June 23 1978, p.7.
7   Allen, 1978.
8   *Petroleum Intelligence Weekly*, June 13 1977, p.2; June 27 1977, p.4.
9   *European Chemical News*, February 24 1978, p.6, plus author's calculations from figures used at the October 1977 meeting of the Euro-Arab Expert Group.
10   CEFIC, 1977a, pp 1-2.
11   Tovias, 1977, pp 61-83 describes how the EC dressed their offer up with sections on 'co-operation' and 'development aid' to get round GATT rules.
12   Tovias, 1977, p.75.
13   *Petroleum Intelligence Weekly*, August 7 1978, p.1.
14   *Financial Times*, September 1 1978, p.9.
15   *European Chemical News*, July 28 1978, p.4.
16   *European Chemical News*, June 23 1978, p.6.
17   Zysman, 1978.
18   *Financial Times*, July 7 1977.

8 The issues for the United States and the 'Western' camp

In contrast to the Europeans, for whom Middle Eastern industrialisation means problems, the United States has little to lose and quite a lot to gain. Some of the potential benefits are shared with the OECD world in general, but others are peculiarly American advantages.

Benefits — corporate

In the Saudi case, one obvious potential benefit is that the industrialisation process is taking place primarily in conjunction with US companies, thus maintaining the special US- Saudi relationship which has held in the corporate sector from the days when Socal first obtained its concession to search for oil in the Kingdom. In particular, it is noticeable that all four of the Aramco partners are negotiating to join in export-oriented ventures with the Saudis, although Mobil has clearly the most ambitious plans. Of the major chemical companies, Dow, Celanese and Texas Eastern are striving to keep the US corporate interests represented. At a less obvious level, the American orientation of the Saudi industrial structure shows in the fact that the major construction jobs are carried out by companies such as Bechtel and Fluor, to say nothing of the role played by the ubiquitous US Corps of Engineers.

As we have already seen in chapter 4, US companies were conspicuous in not trying to take a leading role in Iranian industrialisation, for the unspoken reasons that they knew Saudi Arabia better and felt that Saudi oil potential more than made up for the relatively small domestic market. This is an understandable strategy which has worked so far. The main achievement of US interests is that they have succeeded in keeping the Saudis from turning to radical measures in the slow process of nationalising Aramco. As we write, the final terms of these negotiations have still not been made public, but what is known shows that the US partners will continue to have preferential access to Saudi crude, in return for certain specified services. In 1977, Exxon, Socal, Texaco and Mobil were still able to report aggregate profits of $810 million which directly stemmed from their interest in Aramco.[1] Thus, these companies still have access to a source of profits found in very few

129

other places in the oil world (probably, only BP's North Sea and Alaskan finds, and Shell/Exxon's Dutch gas production come in the same league). Inevitably, this can only help the Aramco four in an era in which oil companies are diversifying to become more general mineral and energy companies. If other US companies which have not been previous investors in Saudi Arabia (such as Dow, Celanese and part-American Shell Oil) can also have their future development strengthened by becoming involved with the Kingdom, then so much the better.

A further, more strategic benefit for the US authorities, stemming from the maintenance of a strong American corporate presence within Saudi Arabia, is that Washington will still have some leverage in future oil supply crises, should the International Energy Agency's Emergency Allocation scheme fall to pieces because of disunity among the industrialised countries. As the lessons from the 1973 oil embargo show,[2] being the parent authorities of the international oil majors does not necessarily guarantee favourable treatment. However, in case there should be significant political disarray within the OECD world, the greater the amount of oil still flowing through US corporate channels, the more weight Washington will have with these companies to stiffen their resolve, if they came under conflicting instructions.

Trade benefits

An obvious benefit from helping the Middle Easterners create capital-intensive industries is that this will help the US economy claw back a good part of what it has been paying the Middle East for oil. As can be seen from table 8.1, the US has been rapidly increasing its import of oil from the Middle East throughout the post-1973 period. Taking into account the fact that oil prices have been rising along with the quantities of imported oil, we find that US payments for Middle Eastern oil went up 19-fold to around $12 billion between 1973 and 1977.

The US has been moderately successful in redressing this oil balance with the Middle East. Within Saudi Arabia it has about one-fifth of the market, despite its historical connections. In Iran, its sales stagnated, and its sales to the general world of the Middle Eastern oil producers have started to grow more slowly. The fall in the value of the Dollar during 1978, and the growing impact of Alaskan production on oil imports mean that the US trade balance with the Middle Eastern oil producers should move towards balance within the next couple of years — due as much to the slow growth of crude imports as to a spectacular

Table 8.1
US-Middle Eastern trade flows: 1973-77 (excluding invisibles)

Year	US imports of Middle-Eastern crude		US exports in $ billion to		
	million b/d	$ billion	Middle East	(Saudi Arabia)	(Iran)
1977	2.6	12	7.6	(3.6)	(2.7)
1976	1.9	8	6.9	(2.8)	(2.8)
1975	1.1	4.5	5.9	(1.5)	(3.2)
1974	1.0	3.6	3.4	(0.8)	(1.73)
1973	0.8	0.6	1.5	(0.4)	(0.77)

Sources: Various issues of BP Statistical Review of the World Oil Industry, Directions of Trade, Yearbook of International Trade Statistics.

increase of exports.

The involvement of US companies in Saudi export ventures will be contributing only moderately to this improvement in the US-Saudi trade balance. They are of importance if they encourage the Saudis to award the construction contracts for these export ventures to US contractors, but they will be spread out over the decade and are dwarfed by Saudi commitments in the military (still heavily dominated by US suppliers — particularly in aircraft), and in infrastructural fields (Jubail, itself, is planned to cost around $40 billion over a decade, and the new airport at Jeddah is scheduled to cost $7 billion — in itself, equivalent to three or four ethylene complexes). Then again, even when an American company does become a partner with the Saudis, there is no guarantee that US companies will get the bulk of the supply contracts. Mobil, for instance, has worked closely with the Japanese plant construction company, Chiyoda, over the years.

Thus, direct investment by US companies into Middle Eastern joint ventures will never make up more than a part of US export policy. Admittedly, the various joint commissions in countries such as Saudi Arabia and Iran have a role to play, particularly in areas such as nuclear sales where politics and commerce are very intertwined. On balance, though, what matters most is that the US should have the Dollar at a competitive level. Certainly, it has the advantage of extremely close ties with the Saudis, and it has to be able to capitalise on the dominant strategic role it plays in the region. On the other hand, it does suffer from the disadvantage of being considerably further geographically from this particular market than the West Europeans — and though distance is each year of less and less importance within the world economy, it cannot yet be totally discounted. Also, US law which limits compliance with the Arab Boycott is considerably tougher than anything enacted elsewhere in the OECD world — and this harms its exports to the region, too.

Limited problems

It is unlikely that the US will be faced with particularly large quantities of products from Middle Eastern plants, although the latters' impact on Western Europe may well have some ripple effects across the Atlantic.

Geography

We have already explained in an earlier chapter that transportation costs are a factor which have to be taken into account, in which case the Atlantic should prove quite a potent barrier to Middle Eastern products. Depending on the exact assumption one makes, it would appear that Saudi-West European transport costs through the Suez Canal will amount on average to about half those involved in Saudi-US East Coast trade in base petrochemical products. This should be enough to make their direct impact relatively small.

Transport costs are not, however, so great that Middle Eastern products will have no impact on the US market. For one thing, one would expect quite sizeable exchange arrangements to be made between some of the US foreign partners involved in these projects and US companies with a stronger marketing presence in regions closer to the Middle East. So, the Middle Eastern plants would release products into the North American market — but at one remove. There is also the possibility that Middle Eastern exports to Western Europe will force companies there to look further westwards to take up slack in their own plants.

On the surface, none of this should matter since US capacity ratios are not too much out of line with domestic and export demand. This is particularly true of refining where refinery utilisation reached the high level of 88 per cent in 1978.[3] Because of the strong environmental pressures and government regulations against building new refineries (only two large new refineries have been built in the US since the mid-1960s), there should be plenty of room for imports from new refining centres. One study sponsored by the US Department of Energy claims that imports of oil products from the Middle East could rise from around 100,000 b/d in 1976 to 600,000 b/d in 1990.[4]

Before the Middle Easterners become too excited about this, however, they should do some thinking about the political problems such imports might entail. They might start with the awareness that US policies affecting the imports of oil have always been petty-minded — and will probably remain so. A country which devised administrative lunacies such as the notorious 'Brownsville loop' (in which, for various arcane reasons, Mexican oil would be moved by tanker to Brownsville, Texas, then loaded into trucks which crossed back into Mexico and then immediately re-crossed into the United States, to be loaded back into tankers which could then steam north) is perfectly capable of sabotaging, unintentionally or otherwise, the export plans of any other country in the world. For one thing, US refineries are currently processing American oil which officially comes to them at prices substantially below world levels, thus immediately ensuring that US capacity is utilised first. Depending on President Carter's firmness in decontrolling the price of domestically produced oil, US crude prices should move up to world levels in the early 1980s, thus giving imports rather greater freedom to penetrate the US market. A large slice of these imports, however, will inevitably go to Venezuelan and Caribbean refiners which have come to be the 'swing' suppliers of products to the United States and have borne the brunt of the preferred position given to US refiners. In 1976 they sent 1.5 million b/d of products to the United States under extremely complex regulations, which very much limited them to the heavy (fuel oil) end of the barrel.[5] The US Department of Energy study, mentioned above, suggests that these sources will provide the US market with between 1.9 and 2.1 million b/d of products through the 1980s to 1990.

Given the past arbitrariness of US import policies, one cannot be too dogmatic about how these policies will develop in the future — but one suspects that Middle Eastern products will not be given particularly favourable treatment. On the one hand, would-be exporters can take encouragement from the fact that US refiners will have to become more tolerant of imports in general, since the shortfall between US oil production and demand would appear likely to rise from 8.7 million b/d in 1977 to 10-11 million b/d in the 1980s. Also, attempts to build new refining capacity within the United States (such as at Hampton Roads) to process crude imports are facing all the old difficulties of obtaining the necessary official permits (many environmentally based), so there should be room for product imports to at least double between 1976 and 1990.[6]

Caribbean competition

The Middle Easterners face not only competition for European markets from North African refiners who have shorter transportation links, but even tougher competition for the United States market from the Mexican, Venezuelan and other Caribbean refiners. Of these competitors, the Venezuelans will become less important as their production starts to decline and domestic demand increases. The Mexicans are still difficult to place in context, since the upper limits of their recent oil

133

discoveries have yet to be established, and we have no clear picture of how their export policies will evolve. What we can say, though, is that Mexico is under exactly the same pressures to move into downstream refining and petrochemical investments as are the Middle Easterners. The former, of course, has the irresistible advantage of being just over the border from the United States and so should be able to undercut any products from the Eastern Hemisphere.

Thus, it seems unlikely that the US would support Middle Eastern projects over Venezuelan or Mexican ones, although past US policies have been too erratic to give a clear indication of whether some form of preference might be given to products from these two countries.[7] On the other hand, there are refineries elsewhere in the region which might be viewed as expendable. These would be the ones in the US Virgin Islands, the Bahamas, Trinidad, Puerto Rico, Colombia, Panama and the Netherlands Antilles, which are typically designed to deal with the heavy end of the barrel which US regulations allow into the US East Coast. Just over a third of this capacity is owned by the international majors,[8] so it would be administratively easy for them to phase out these refineries, which are generally producing the less attractive heavy products, should the companies find themselves having to market quantities of products from joint ventures they have in the Middle East. On the other hand, there are the inevitable political distortions which go with US oil import policies, since the Virgin Islands, Puerto Rico and Bahamas all qualify for preferential treatment as far as the US market is concerned, and of the companies involved in these locations, only Socal also has a stake in the Middle East. The companies connected with these islands will certainly fight within Washington against any attempts to remove their privileged status, and such special interests can normally be counted on to delay (if not successfully fight off) concessions being offered to foreign governments.

West Europeans

Even supposing the Middle Easterners can prevent US policy from favouring non-US refineries in the Western Hemisphere, there is still the problem of the West Europeans to overcome. Certainly until the mid-1980s, there is going to be enough spare capacity in Europe to make exports to North America a real attraction. The previously mentioned study for the US Department of Energy suggests that West Europe could be exporting some 500,000 b/d of products to the US by 1980, and that this would vary between 300,000 and 400,000 b/d for the rest of the decade.[9] In these circumstances, the West Europeans should be competitive with Middle Eastern products, because they are significantly closer to the US and will be producing from plant which in many

134

cases will be older (and hence cheaper) than those in the Middle East.

None of this is very optimistic for the Middle Easterners. With US gasoline demand expected to start declining from 1979 onwards with the improvement in Detroit's mileage-per-gallon, the products which will continue to grow in importance are products such as fuel oil, which are precisely the kind of low-value product whose economics are sensitive to transport costs. There are respected figures such as John Lichtblau who argue that US demand for oil products in 1985 will only call for another 1-1.2 million b/d of new refining capacity within the US, the Caribbean or the Eastern Hemisphere.[10] The chances of the Middle Easterners being squeezed out of a share of this incremental demand could be quite high. The main ray of hope is that the US refining industry is badly equipped to deal with high-sulphur crudes — which it will increasingly have to take, as 'sweet' (low-sulphur) crudes are more rapidly consumed. As Lichtblau argues elsewhere, there is going to be a need for a certain amount of investment in desulphuri-sation facilities. This could be located at either end of crude flows, but since desulphurisation is a process which is particularly heavy in its use of hydrogen (hydrogen production can add 80 cents to $1 to the cost of treating a barrel of residual fuel oil), the availability of plentiful low-cost natural gas in the exporting countries will make hydrogen production relatively cheap by US standards, and thus make it logical to build the necessary plant in producing rather than consuming countries.[11] On the other hand, even if this analysis is correct, there is some possibility that it will be the Mexicans or Venezuelans rather than the Middle Easterners who will be best placed to gain further access to the US market by following such a strategy.

Tariffs

In the case of petrochemical products from the Middle East, the barriers are going to be political rather than geographical. For one thing, US tariffs on petrochemical products are high by industrialised world standards. One large category of such imports (the so-called benzenoid chemicals) are kept out by a protectionist device known as the American Selling Price, which has survived unscathed from succeeding rounds of GATT tariff cutting. In the Multilaterial Trade Negotiations, which are taking place within the GATT framework as we write, the US negotiators have proved willing to drop the American Selling Price system, but will still end up with an effective tariff of 10-12 per cent against the average chemical import. If these negotiations do lead to general tariff cuts (and it is by no means certain they will be successful), then the EC countries will reduce their effective tariffs to a much lower 3-4 per cent. If the talks fail, the US will continue effective tariffs of over 20 per cent against many products, a virtually insurmountable barrier to would-be exporters from the Middle East.[12] One barrier which should disappear, however, is the one whereby the American chemical industry has been able to call on gas feedstocks at prices well below world levels. This has stemmed from the long-standing US refusal to accept world-level pricing for domestic oil and gas supplies, and this has infuriated the Europeans whose industry has had to rest on higher-priced naphtha. All indications are that US gas prices will now be decontrolled by 1985, thus increasing the vulnerability of the US chemical industry to imports and, incidentally, increasing the interest of US companies to become involved in parts of the world where gas supplies are still relatively under-utilised.

Politicising US import policies

If one conclusion had to be drawn for would-be exporters to the United States it would be that there is probably no single country whose future import policies are harder to predict. Chemical imports are already a political issue, with a strong industry lobby determined to protect itself from too keen international competition. Oil products are even more complicated, with different regions ranged against each other and special interests running rampant. Since it is still not absolutely clear when US crude prices will finally be allowed to rise to world levels (officially this should happen by 1980), and we cannot tell if the authorities will allow new, worldscale refineries to be built on American soil, it would appear presumptuous to predict how individual foreign countries will be treated during the 1980s.

Confusion on import policies is best exemplified in the field of gas, where the situation has been changing very quickly as US gas supplies suddenly started to fall well behind demand. Some deal might have been struck with the Mexicans, but Energy Secretary James Schlesinger refused to approve the purchase of Mexican gas at $2.60 per thousand cubic feet, even though permission had been given for the import of some Liquefied Natural Gas from Algeria at higher prices. It was only in early 1979 that an apparently coherent gas import policy started to emerge. Schlesinger announced that there was now a hierarchy of alternative gas sources. First would come Alaskan gas, followed by pipeline gas from Canada and Mexico, then by short-haul LNG with 'long-haul, high-cost, possibly insecure' LNG taking last place.[13] This should bring a long period of uncertainty to an end. In the meantime, at least two major LNG deals (the Algerian Eascogas and the Iranian El Paso ones) had collapsed in the face of seemingly endless procrastination by the Federal Power Commission and its successors. The Middle Easterners can take no comfort from the newly-emerged policy, for they are the most significant potential long-haul suppliers to the US market.

US economic decision-making will continue to play havoc with the plans of potential trade partners, but it is doubtful if there will be any serious centralisation or rationalisation of this process in the foreseeable future. The consumer interest in low prices will continue (through bodies like the Federal Energy Regulatory Commission) to bedevil import deals which raise American energy prices. The environmental interest groups which have blocked virtually all serious refinery projects since 1970 will continue to regard import terminals for LNG, oil and chemical products with the utmost suspicion. The result will be that the more desirable and valuable products which the oil-producing countries may choose to produce are precisely the less stable and more environmentally troublesome ones. So, even if would-be Middle Eastern exporters to the United States can defeat the special interests which may fight them on Capitol Hill, they may well find themselves bogged down in planning hearings which will sorely test their patience. Although the motives of planners and environmentalists will be pure, the effect will be to deter would-be exporters to the United States and to force them to follow the path that the Algerians are treading, i.e. seeking alternative markets in economies in which decisions can be made relatively promptly. On the other hand, the fact that environmental worries may continue to stop the construction of the necessary import shipping terminals will mean that domestic processing capacity will be blocked as well. This will certainly encourage companies to look outside the United States for countries with speedier or less onerous decision-making processes.

A rather curious picture thus emerges. The US implicitly stimulates American companies to invest in productive facilities in the oil-producing world, without offering any guarantees that the products will be accepted back into the United States. To fellow governments within the industrialised world, this may pose some extra burdens if they are already wrestling with problems of industrial over-capacity. Ultimately, though, there will be an indirect economic impact on the United States. There is not a great deal that the US can do about the plateauing of its oil and gas production, but its refusal to come to terms with the implications of this for its hydrocarbon-processing industries is damaging. Under-pricing hydrocarbons today (which encourages consumption) will only increase the rapidity with which such industries will corner remaining oil and gas supplies; they will be willing to pay premium prices which will be out of the reach of those wanting to use such sources for heating or ground transportation purposes. Restricting refinery construction merely ensures that increased oil imports will inevitably take the form of more expensive and environmentally dangerous oil products rather than crude. Restricting gas imports will tempt industrialists to migrate to countries where gas supplies are more readily available.

Past and present policies suggest that the US will resist allowing itself to become too affected by product imports, be they from the Eastern or Western Hemisphere. Clearly, though, whatever countries do manage to provide the relevant products, the Middle Easterners are going to be in an extremely marginal position. Therefore, one might go on to argue that the US has no real policy interests in Middle Eastern industrialisation beyond the specific ones of backing US corporate interests and pushing American exports into the area. But policy-makers in Washington would be wrong to take too narrow a view since there are broader, OECD-wide concerns.

'Western' interests

Washington is not only the capital of the United States, but it also gives leadership to the non-communist, industrialised world. In this wider role, there are one or two further considerations which need to be taken into account.

Petrodollar absorption

One strong argument for encouraging the oil producers to push ahead with industrialisation is that there are few more potent ways (other than selling armaments) of making the oil producers spend their petrodollars, thus further reducing the spectre of international financial collapse which stared the OECD world in the face in 1974 (when the oil producers ran a current account surplus of $68 billion – up from $3.5 billion the year before). The absorption of these petrodollar surpluses has gone on apace, even before export-oriented industrialisation has had a chance of playing any but a rather minor role. Quite simply, direct demand for consumer goods, and expenditure on weapons and infrastructure (though a fair amount of the latter is for pre-industrial activity) have lapped up far more money than the pessimists feared. The absorptive process has also been helped by OPEC's unwillingness to price its oil in a 'basket' of currencies, thus leaving it exposed to the ravages of the falling Dollar, and by the fact that economic growth (and the world's resultant demand for oil) slowed down after 1973, reducing oil income still further below what the pessimists would have predicted.

The result has been that OPEC imports grew from $29 billion per annum in 1973 to some $142 billion in 1978, or an average nominal increase of over 37 per cent (in real terms, OPEC as a whole increased imports by some 25 per cent per annum during this period). Saudi

Arabia easily outpaced the average OPEC member, raising its imports by 55 per cent per annum during this period to an estimated $33 billion in 1978.[14] This meant that the Saudis came perilously close to failing to cover their import bill from oil income for the first time since 1973. Needing an annual export achievement of over 7 million b/d to cover a $33 million import bill, the country was averaging only 7.6 million b/d from January to July, and its balance of international payments actually went into deficit to the tune of $1.1 billion in the first quarter of 1978.[15] Ultimately, however, its export earnings surged ahead of its import bill thanks to the end-of-year pre-OPEC meeting surge in oil purchases, helped by the collapse of Iranian production, which extra Saudi production partially replaced. It was, however, a year which must have reminded the Saudis that their import needs are inexorably climbing and that they must keep their oil income climbing by combining steadily increased crude exports with real increases in the OPEC-determined price for crude oil.

Now, obviously, Saudi imports cannot keep rising at 55 per cent per annum in nominal terms, but it is equally obvious that their annual rise is not going to slow down to, for example, 10 per cent per annum, which is the probable annual rise in crude prices in the early 1980s.[16] Any further increases in Saudi income, therefore, will have to come partially from increased crude production. This is the reason why at least one of us feels that concern about Saudi Arabia refusing to lift crude production levels through the 1980s to those needed by the world economy is perhaps overdone. Saudi import demand, even before the construction of the kind of projects which this book has been considering, is proving so buoyant that the Saudis will have to increase their annual production of crude, even if OPEC manages to keep oil prices moving somewhat ahead of world inflation rates. The construction of export-oriented plants can only strengthen this propensity to import (and thus to produce crude), particularly since the products are not likely to become significant as a source of revenue until well into the late 1980s. A further benefit to be gained by the OECD world is that once such ventures are in operation, they will generate a demand for gas which will tend to ensure quite substantial production levels for the associated crude. In 1973, Saudi Arabia could cut back crude exports without doing any incidental harm to its economy, thereby foregoing only 'lost' oil revenues. As each year goes by and electricity systems, desalination plants, petrochemical complexes and, even, (for their energy) refineries, come to be dependent on associated gas, cutting back crude production for whatever reason may have a broader, more damaging impact on the wider Saudi economy. The expected Saudi move would be to develop some 'dry' gas fields — i.e. not associated with oil production — to cover a higher proportion of their internal fuel needs.

Social implications of capital-intensive industrialisation

These are uncompromising arguments, but ones which the OECD world must inevitably listen to. There is, however, at least one serious set of counter-arguments. The massive unrest experienced in Iran suggests that 'growth' which relies excessively on capital-intensive investment is inherently unstable. Obviously, a country's long-term balance of payments matters, so oil producers must be concerned with trying to ensure that there is industry in place when their oil dries up. However, over-emphasis on capital-intensive industrialisation may cause as many problems as it solves. Technological complexity means that increasingly scarce capital is used to create a few thousand jobs, the most demanding of which will tend to be given to foreigners. Because there is not much evidence of really significant links between these capital-intensive complexes and the local economy, not much is done to create jobs among the indigenous population in the short-to-medium term. The Iranian case clearly demonstrates that, in a relatively populous society, an insensitively-run, capital-intensive industrialisation programme can cause so much resentment among those who do not directly benefit, that the whole modernisation plan can be put in jeopardy.

In the Saudi case, the immediate dangers are rather less as the House of Saud has greater legitimacy in Saudi Arabia than the Pahlavis had in Iran. Thus, the strains caused by over-rapid industrialisation would tend to show up as disputes within the Saudi ruling family, rather than as a challenge to their whole regime. On the other hand, there is a real possibility that the growing numbers of expatriate workers will pose problems for the Kingdom. Such numbers are difficult to estimate, but there could be anything up to 1.5 million Yemenis working in the country, while the 1976-80 Plan called for at least 500,000 other expatriate workers.[17] The argument put forward by officials such as the Industry Minister, Dr al-Qusaibi,[18] is that this is a passing problem, since the basic industries being planned will not use more than 20,000 workers; to start with at least a quarter of these will be Saudis, increasing, it is hoped, to 75 per cent after the first ten years of operation. He could be right, but any Westerner who argues that Saudi industrialisation should be encouraged at all costs must bear in mind that the problem with expatriates could prove much more serious than the Minister is willing to accept. It is unlikely that the Kuwaiti situation will be repeated, in which indigenous citizens are outnumbered by foreigners. But there is a real possibility that expatriates will gradually make up about 40 per cent of the country's population at any one

140

time. Probably, the highly-paid expatriates from the OECD world will not matter too much, since few of them will want to make a long-term commitment to the Kingdom. The problems will be caused by expatriates from the immediate region who will increasingly want stability of employment and political rights which the Saudis are unlikely to give them.

The anti-Soviet angle

Accepting that there is an upper limit to the speed with which capital-intensive industrialisation within the Middle East can be carried out without destroying the social fabric of the countries concerned, there are 'Great Power' considerations which must also be taken into account. One can certainly argue that a major Washington goal is to keep the Soviet Union in a minor role within the Middle East. The US has been largely successful in this policy, although geography plays into the hands of the Soviets and the US has been historically allied to Israel. The Camp David summit in September 1978 indicates how protection of Middle East oil is worrying the US to the extent of taking further considerable risks in pressing for a Middle East peace formula. Even though the Soviet Union has experienced some success in various countries of marginal importance (Afghanistan, the PDRY and Ethiopia), it has totally failed to regain the influence it had in the region in the days of President Nasser. This is despite the fact that there are countries such as Libya, Syria and Iraq whose position on the Israeli-Palestinian issue has pushed them in an anti-American direction.

It is possible that the Soviet Union's apparent lack of impact is illusory. Certainly, one can argue that the Soviet Union does have a somewhat opportunistic strategy aimed at strengthening the position of its allies towards the oil-rich Gulf countries,[19] but then one is struck by just how little the Soviet Union has to offer the region in any area other than arms. Despite the fact that it has a long common border with Iran and that there has been a friendly regime in Iraq since the early 1960s, the Soviet Union and the East European countries have an abysmal trade record with the Middle Eastern region. In 1975, these countries contributed only 9 per cent of Iraq's imports, 4 per cent of Iran's and 1 per cent of Saudi Arabia's — a performance which individual countries such as West Germany and the United Kingdom easily surpassed.[20]

Quite clearly, the Soviet Union has proved incapable of supplying the good quality technology which the oil-rich Middle Easterners need. Certainly, there is a handful of major Soviet deals such as the Iranian blast-furnace complex at Isfahan (pre-dating the oil price rise), but otherwise the Eastern Europeans are conspicuous by their lack of involvement in such projects. Instead, it is the West Europeans, Japanese and Americans who have won the overwhelming bulk of such projects, indicating that the Soviet Union and her allies have very little to offer outside the military field.

This does not mean that the Eastern bloc will be without political importance in the region, but there is something very unbalanced about its potential contribution — so strong in military matters and so weak in commercial ones. There is now so much industrial activity within the region that no oil-producing country can turn a blind eye to failures in its own technology. One can, therefore, be confident that, if any of the major Middle Eastern powers were tempted to take an anti-Western attitude, the technological factor would still pull it back towards the OECD world. Obviously, we are not arguing that the US any longer dominates the world industrial scene, so that technological needs inevitably throw a country into American arms. On the other hand, it is clear that the OECD members, in general, do possess a technological lead over the East Europeans. They also have the hard currency markets where products can, it is hoped, be relatively easily disposed of. All told, then, the kind of export-oriented projects we have been discussing in this book will tend to reinforce this lead of the OECD world within the Middle East.

A possible backlash?

One final consideration which needs to be taken into account, is what will happen if the ambitions of the Middle Easterners are thwarted. In the course of this book we have suggested various reasons why the bigger projects might be delayed — disappointing markets, tariffs, outright protectionism and, in the case of joint ventures, a growing caution on the part of the foreign corporate partners. There are already some indications on the Saudi side of growing impatience with OECD excuses about why Middle Eastern ventures make little economic sense. There is the danger that this resentment, which is only just surfacing, could grow worse as time goes on.

To the individual corporations concerned, such resentment could be of great importance. After all, the Saudi projects involve access to well over 250,000 b/d of crude oil in an era when oil production will be reaching its peak. Secondly, the oil-producing economies are going to be wealthy by the standards of many LDCs, and no company wants to be excluded from selling products to them or from picking up the smaller import-substituting projects which, spread across a number of such countries, can cumulatively be quite important. Either way, the companies which are negotiating the relevant joint ventures will be aware that commercial necessity may force them to drag their feet at a time when the governments concerned may want to press ahead. Just as Mitsubishi ran into a great deal of anti-Mitsubishi, anti-Japanese sentiment, when the company originally decided to pull out of the proposed ethylene complex in Saudi Arabia, equally some very emotionally-charged times may lie ahead, if the other joint ventures are continually postponed.

The industrialised world will have a greater worry that Middle Eastern resentment may culminate in the mid to late 1980s, when some of these projects will actually be in operation and may have considerable difficulties in finding markets. The timing of the growth of such resentment could be extremely important, because this may be the time when OPEC oil production would be at its maximum permitted levels; thus, much could hinge on the production policies of Saudi Arabia, the one country with the potential to produce more than 14 million b/d, if it would be willing to make the necessary investment. Tough OECD policies to restrict oil demand may reduce the need for a really huge increase in Saudi production, but policy-makers would be mad to ignore the possibility of encouraging the Saudis to produce more. Officially, reports that the Kingdom will produce 20 million b/d are, to quote Sheikh Yamani's words, 'figments of the imagination which we must not take seriously'.[21] There is a danger however that the Saudis may not even invest in facilities which would permit a production rate of 15 million b/d.[22] OECD diplomatic options, therefore, have to be left open. This may mean encouraging companies to go ahead with marginal investments they might otherwise consider dropping, or developing a consensus among OECD members about how much tolerance should be given to Middle Eastern (particularly Saudi) products as they come on to the world markets of the 1980s. It might even mean using channels such as the US-Saudi Joint Economic Commission or the Euro-Arab Dialogue to come to some agreement, whereby Saudi willingness to expand productive capacity beyond the currently contemplated 14 million b/d would be rewarded with a detailed understanding about how Saudi or Middle Eastern oil and petrochemical products will be received by the OECD world. What should be avoided at all costs is for the proposed ventures to fade away in an atmosphere of bickering. It may well be that the world will never call on Saudi Arabia to pump more crude than it is willing to produce for sound commercial reasons, but the OECD countries cannot count on this. Outside the Israeli-Palestinian issue, there is probably no single potential source of discord more potent than the fate of the projects this book has been discussing.

Notes

1   *Petroleum Intelligence Weekly*, May 1 1978, pp 3-4.
2   Turner, 1978a, chapter 9.
3   Department of Energy (US), 1978b, p.6; Lichtblau, 1978a, p.45.
4   Department of Energy (US), 1978a, table 9.
5   For an enjoyable introduction to the intricacies of US oil import policies, see Bradford, 1975.
6   Department of Energy (US), 1978, table 9.
7   As late as 1972, the US was still refusing to give the Venezuelans preference over supplies from the Eastern Hemisphere, choosing to rely, for security reasons, on Canadian supplies. (Tugwell, 1975, p.135).
8   Department of Energy (US), 1978a, p.217.
9   Department of Energy (US), 1978a, table 9.
10   Lichtblau, 1978b, p.8.
11   Lichtblau, 1978a, p.47; Department of Energy (US), 1978a, pp 12-13, 84-5.
12   *Economist*, August 12 1978, p.75.
13   *Petroleum Intelligence Weekly*, January 15 1979, pp 3-4.
14   *Middle East Economic Survey*, August 14 1978, p.6.
15   *IMF Survey*, September 4 1978, p.265.
16   Some people argue that the Saudi import capacity will grow more slowly, once the current burst of infrastructural investment is over. We feel this argument can be given too much emphasis.
17   Official Saudi advertisement, *Guardian* (London), August 22 1977.
18   *Middle East Economic Survey* Supplement, May 8 1978, pp 5-6.
19   Klinghoffer, 1977; Yodfat and Abir, 1977.
20   Bedore and Turner, 1977, p.333.
21   PIRINC, 1978, pp 6-17.
22   In 1976, the Saudis were intending to invest sufficiently to increase their output capacity to over 14 million b/d. In late 1977 or during 1978, these plans were cut back for financial reasons; after all, the early 1980s looked then as though they would be marked by an oil glut, thus making immediate expansion a wasteful investment. There has also been a downward revision of estimates of sustainable production levels given the *existing* productive facilities. Weighing the evidence from Saudi performance during the Iranian crisis, *Petroleum Intelligence Weekly* cut its estimates of the Kingdom's current output capacity from 11.8 million b/d to 10.8 million (*Petroleum Intelligence Weekly*, May 14 1979, p.11). It is thus not at all certain what the Saudis could produce during the 1980s if they chose to. What is undisputed is that they could produce more than 10.8 million b/d if they made the necessary investments. That is what has to be bargained for.

9 The issues for Japan

It was inevitable that Japan would move rapidly to cash in on any Middle Eastern economic boom. Throughout this century, the country has been particularly dependent on imported raw materials and this dependence became worse with the switch to oil. By 1972, only Finland, Ireland, Luxembourg and Denmark amongst the OECD member countries were more dependent on imported energy. Japan was 90 per cent dependent on such imports, compared with the British and West Germans, who could provide half their own energy needs, or with the Americans who were 86 per cent self-sufficient.[1] To make matters even worse, Japan was particularly dependent on oil as a source of energy and so, because of its geographical position, had come to rely heavily on the Middle East, since only Indonesia among non-Middle Eastern oil producers was in a position to provide any serious quantities of crude. By 1973, Japan was taking more than four times as much oil from the Middle East as the United States.[2] In Dollar terms, the impact of the oil price rises meant that its import bill for Middle Eastern crude went up from $3 billion in 1973 to $14 billion in 1974.

Table 9.1
Japan-Middle East trade flows: 1973-77 (excluding invisibles)

Year	Japanese imports of M.E. crude		Japanese exports in $ billion to		
	million b/d	$ billion	Middle East	(Saudi Arabia)	(Iran)
1973	4.4	3	1.2	(0.3)	(0.5)
1974	4.1	14	2.3	(0.5)	(0.8)
1975	3.7	15	4.9	(1.5)	(1.7)
1976	3.9	16	6.4	(2.1)	(2.1)
1977	4.1	19	7.9	(2.6)	(2.1)

Sources: Various issues of BP Statistical Review of the World Oil Industry, Directions of Trade, Yearbook of International Trade Statistics.

As can be seen from table 9.1, Japan has still not come near to balancing its trade flows with the Middle Eastern oil producers, nor does it have the 'services' cushion which makes the American and British current accounts position better than the trade flows indicate.

145

On the other hand, Japan successfully raised its share of the Middle Eastern oil producer's market from 14.5 per cent in 1973 to nearly 18 per cent in 1975. Its share dropped slightly after that peak, but still ran at over 17 per cent in 1977.

Corporate vulnerability

As Japan has had no historic ties with the Middle East region, and because the Yen has risen fast since 1975, this has been a creditable performance. Much of the result has been achieved by Japanese exporters spotting openings in markets for cars, consumer durables and, even more so, for industrial plant. This latter sector was apparently identified by MITI in the early 1970s as an area of some priority. It is, therefore, very gratifying that Japanese companies such as Chiyoda, Kako Kensetsu and Toyo Engineering have done extremely well in the desalination plant field, that Japanese companies have proved themselves effective contractors in a number of Saudi projects, and that the Iraqis turned to Japan for a number of fertiliser and refinery projects.

On the other hand, precisely because they have no historic ties with the region, they cannot afford to be satisfied with temporary trading successes. There are already signs that the rising Yen is pricing the Japanese out of business in the area, and the fact that their market share in the Middle East reached its peak in 1975 must give them some cause for alarm. Their hope must be that, being such a massive customer for Middle Eastern oil and gas (which is growing more and more important), they will merit considerate treatment from these oil producers. But the Japanese, who put some effort into 'petro-diplomacy' in early 1973, know only too well that in times of crisis, the Middle Easterners will give them no priority treatment. In fact, the Japanese fears go deeper. They suspect that in a future panic the Americans will always be tempted to use their diplomatic leverage on the region to get preferential access to oil and gas supplies. The Japanese are particularly aware that they are vulnerable, since they are not in the armaments business.

One way to strengthen relations between Japan and the Middle East is for the former's companies to invest there, thus building permanent links which will remain — irrespective of the fate of trade flows. It is still unclear, however, just how effectively the Japanese will be able to follow this particular strategy. Alternatively, the Middle Easterners can be encouraged to buy Japanese stocks, and there is some satisfaction in Tokyo due to the fact that there have been purchases of Japanese Public Bonds by some Middle Easterners.

On the one hand, the government and corporate sectors have been united since the late 1960s in their belief that Japanese companies should be investing much more heavily abroad. By 1973, such direct investments were running at more than eight times the amount they had been five years earlier.[3] There are a number of general factors which have played a role in this process — such as the growing scarcity of cheap labour, worries about pollution and escalating land prices. In particular, the Japanese petrochemical industry has had very strong motives for investing outside Japan, since naphtha prices at home have been deliberately kept above world levels in order to keep down the prices of other, more politically-sensitive parts of the barrel (particularly fuel oil and kerosene). In 1977, for instance, domestically produced naphtha was costing the petrochemical companies a quarter more than the price charged in Europe, and 40 per cent more than US levels. Not only were naphtha imports officially limited by the Japanese authorities, but importing rights were reserved for refining companies only. It is small wonder, then, that the Japanese petrochemical companies were anxious to invest overseas; this would at last give them access to feedstocks at world prices and would free them from the strict environmental regulations in Japan.

On the other hand, the petrochemical companies concerned are small and poorly financed by world standards, and there are real doubts as to whether they are sufficiently strong to play the kind of investment role which the Japanese authorities would like. This weakness stems partly from the policy decisions described in the previous paragraph, favouring heavy industry at the expense of most of the industries supplying the necessary energy, the very strong electric power companies being the main exception. In the case of petrochemicals, official policies favoured energy-intensive, heavy industries which had privileged access to refined oil products.[4] This weakness also relates to the way in which Japanese trading companies have followed an excessive policy of 'me-tooism'. Each major group insists on having a petrochemical venture within it, even if this means that the industry becomes excessively fragmented. The general picture is that the Japanese may have around twice as many chemical producing companies per head of population as do the Americans or West Europeans.[5]

Because this fragmentation of the industry is imposed on a structure in which trading company 'families' (for example, Mitsui, Mitsubishi, Sumitomo) are of considerable importance, the picture is very confused. On the one hand, the two largest Japanese chemical companies (numbers 22 and 25 in 1977 world sales rankings) are tiny by world standards; in 1977 Mitsubishi Chemical had 8,800 employees and Sumitomo Chemical had 11,200, compared with ICI and Hoechst, which both had over 180,000 employees. On the other hand, each trading group's chemical interests are spread over a number of distinct 'family' companies; Mitsubishi Chemical is in the same loose confederation as Asahi Glass, Mitsubishi Rayon, Mitsubishi Monsanto Chemical, Mitsubishi Petrochemical, Mitsubishi Gas Chemical and Mitsubishi Plastics Industry.[6] This grouping of companies with chemical interests obviously makes each trading company confederation rather stronger than the analysis of any one of its parts might indicate. Conversely, this is at the expense of a complex decision-making process which may be unsuited for the stresses and strains of overseas investment in the 1980s. A further consideration worth bearing in mind is that the average Japanese chemical company is financially very exposed, compared with its Western competitors. In general it appears that the former's debt equity ratio is around 80:20, compared with the 30:70 ratios found with many US chemical companies.[7]

It is probably a combination of the relative smallness of the Japanese petrochemical companies and their high debt-equity ratio which explains why they have had a distinctive history in Saudi Arabia and Iran. We have explained in chapter 4 that both Mitsubishi and Mitsui became interested in Middle Eastern investments independently of any encouragement given by the Japanese government. The distinctive element in both cases, however, is that when they ran into trouble (Mitsui in 1973-75 and 1978-79 in Iran; Mitsubishi when it was forced back into Saudi Arabia), they naturally turned to the Japanese government for financial help and, in the Mitsubishi case, for finding other Japanese companies with which the risk could be shared. This contrasts significantly with their Western competitors who either chose not to become involved or, if they decided to keep negotiating, have resigned themselves to financing, through normal commercial channels, any parts of the ventures which they could not persuade the host governments to cover.

Inevitably, then, the relative weakness of the Japanese petrochemical companies means that the Japanese government is going to be far more entangled with the investment decisions of her corporate sector than are the other OECD governments. In an age which puts greater stress on intergovernmental negotiations in economic issues, this may not be of great concern — though there has been some expression of unease by the Saudis about the idea of any of the joint ventures involving foreign governments. On the other hand the Saudis are as aware as any other Middle Eastern government of the value in diversifying markets. At a time when the West Europeans are crying out that their economies are so plagued with over-capacity that they cannot guarantee to accept future Middle Eastern products, the existence of a few projects which look eastwards for their markets is attractive. It should be noted, however, that the Japanese authorities insisted that the IJPC partners in Iran commit themselves to consult with MITI before starting exports to

Japan.

The spread of Japanese private investment means, however, that this country will now be exposed to the type of investment disputes in the Middle East with which more traditional parent governments of multinational companies have had to wrestle for years. To take but one example: whatever the fate of the Shah by the time this book is published, there is a strong possibility of a more xenophobic reaction to foreign businesses operating within Iran. Under the Shah this would have manifested itself in efforts to reduce the role of the oil Consortium even further from its present, ambiguous position. This would have been a problem for the British, American and Dutch governments, but would not have involved the Japanese. The Mitsui stake in the Iran-Japan Petrochemical Company, however, means that the Japanese are now for the first time very exposed to any xenophobic backlash in the Middle East. It is problematic whether Tokyo will be able to handle such a crisis. There is at least one Japanese author[8] who argues that his government is still extremely inexperienced in handling the diplomacy surrounding Japanese investments. Based on our rather limited evidence from the Middle East, we see no reason to dispute his judgement. Tokyo is undoubtedly learning that overseas private investments bring their headaches, as well as their expected economic benefits.

Capacity problems and rationalisation

On the surface, Japanese problems with over-capacity in our two main industries are quite similar to those facing West Europe. Ethylene production at home has, for instance, run stubbornly at 70 per cent of capacity during 1977 and 1978 (compared with 92 per cent in 1973).[9] On the other hand, compared with their West European competitors, the Japanese chemical companies have been relatively restrained in recent years. They have built only two new plants since 1972. Showa Denko's ethylene cracker became operative in August 1977 and was allowed to begin operations only after the firm had closed an older and smaller plant down for a year,[10] so avoiding further aggravation of the industry's capacity problems. In early 1978, in marked contrast to Western Europe, which faces a similar position of over-capacity, there were no further ethylene crackers under construction. The relatively fast reactions of the Japanese industry probably reflect a combination of its cash-flow problems and its growing lack of enthusiasm about investing on the Japanese mainland.

The Japanese, then, might be in a good position to take advantage of Middle Eastern industrial developments, with the next generation of plants being designed as complementary to the Middle Eastern base chemical projects. There are even signs that companies are indeed thinking this way. The Mitsui group, for instance, is starting to plan a petrochemical complex in the Northern Japanese island, Hokkaido. Although there is no certainty that anything will come of the discussions, planning is proceeding with the knowledge that Mitsui and other Japanese companies may well have built ethylene complexes in Saudi Arabia, Iran and Singapore by the time any Hokkaido development comes to fruition. Thus, Mitsui is reputedly giving serious consideration to using this new complex for specialised chemical production.[11] This is exactly the kind of complementary investment which the Arabs would like the West Europeans to consider.

The fragmentation and over-competition in these sectors, however, does threaten any such policy aimed at the inclusion of Middle Eastern imports in the home market. As previously noted, Japanese industry is still plagued with a 'me-too' investment philosophy. Every economically superfluous company increases the danger of another round of investment in Japanese capacity, perhaps triggered off by just one or two companies with refining interests whose future would be threatened by a decision to give the green light to a Middle Eastern export refinery such as the projected Irano-Japanese one at Bandar Shahpur. Similarly, there are around 12 ethylene producers in Japan, and MITI believes that only three or four of these could have an assured future.[12]

So, the Japanese authorities will have to work out any market access agreement with Middle Eastern producers against a background of considerable corporate reorganisation at home. Japan has one advantage over the Europeans because it has no worries concerning the nationalistic rivalries which have made the rationalisation of the European synthetic fibres industry so difficult. On the other hand, it is faced with the problem that its whole business philosophy makes drastic amalgamations within industries extremely difficult. Although there are signs that in certain industries the principle of closing down plants is gradually being accepted (e.g. in shipbuilding, where it is no longer a matter of course that the redundant workers are found other jobs within the company), Japanese companies have not yet learned to accept the cold-blooded takeover bid of failing companies — which is Europe's and America's most ruthless way of lopping off unwanted industrial capacity. Rather, where Japanese mergers do take place, they tend to resemble those found in Western Europe of the late 1950s and early 1960s. Neither of the merging companies takes command, and one is left with dual management and employment structures.[13] Certainly, MITI's one big attempt to rationalise part of the chemical industry (synthetic fibres) has so far not been very successful, precisely because the companies involved refuse to merge, arguing instead that the creation of joint overseas sales companies would be sufficient.

On balance, though, the Japanese ought to find it slightly easier than the West Europeans to make room for Middle Eastern products in the 1980s. After all, they have already partly sacrificed the refining and petrochemical sectors to wider national goals. These are potentially polluting industries which are less and less welcome in Japan (the fact that Mitsui is discussing Hokkaido as a site for a petrochemical complex, however, suggests there are still peripheral, sparsely-populated areas of Japan that prove willing to take such industries). In general, the rise of the Yen also makes both companies and the central government happy to see more overseas investment (the Ministry of Labour is an exception, warning against job export at a time when Japanese unemployment is at record levels). However, the number of Japanese companies which will be left without any viable future by such emphasis on the Middle Eastern projects will be high by European standards. In the West, a substantial part of the sectors under pressure is in the hands of multinational companies; these are prepared to move into more highly-skilled parts of the industries in question, or even to diversify in other areas, should the threat from the new industrial challengers be too strong. The Japanese, on the other hand, have gone out of their way to stop their refining companies from integrating either forwards or backwards — hence these companies have developed none of the adaptive skills the present problems require. Again, although the trading companies have the breadth of experience to move out of the most threatened sectors, the financial strength of the average petrochemical company in Japan remains open to question. It could just be that the rising Yen will tip many companies into such a situation that they have no cash to buy themselves into new businesses — and must therefore slide inevitably into the hands of the banks or the government. Only time will tell.

Regional trade-offs

Just as the West Europeans have to weigh any reaction to Middle Eastern industrial projects against the interests of North African and East European competitors, so the Japanese, too, have other outside interests to consider. For Japan, the problem is to reconcile Middle Eastern ambitions with those of its Asian neighbours such as Singapore, South Korea and Indonesia. The latter's oil may not be as crucial as the Middle East's, but Japanese diplomacy is more involved on a routine basis with Djakarta than with Riyadh, Teheran or Baghdad. In particular, Japan has a vested interest in keeping on good terms with South Korea and the countries (Indonesia, Malaysia, the Philippines, Singapore and Thailand) belonging to the Association of South East Asian Nations (ASEAN), which is the area's best hope for the emergence of a stable and prosperous bloc of anti-communist states. So, although Premier Fukuda toured the Middle East in autumn 1978, this visit came over a year after a six-nation tour of South East Asia had ended with the announcement of the 'Fukuda doctrine', stressing the need for mutual co-operation between Japan and the ASEAN group. In particular, he pledged $1 billion in assistance for joint development projects within ASEAN.

Luckily, the Japanese will never have to choose between the Middle East and South East Asia, but the interests of the two regions will sometimes clash. For instance, in the summer of 1977, Sumitomo put together proposals for a joint (fifty-fifty) venture (an ethylene complex) with the Singapore government and, by means of some hard politicking in Tokyo, had this denominated as a 'national' project, thus becoming eligible for some extra government aid. The proposal was by no means foolish because Singapore has an established refining industry and considerable industrial skills. It is also well located to serve as a trading centre in both oil and chemical products for much of South East Asia and Oceania. Shipments can either go north to markets such as Japan, the Philippines and Hong Kong, or south east to Australia. Certainly, Singapore will have a freight advantage in serving markets to the East,[14] and, with its well-developed industrial infrastructure, will not face the construction and operating disadvantages that exist in the Middle East.

Should the Sumitomo project finally come to fruition, however, it will play havoc with many of the initial assumptions made by Mitsui and Mitsubishi when they first looked at petrochemical investments in the Middle East. Quite clearly, the development of Singapore as a petrochemical centre would mean that one of the most logical markets for Middle Eastern products will be blocked. Again, the fact that Mitsui is entering an ethylene investment in South Korea as well as in Iran is not very conducive to reassuring Middle Easterners that their Japanese partners will be able to find markets to the East.

Of course, it could be that the Japanese will never really be faced with the problem of balancing the conflicting aspirations of the various Middle Eastern and East Asian claimants in the refining and petrochemical fields. The Mitsui project in Iran, the Sumitomo complex in Singapore or one of the Mitsubishi projects in Saudi Arabia could fade away or be badly delayed, thus reducing the all-out competition between them (it should be noted that the Saudi methanol proposals are relatively immune from such competition). Again, the development of various Asian markets may take place quickly, thus providing plenty of space for these various plants. But the way Sumitomo and Mitsubishi have chosen to become involved with projects in Saudi Arabia and Singapore, as though to counter Mitsui's investment in Iran, reminds one uneasily of the duplicate investment strategies which these companies followed within the domestic Japanese market. It is questionable whether their strategies reflect a careful analysis of the economic pros and cons of any particular project — or are an emotive reaction that what Mitsui has done, they too must do.

A second point that needs to be stressed is that petrochemical products are already entering Japan from countries such as Taiwan. As yet this is a trickle, but Taiwan no longer imports significant quantities of Low Density Polyethylene from Japan; instead it now exports the product back to Japan and is adding yet further capacity.[15] Japanese producers are also importing synthetic rubber, polyvinyl chloride and styrene monomer from the same country. So, just as the North Africans and East Europeans are penetrating the West European market before the main Middle Eastern industrial projects come into operation, so too are the East Asian 'super-competitive' economies starting to penetrate Japanese markets in advance of them, thus making it all the more difficult for the Middle Eastern exporters when they finally start moving.

Like the rest of the OECD world, the Japanese undoubtedly hope they will never have to choose between the aspirations of the Middle Easterners and those of countries rather closer to end-markets. As noted, although the Japanese are scared of offending the Middle Easterners lest they harm their chances of obtaining trouble-free access to oil, one should not discount how sensitive the Japanese are to their fellow Asians' suspicions. If the Japanese can avoid it, they would prefer not to disappoint the aspirations either of the Saudi leadership or of Singapore's Lee Kuan Yew.

The Japanese 'model'

The Japanese were the first non-Western country to become a major industrial power. Hence the history of their development must be of interest to any Third World country seeking to follow in their footsteps. In fact, one distinguished Japanese, Mr Yasuji Torii, Chairman of Mitsui Petrochemicals, using the petrochemical industry as his example, drew attention, at an OPEC conference,[16] to the lessons to be learned from the Japanese experience.

To all intents and purposes, Japan had no petrochemical industry before World War II. In the mid-1950s, which was the earliest the authorities could justify moving on from more immediate problems of industrial reconstruction, the industry ministry (MITI) instituted a tax and financial system under which the first significant plants were constructed between 1956 and 1958. MITI also kept a keen eye on the agreements under which foreign technology was imported.

This first wave of investment was almost entirely dependent on imported western technology, with about one quarter of the construction costs being made up of imported components. Gradually, however, the technological expertise of the Japanese companies improved and, by the early 1960s, the time-lag between commercial use of a technology in the West and its application in Japan had been narrowed to one or two years. By the mid-1960s, though, it was still extremely rare for a Japanese company to produce its own indigenous technology for a given process; this had happened in only two cases in a list of eleven products.[17]

This first wave of plants was also quite small by world standards, reflecting the general shortage of capital which then faced Japanese industry. From the start, though, MITI followed a deliberate policy of increasing the minimum size requirements that proposed plants had to meet if they were to be given permission to go ahead. This was a policy deliberately aimed at getting full economies of scale, thus bringing product prices down to world levels. By 1968, the Japanese were second only to the United States in their production of ethylene.

Obviously, this Japanese experience is distinctive in some ways from that facing the Middle Eastern oil producers today, even if the latter are faced with the same basic problem of building a petrochemical industry from scratch. Firstly, the Middle Easterners have the oil and gas feedstocks under their own soil. Secondly, they have few of the capital constraints which held the Japanese back in the very first stages of their petrochemical investments.

On the other hand, Mitsui's Mr Torii spelled out some of the circumstances which were relatively favourable to the Japanese and, since his company is actively involved in the giant Iranian IJPC petrochemical complex, his views command respect. Firstly, he stressed the high educational levels of the Japanese labour force (the illiteracy rate was negligible), and the relatively well-developed supporting industries which helped in the smooth running and maintenance of the new petrochemical industries. In the case of the oil-producing world, he pointed to the existence of relatively long-established refining industries, and suggested that the existence of a supporting infrastructure and industry around them should help the petrochemical sector once it started. He was considerably less happy about the existence of adequately trained and motivated middle-level supervisors and general workers. The fact that the OPEC states have to fall back relatively heavily (by Japanese standards) on expatriate workers, is a sign that the petrochemical industry is not yet taking firm root in the oil-producing world. In particular, he stressed that technology transfer is something more than buying the best of existing technology. Until the oil producers are capable of assimilating such technology, of reproducing it and, even, of starting to anticipate future developments, he judged that the technology cannot truly be said to be transferred.

Finally, he pointed to the advantages Japan gained from having a large population (approaching 100 million) at a time when the optimum size of chemical plants was relatively small (say, 20,000 tons/year for an ethylene plant). This meant that quite a small increase in the penetration of petrochemical products into people's lives justified new, more modern capacity. The oil producers, however, have much smaller populations, and they are trying to break into the chemical industry at a time when the optimum scale of plant is around 20 times the size (in the case of ethylene) of that which the Japanese were having to handle in the mid-1950s. To justify such huge plants, the Middle Easterners will have to change the patterns of consumer demand in domestic markets far faster than the Japanese ever had to contemplate. They will also have to turn to export markets almost from the start — while the Japanese were able to ease their production costs towards comparative world standards over a number of years (it was at least fourteen or fifteen years after completion of the first post-war petrochemical plants before the Japanese felt able to start dismantling the protection policies granted to the infant industry).

Obviously, the oil producers will go ahead with their industrialisation regardless of what has happened elsewhere in the world, but the fact that the Japanese have created a petrochemical industry from next to nothing since the mid-1950s should cause the Middle Easterners to reflect on possible lessons to be learned. Firstly, it is clear from the Japanese case that industrialisation is a long, hard slog involving a whole national culture — from the structure of basic education to the decisions of top policy-makers. It certainly requires very clear analytical thinking and policy-making on the part of a major planning or industry ministry such as MITI; any young, industrialising country might well study and re-study the history of this particular ministry which has been so important within the Japanese context. Secondly, it is fair to note that the Japanese approach has been both xenophobic and cosmopolitan. On the one hand, they have never hesitated to use the best of non-Japanese technology. On the other hand, they have generally acquired such technology through licensing or by the straight purchase of processes, in preference to a transfer of technology by foreigners through joint ventures with Japanese partners or wholly-foreign subsidiaries. There has, perhaps, been an element of xenophobia in this restriction on foreign investors, but it also reflects a certain amount of logic. The fact that no foreign investors have been involved (in most cases) means that the Japanese were able to devote their full attention to absorbing the new technology, learning from their mistakes and gradually moving towards producing innovations of their own. The fact that they have not been particularly successful in the area of petrochemical innovation should be noted by all those who feel that the Japanese are invincible in all industries — but the speed with which their industry grew (despite some MITI-imposed handicaps in the area of naphtha-pricing) is an indication of just how effective the Japanese have become at absorbing the best of the world's technology.

This would, therefore, suggest that it may be the more self-sufficient oil producers, such as Iraq and Algeria, who are following a strategy closest to that which proved effective for Japan. We should again take note, however, that the Japanese were able to build their industry with little dependence on export markets. It is still possible to argue, then, that joint ventures with foreign partners might have been called for if penetration of export markets had been as crucial to the industry's development as it will be to Saudi Arabia. But, if the Saudis' strategy can be so defended, they still need to make sure that they are not depriving themselves of a learning process which may prove invaluable in the long term. The lesson to be learned from Japan is that technology transfer involves learning. The role of the foreign partner in any national learning process needs very close attention — particularly in industries which are so essential to the future of the Middle Eastern oil producers.

Notes

1   Turner, 1978b, p.105.
2   *BP Statistical Review of the World Oil Industry, 1973*, p.10.
3   Kitamura, 1976, p.162.
4   Tsurumi, 1976, p.59.
5   *Chemical Insight*, no.147, early April 1978, p.7.
6   *Chemical Insight*, no.156, late August 1978, pp 14-5; no.158, late September 1978, p.5.
7   *Chemical Insight*, no.143, early February 1978, pp 2-5.
8   Tsurumi, 1976, chapter 10.
9   *Japan Economic Journal*, April 25 1978, p.9; *Chemical Insight*, no.143, early February 1978, pp 2-5.
10   *Japan Economic Journal*, July 11 1978, p.15.
11   *Japan Economic Journal*, April 25 1978, p.9.
12   *Chemical Insight*, no.143, early February 1978, pp 2-5.
13   *Chemical Insight*, no.156, late August 1978, pp 4-7.
14   Department of Energy (US), 1978a, p.228.

15 *Japan Economic Journal*, July 11 1978, p.15.
16 Torii, 1978.
17 Torii, 1978, p.144.

10 Options for the Middle East

It was not our intention to write a pessimistic book. As will be obvious, however, the more closely we have scrutinised Middle Eastern plans for refined oil and petrochemical exports, the more evident the marketing problems facing the Middle Easterners have become. The fact that petrodollar surpluses are speedily absorbed means that the Middle Easterners have less freedom to push through capital-intensive projects regardless of economic realities. Finally, even at the time of writing, the ever-worsening political crisis in Iran has shown the vulnerability of such ventures to a popular backlash against accelerated modernisation. Despite this, there are policy recommendations which can be made to speed up the development and international acceptance of such ventures.

Industrialisation in perspective

We should probably start with an acceptance that national development does not necessarily depend on industrialisation at all costs. Giving the go-ahead to billion-dollar, hydrocarbons-based, industrial plants is not the only way of increasing one's social returns from spare capital and gas. For one thing, as we have argued in chapter 6, natural gas can give strong positive returns to the national economy even if it is not liquefied or used as a feedstock for petrochemical plants. The Venezuelans, for instance, reinject over 50 per cent of their gas into crude oil fields as a matter of long-standing policy.[1] Mexican officials talk about using their gas domestically as a substitute for fuel oil; the latter can then be exported either as product or as crude.[2] Within the Middle East, Kuwait uses substantial amounts of gas for its desalination programme; Iran is just starting to substantially use gas for reinjection purposes (some 17 per cent of output in 1978), and over half the gas that Saudi Arabia currently gathers (less than a quarter of what it produced in 1977) is also used for reinjection.[3] Insofar as these applications of gas permit greater exports of higher-value crude, the relevant national economies are net gainers.

Again, it may be possible for some of the smaller Gulf states to virtually skip industrialisation altogether. Bahrain and Dubai, for instance, are making a strong challenge to take over a good part of the service role which Beirut used to play. The Saudis and Kuwaitis might also be tempted to develop such a service sector on the strength of their financial surpluses. After all, experience around the world suggests that people prefer to work in offices and government bureaucracies rather than slave away in industrial plants. We doubt if Saudis and Kuwaitis are any different. Certainly, there are countries such as Switzerland or cities such as London, New York and pre-civil war Beirut which show that a thriving service sector can flourish, relatively divorced from an industrial base.

However, financial services such as banking and insurance are just the kind of industries the Saudis would find it ideologically difficult to enter. This is chiefly because financial activities rest heavily on the principle of charging interest which is so much a bone of contention within the Islamic world. Admittedly, there are ways round charging interest, such as charging fees for services rendered or by tying repayments to a project's profitability, but the Saudis have decided that such industries are not for them. This, therefore, means that the Kingdom has to rely on capital-intensive industrialisation as the best means of creating good quality jobs for its citizens.

Choice of products

At the moment — and events in Iran must give them pause — the Saudis are not convinced by such arguments and are pushing ahead with their plans for Yanbu, Jubail and the associated industrialisation. What can be done to smooth their entry, along with that of the Iranians and other Middle Easterners, into world markets?

Obviously, there is not a great deal the Middle Easterners can do about the fact that world markets are facing serious over-capacity in many sectors, even before Middle Eastern plants are operative. Much of this over-capacity is a function of the relative weakness of the world economy and, unless the Middle Easterners moderate their oil-pricing policies to avoid damaging world industrial confidence, they will have to accept these capacity problems. Later on in this chapter, we shall suggest some diplomatic moves they might take to encourage OECD economies to adjust to their plans. For the moment, however, the problem is of finding those sectors which will give the Middle Easterners their best chance of penetrating relatively glutted world markets.

Although independent commentators remain pessimistic about the general prospects facing the Middle Easterners, some consensus seems to be emerging about how they might make the most of a somewhat depressing situation. On the refining side, there is interest in the idea

159

discussed in chapter 6, that the Middle East might specialise in producing made-to-measure feedstocks by carrying out the cracking, viscosity reduction and desulphurisation — especially since the latter process is a heavy user of hydrogen which could be economically provided from flare gas. A study for the US Department of Energy on desulphurisation points out that hydrogen alone contributes 80 cents to $1 to the cost of treating a barrel of residual fuel oil; it also points out that the rate at which US and Caribbean refineries are being converted to treat sulphurous crudes is definitely inadequate.[4] Though it does not say so, this analysis suggests that there is room for desulphurisation plants to be installed outside the United States. Another study for the same Department goes further and specifically states: 'If . . . the producer refineries confine themselves to an oil topping and desulphurisation operation they may well have a useful role to play . . . the residual fuel oil could be desulphurised at a much lower cost than in the countries of destination, on the basis of hydrogen obtained from natural gas which may otherwise be flared and could therefore be made available at low cost.'[5] There are dissident voices, such as that of Chem System's Peter Spitz, but his case is not an overwhelming one.[6] In general, though, the fact that there has been preliminary discussion within the Euro-Arab Dialogue about the possibility of basing some form of complementary investments on gradually locating more desulphurisation operations in the Arab world, shows how the argument is moving. Transportation costs will still be relatively high, given the value of the product, but there is a certain logic behind the arguments.

As far as petrochemicals are concerned, the advice seems to be that the Middle Easterners should start by keeping to the simpler base chemicals, only gradually moving downstream into the more complicated products. Peter Spitz, for instance, told an OPEC meeting that ammonia production would make sense for gas producers from a number of viewpoints, including economics and availability of regional markets. He further suggested that instead of producing ethylene and then converting it into more specialised, intermediate chemicals, they might consider manufacturing cryogenic ethylene for export. This would remove the problem of co-ordinating the production from a whole cluster of ethylene-based plants within the Middle East. It would simplify the marketing, because it would be possible to sign a few long-term contracts. It would also solve the problem of having all stages of the chemical transformations done within high-capital cost plants, although a limited amount of ethylene could still be converted locally for regional markets.[7] His general points were taken up at the same meeting by Mr Yasuji Torii of Mitsui Petrochemicals. After pointing out how the Japanese industry has evolved over several decades and owes much to the general sophistication of supporting companies within the

Japanese economy, he concluded by suggesting an order of priorities:

> . . . I feel that it is advisable for OPEC Member Countries, as they embark on the petrochemical business, not to aim at completion of a grand complex in a single effort, but to start first with solvents, aromatics or bulk products going a step further than oil products; then to go into quantity production of monomers such as ethylene glycol, methanol, cumene and phenol; and finally proceed to polymers including polyethylene and polypropylene.[8]

For non-chemist readers, this means that he is arguing that the oil producers should start by concentrating on products which use standard technology and which primarily call for attention to chemical quality. Only when this quality problem has been conquered should the producers go on to the polymers (i.e. plastics, rubbers and fibres). The latter are much more likely to involve after-sales technical servicing, and also start to need some research backing in order to improve production processes and to modify properties to meet specific market needs.

This is all pretty general advice, but it has to be made. There is a temptation to want 'instant industries', when an evolutionary approach is wiser. In arguing this, we are not using a double standard, for a company breaking into a new market will nearly always proceed in steps (Dow, for instance, first entered West Europe with end-products using imported feedstocks; then, after building up markets, gradually increased capacity to produce ethylene and whatever else was needed as feedstock).

One point which requires particular emphasis is the need to give a great deal of attention to marketing. All the products we consider in this book involve more complicated marketing than crude oil, which should, in theory, be easy to sell. Regardless of this, the Middle Eastern national oil companies are only slowly expanding their market share of crude, despite the fact that there has been no political reason why they could not have thrust the international oil companies aside if they had so chosen. Crude oil, however, has to be sold to refiners and these are still quite heavily dominated by the international companies. The result is that the Middle Eastern companies still sell a lot of their crude through long-term marketing contracts with western corporations. If this is true of selling crude oil, then it will be even more so for chemical products; Middle Eastern state petrochemical companies are unlikely to manage their operations so well initially, that they will be able to eliminate the traditional chemical companies and sell directly to end-consumers. Instead, the marketing problem of the Middle Easterners for the coming decade is to persuade a limited number of oil and chemical companies to take increasing amounts of Middle Eastern base chemicals on long-term contracts. This will involve only a limited number of contracts, but it is going to take time — because of the industry's traditional obsession with security of supplies and quality control. This, therefore, suggests that it would be wise for the Saudis and Iranians to involve foreign companies as partners in chemical joint ventures, thus benefiting from immediate access to the partners' marketing network all over the world.

At the same time, there is growing awareness of the potential of non-OECD regional markets. This is, in fact, a major change in thinking since the 1975-76 era when it was generally accepted that the OECD world would take the bulk of such products. *Chemical Insight*'s Mike Hyde was, for instance, then estimating that 70 per cent of the products from Middle Eastern plants would be aimed at West Europe — a belief which was reinforced at one of the earlier meetings of the petrochemical and refining sub-group of the Euro-Arab Dialogue. The Arab delegation at that meeting stated that they expected West Europe to absorb the production from Arab plants not needed in the Middle East. However (partly as a result of the analytical work done within the Dialogue) there is now a much greater awareness that over-capacity within the OECD world is a continuing problem, with which the Middle East must come to terms.

There are now clear indications that both the foreign partners and the various Middle Eastern authorities are examining potential non-OECD markets very carefully. An intervention from a Dow Chemical manager at the October 1978 OPEC conference on 'Downstream operations in OPEC member countries' shows the way in which people's thinking is evolving. While admitting that it was probably inevitable that Middle Eastern glycols would have to find markets in West Europe and, perhaps, Japan, he argued that there was a growing opportunity to create new markets for the polyethylenes within the Middle Eastern and Indian Ocean regions. There is, in his view, a huge, undeveloped market for plastics. In Africa, for instance, per capita consumption is 1 kilogram, compared with West Germany's 84.5 kg per head in 1976, or the USA's 61.8 kg.[9] He pointed to the fact that most of the LDCs in the region are building huge cement plants with capacities of around 10 million tons/year; this immediately presents the opportunity of substituting plastic bags for paper ones, particularly in those countries without plentiful forests. He also mentioned that Dow had entered an African joint venture (as a minor partner) to replace cardboard with a plastic equivalent.

These arguments reinforce points made in off-the-record remarks by other potential partners. Relatively populous Egypt and the Sudan, for instance, will be separated from Mobil's plants at Yanbu by a mere 100 miles of Red Sea. Even more populous India and Pakistan are within

1,500 miles of Jubail and Bandar Shahpur — and there are signs that the Middle Eastern oil producers can find markets there. The Saudi fertiliser plant, SAFCO, for instance, signed two major export contracts in 1978 — a 30,000 ton urea order with India and a 100,000 ton one with Pakistan.[10] This is not to say that such LDCs will be delighted at the prospects of becoming dependent on chemical imports from their oil-rich neighbours. Obviously, the Egypts and Indias of the world will continue to protect their own infant industries and, where a country has found its own oil and gas (as both these countries have), the Middle Easterners will have to fight their way past increasingly organised local competitors. But then, the transportation logic which works against the Middle Easterners when they look North-West to Mediterranean or North American markets, works more in their favour when they move products towards Africa or East Asia and Oceania. In both these cases, it will be the Middle Easterners who have shorter lines of communication than their European and American competitors. They also have the further advantage that they will be the strongest financial powers in a part of the world where per capita income is desperately low. Egypt may eventually return to relying on Saudi aid too much to turn down proposals to make the chemical industries of the two nations more mutually complementary. An Islamic country such as Pakistan has been doing well out of aid from its oil-producing fellow Moslems. Also, populous countries such as India, Pakistan and Egypt, whose nationals are widely used as expatriate labour within the oil-producing economies, are reaping such benefits from this ($2 billion in foreign exchange remittances for India in 1976, $1.11 billion for Pakistan in 1977), that they are not likely to risk disturbing this relationship by creating problems for the oil-producers' petrochemical aspirations.[11]

Regional co-operation

There is also general acceptance of the idea that anything which can be done to increase regional co-operation should improve the economics of the massive projects under consideration. Peter Spitz has argued[12] that the Middle Easterners should explore the possibility of 'shared' projects which would permit the pooling of markets. He mentioned a proposed linear alkylbenzene plant which, when designed for a combined Arab market of 150 million, justifies being built on a world scale, thus making economic sense. He also suggested that the OPEC members might apportion different chemical specialities to specified countries, so that one might specialise in polyethylene, another in styrene, etc. Spitz even suggested that OPEC members might combine with low-cost labour states, with the former providing the feedstocks and the latter the more labour-intensive conversion facilities necessary to move into the cheap plastic, fibres and clothing markets.

All these proposals are fine in theory, but to overcome nationalistic self-interest is not easy. We are, for instance, not aware that negotiations within the Andean Pact have actually led to significant specialisation among its members' chemical industries, while Kuwait's attempts to find Middle Eastern partners for an ethylene complex at Shuaiba have so far been unsuccessful. On the other hand, OAPEC has drawn up a five-year work programme, which includes the establishment of joint-venture petrochemical projects. They specifically discuss the possibility of such initiatives in the manufacture of lube-oils, carbon black, detergents and synthetic rubber, where it would be desirable to join economies of scale to an integrated Arab market.[13] Admittedly, such ventures are still at the talking stage, but OAPEC is emerging as quite an important body in the industrial politics of the Arab world. The logic behind its case is impeccable, so we must wait and see whether the Organisation can push regional co-operation beyond the Arab Shipbuilding and Repair Yard in Bahrain, the Arab Maritime Petroleum Transport Company and the Arab Petroleum Services Company. With the support of a key member such as Saudi Arabia, there is no reason why OAPEC should not get at least one or two of the proposed petrochemical joint ventures into operation.

Downstream investments

Despite the foregoing strategies, the odds are that there will still be Middle Eastern and North African states which want to export chemical and refined oil products into OECD markets, but will find that they are denied full market access, either openly or implicitly. Again, where countries have opted for the joint-venture approach, there is a possibility that national aspirations will be held back by the fact that the foreign partner's investment decisions are taken exceedingly cautiously. What else can be done?

There may be quite a strong argument for selective buying into the downstream operations of companies within the OECD world. Such extension by acquisition is a well-tried strategy of multinational companies, since it is often more economical of time and money to take over existing manufacturing and marketing operations rather than trying to compete by setting up new operations from scratch. There is, moreover, some evidence that some governments and individuals within the oil-producing states are starting to think this way, even if Saudi Arabia continues to reject it in favour of a home-based industry. Thus, Venezuela's Petroven has apparently approached Exxon and Shell about possibly buying a share in their big refineries in Aruba and Curacao.[14] Such deals would give Venezuela a secure outlet for her heavy crudes, while it launches a $1.1 billion improvement programme for the refineries on its own soil. Then there is the bid from First Arabian (a Paris-based group of Arab investors) for the bankrupt Canadian refinery at Come-by-Chance, Newfoundland. At the time of writing, it was unclear whether this deal would get the necessary approval of the creditors and the governments of Newfoundland and Canada, but if it does, then a refinery, which originally cost $189 million to build, will be bought for a sum around $35 million − a clear indication of the investment opportunities arising from the current over-capacity in key OECD industries.[15] In a different corporate guise (this time via Luxembourg-based Arabian Seaoil Corporation), Roger E. Tamraz has put in a bid for the virtually bankrupt Commonwealth Refining, which has a refinery and petrochemical complex in Puerto Rico. Once again the negotiations are complex, involving, in this case, a debt of $400 million. But merely by making the bid, Tamraz is showing that there are 'bargains' to be found around the refining and petrochemical industries.[16] Finally, the purchase by private Saudi interests of a 10 per cent share of the Italian chemical company Montedison should presumably be seen in the same light. With accumulated debts of over $4 billion (firm evidence that corporate incompetence is not the prerogative of the non-OECD world), Montedison was ripe for such a move. Admittedly, as we write, the motives of the new investors are not totally clear (they have, for instance, obtained the option to buy into the company's profitable banking and insurance interests), but it is significant that the agreement includes the formation of a fifty-fifty company 'to develop commercial operations in the field of raw materials, oil included'. At the same time, however, the new company has not been given sole rights to handle the roughly 100,000 b/d of oil which the company consumes. This exclusion is seen as a gesture to the Italian state oil company, ENI, which is Montedison's largest public sector shareholder.[17] Whatever the short-term aspects of this bid, it is clear that it is a logical buy into a chemical company whose investment strategies can probably be co-ordinated with Middle Eastern ones. The Italian economy, in particular, is littered with refineries and petrochemical plants which might be picked up for a song, so we expect much more such moves. It should be stressed, however, that these Saudi investors are private ones, and their initiative should not be taken as a sign that official Saudi policy may change on downstream investments.

Buying up plant from impoverished competitors for knock-down prices is a well-established way of rationalising industries plagued with over-capacity. It means the purchaser need not spend more money to build new capacity, and the vendor withdraws more or less permanently from some region or some range of products. But the strategy does have its risks. The prime one is that the reasons which led to such a plant's unprofitability could be endemic, and there is no guarantee that the new owners will find any better solution to such problems. For instance, it is estimated that eastern Canada is already plagued with 300,000 b/d surplus refining capacity, and this could become worse if plans to move natural gas into the area go through.[18] There is then a real possibility that no owner of the Come-by-Chance refinery will be able to get it operating in the black. Again, there is a long history of non-Italian companies which have found that investing in Italy is like putting one foot into the quicksands. The fact that companies such as Shell and BP have deliberately pulled out of this economy should give anyone looking there for easy profits serious cause for thought. On balance, then, the apparent Venezuelan strategy with regard to the Antilles refineries seems rather safer. Instead of buying into corporate disasters, they are taking only a share in the Exxon and Shell refineries, thus ensuring that these giant companies have a vested interest in seeing that the plants continue to run reasonably efficiently. This seems a far safer first step away from home than taking sole responsibility for running plants of small, bankrupt companies. The latter strategy is one which is extremely risky, involving strong nerves and, probably, a long purse.

In general, though, a Middle Eastern strategy of gradually increasing shares in overseas downstream production, distribution and marketing is desirable. Only a few exceptional companies are able to run manufacturing operations thousands of miles from their end-markets, without having a strong marketing operation near the customers. The point here is that technology is not developed in a vacuum. A product is worthless unless it fills some social and/or commercial need. Now, there is no immediate reason why the Saudis should not follow a policy of buying refineries and petrochemical plants from OECD suppliers, which would permit them to turn out substantial quantities of products from outside the Kingdom. If they leave all the downstream marketing to foreign partners, however, the Middle Easterners will remain in perpetual dependence on the foreigners, as it will be virtually impossible to generate their own, commercially-attractive technologies. This is a capability which generally comes only when there is a strong link between researchers and a company's marketing efforts. The faster a technology is moving, the more essential it is that the researchers have sufficient market knowledge and an instinctive feeling about which new developments might or might not have commercial potential. Achieving this happy state of affairs will take time. In the meantime, the need is to develop a core of national citizens with deep experience of downstream overseas activities. In the short term, this core may be best developed by insisting that foreign partners give such citizens every opportunity to learn this end of the business. In the medium term, direct acquisition of foreign assets, though a risky strategy, is the one guaranteed way to speed up the learning process. Undoubtedly, there will be disasters, with the probable purchases of some operations that are beyond recovery. But it will always be possible to ensure that the risks taken are not so great that the entire health of the parent enterprise is threatened. Without taking such risks, however, Middle Eastern oil and chemical companies will remain in a permanent stage of dependence on their OECD opposite numbers . . . and the whole aim of their strategy should be to reduce this dependence, slowly but steadily.

After all these arguments, however, we have to note that the oil producers, in general, remain opposed to such a strategy.

Tying products to crude

Underlying all the arguments in this book is the threat that the oil producers will finally insist that OECD crude importers should take a proportion of oil or petrochemical products along with their crude purchases. This was expressed in an editorial of OAPEC's bulletin which, after dismissing OECD arguments about excess capacity in the refining industry, went on to say: 'It must be emphasised that demand for crude oil is, after all, a desired demand for products. Hence the consumers' net imports of petroleum in the intermediate term will have to include products at any given level of supply. The producers may have to determine this level themselves to make it consistent with their need to export surplus refined products.'[19] A slightly different point was made by the Kuwaiti Oil Minister, Sheikh Ali Khalifah al-Sabah, at the OPEC-sponsored seminar on 'Downstream Operations in OPEC member countries'. In discussing the various restrictions and hostile attitudes found in the OECD world toward OPEC's industrial aspirations, he went on to say: 'These restrictions and attitudes will not be pacifically accepted by OPEC. In fact it falls within the framework of the OPEC Ministerial Strategy Committee to look into the long-term implications of such practices. It may not be long before the removal of such practices becomes a condition of supply of crude oil. However, it would be much better if these problems were resolved through dialogue rather than confrontation.'[20]

In general, discussion of such linkage of crude to product sales is not held publicly. It is very common, however, in private conversations one has with Middle Eastern individuals from policy-makers downwards. There is already an example of linkage (connected with crude sales) which may show the way thinking is moving within the oil-producing world; this is the Saudi decision (February 1978) that Aramco must increase the rate of its heavy (and commercially less-attractive) crude flow to 35 per cent, while keeping the light crude share down to 65 per cent. Saudi policy is to insist on a further step during the 1980s which will shift the balance between light and heavy crude exports to around fifty-fifty, which corresponds to the reserve ratio of her crude oils. [21] Obviously, we are not talking about oil products here, but the principle behind such Saudi moves — and that behind the OAPEC editorial's theme — is the same. A crude or product which is otherwise commercially unattractive is forced on to world markets by insisting that consumers wanting to take desirable crudes (particularly the light ones) have to take a certain proportion of the undesirable products as well.

Superficially, this seems a very serious threat. Much will depend on whether the 1980s produce a sellers' or buyers' market, and whether OPEC has the ability to co-ordinate its members' selling strategies in a situation which will be very much more complex than the selling of crude. If crude oil becomes a sellers' market, then the threat to tie products to crude is indeed serious — particularly in the case of Saudi Arabia, which will be overwhelmingly important as the world's largest exporter.

On the other hand, whether or not the state of crude markets permits such linkage of sales, the fact that it is necessary may mean that the oil producers are taking an economic loss on the transaction. Readers in the OECD world should perhaps note that this is not an inevitable conclusion. For instance, if such means are used to force products through high tariff barriers, then the oil producer is transferring the cost of jumping these barriers on to the importer instead of bearing the cost himself. Such a strategy is not necessarily bad economics for the would-be exporter.

Conversely, if world oil becomes a buyers' market, this type of linkage approach will be dangerous for the oil producers, because the interplay of a widening variety of both productive locations and product qualities will inevitably lead to greater *de facto* competition between crude oil prices. As a study for the US Department of Energy puts it, potential competition will be strengthened because there is every incentive to use one's refining (and, implicitly, petrochemical) capacity since '. . . oil can be left in the ground for tomorrow, but an idle asset is a wasting proposition.'[22] In these circumstances, much would depend on the economic rationality of the oil producers (whether or not they recognise that there are points beyond which tied sales give a negative return to their economies) and on OPEC's ability to monitor the increasingly complex, competitive strategies available to its members. Should the oil demand-supply relationship stay relatively loose during the 1980s, then the chances that product-linkage will lead to serious strains within OPEC are quite high. Certainly, the industrialised, oil-importing countries will be extremely unhappy at being forced to buy products in this way and there will be a very serious preference for crudes which are sold on price alone.

Clearly, should Middle Eastern products be unable to find markets within the OECD on their own merits, then the state of world oil markets is going to be the key factor which determines what extra amount of sales can be provided by linking them to crude sales . . . and here we are in the hands of the oil forecasters. It would be fair to say that forecasts for the next ten or fifteen years were becoming less apocalyptic as time passed; world growth shows little signs of reverting to pre-1973 levels; the amount of energy and oil conservation has taken most forecasters by surprise; and there were indications that even the supply of energy was proving to be more price-responsive than expected. Also, there seemed little doubt that the *technically* feasible production could be enough to satisfy nearly any demand for oil until well into the 1990s (see figure 10.1). On the other hand, it is now clear that for poli-

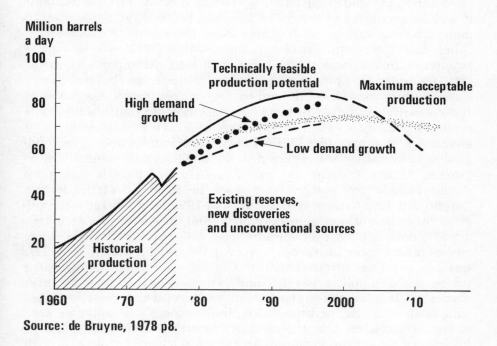

Source: de Bruyne, 1978 p8.

Figure 10.1   The oil era (world outside communist areas)

tical reasons, oil will never be pumped at that rate, so that we now have to project a lower figure of 'maximum acceptable production'. Many analysts were assuming that OPEC would produce between 40-50 million b/d in the 1980s and 1990s but conventional wisdom is now that OPEC will find it difficult even to produce at 3-5 million b/d.

Our own bet is that the 1980s and 1990s will be an era of mini-crises,[23] in which there will be quite a lot of potential slack in the system. However, miscalculations about the height of the oil supply ceiling, faster than expected oil demand growth, or sudden supply crises (such as that caused by the Iranian turmoil of 1978-79), will lead to demand hitting the supply ceiling, triggering off a price rise which, in turn, will lead to a dampening of demand and the re-emergence of a buyers' market. If we are right in suspecting that OPEC will not gain a consistent whip-hand in oil markets, the chances of linking products to crude sales will be considerably reduced.

There are, however, two further points to be made. Firstly, even in such an era of sporadic oil crises, Saudi Arabia is going to be by far the most important crude supplier within OPEC. It really does not matter if it will be producing as low as 14.5 million b/d in 1990,[24] or over 20 million b/d as various studies have suggested might be called for.[25] Quite simply, no other crude producer within OPEC will be half as important, so that Saudi Arabia has such a crucial importance to the OECD world that — however diplomatically dangerous concessions to a single country may be — it is hard to imagine that importing companies and countries will refuse to bend over backwards to find a home for its products. Secondly, even within the wider OPEC grouping, it is increasingly accepted that OECD-based oil companies operating in oil-producing countries are expected to undertake certain minimum obligations. At the moment, the negotiations on what such obligations should include are mostly about crude oil liftings, but the Iranian Consortium negotiations during the mid-1970s were already complicated by questions concerning products from the Abadan refinery. One would, therefore, expect negotiations to gradually include some commitments about marketing certain products. Perhaps they will be smallish quantities to start with but, if we are miscalculating and if future crude supply crises become extremely severe over the next couple of decades, the proportion of products which must be taken with crude will rise, perhaps slowly, but inexorably. Finally, we need to remind ourselves that the onus of marketing strategy does not lie solely with the oil producing countries. For the largest projects in both Saudi Arabia and the Shah's Iran, for example, the foreign joint-venture partners were to have overall marketing responsibility (at least initially) for the resultant products from these new complexes. Thus it is the companies, rather than the Middle Eastern governments, that will go a long way in determining the location and conditions for the selling of these products. The individual reader can consider for himself whether this fact increases or decreases the probability of tied crude/ product sales.

Conflict or accommodation?

It is important to note that it is by no means clear that it will be necessary to force such products on an unwilling OECD. In the final chapter, we shall examine the chances of these problems disappearing of their own accord. We shall also look at possible diplomatic initiatives that may defuse residual conflicts between OPEC and the OECD.

Notes

1   *Petroleum Intelligence Weekly*, October 30 1978, p.3.
2   *Petroleum Intelligence Weekly*, October 16 1978, p.10.
3   *Petroleum Intelligence Weekly*, October 30 1978, pp 3-4.
4   Department of Energy (US), 1977b, pp 2-3, 12-13.
5   Department of Energy (US), 1978a, pp 100-1.
6   Spitz, 1978.
7   *European Chemical News*, October 27 1978, pp 8, 42.
8   Torii, 1978, p.151.
9   Waddams, 1978, p.318.
10 *European Chemical News*, September 15 1978, p.14.
11 *Financial Times*, September 15 1978.
12 Spitz, 1978, p.47.
13 *Middle East Economic Survey*, August 7 1978, p.3.
14 *Petroleum Intelligence Weekly*, October 9 1978, pp 4-5.
15 *Business Week*, October 23 1978, p.62; *Petroleum Intelligence Weekly*, October 30 1978, p.9.
16 *European Chemical News*, October 6 1978, p.6.
17 *European Chemical News*, October 6 1978, p.4; *Middle East Economic Survey*, October 9 1978, p.16.
18 *Petroleum Intelligence Weekly*, October 30 1978, p.9.
19 *Middle East Economic Survey*, February 13 1978, pp 8-9.
20 *Middle East Economic Survey*, Supplement, October 16 1978, p.ii.
21 *Petroleum Intelligence Weekly*, February 27 1978, p.3; October 16 1978, p.5.
22 Department of Energy (US), 1978a, p.98.
23 de Bruyne, 1978, pp 12-14, develops the idea.

24   Department of Energy (US), 1978a, table 5.
25   PIRINC, 1978, pp 6-12; Congressional Research Service, 1977, p.60.

11 Adjustment or conflict?

It is almost inevitable that people like ourselves who write about a particular industrial sector become over-pessimistic and slide imperceptibly into the protectionist camp. By concentrating on a specific industry or country, it is very easy to lose sight of the macro-economic situation in which there may be developments that go a long way towards mitigating problems arising at a sectoral level. In this final chapter we are, therefore, deliberately challenging the pessimism which may seem to run through this book. Will the problems we have encountered be ameliorated by the 'automatic' workings of the world economy? Or will certain core problems remain as an irritant to the smooth working of the international trading system? Is there anything that governments or international organisations can do?

Spontaneous adjustment

Plant closures

The most obvious form of adjustment is for OECD-based companies to scrap plants in industries plagued by over-capacity. This is starting to happen in Western Europe, particularly in the refining and synthetic fibres industries. In the refining case during 1977, some 8 per cent of West Europe's refining capacity was either scrapped for good (80,000 b/d), withdrawn for conversion (420,000 b/d) or stopped indefinitely (1,140,000 b/d).[1] Further closures occurred in 1978 with, for instance, Occidental suspending all its refining activities in West Europe by closing a 100,000 b/d Antwerp refinery and indefinitely deferring any further work on a partly built project in Britain. Much the same thing is happening in synthetic fibres, although here the picture is complicated by the West European producers' determination to create a cartel to control the rationalisation process. In basic petrochemicals, there are now cases such as Shell's decision to close its Pernis ethylene plant in order that other European ethylene units should run closer to capacity.

Intra-OECD divestments and mergers

The second way in which macro-adjustment takes place is by a series of apparently isolated deals in which companies trade plants and subsidiaries, effectively reducing the exposure of the vending company and allowing the purchasing company to do the necessary rationalisation within its own corporate strategy. Typical of such deals which occurred in 1978 were Conoco's disposal of its UK chemical interests to Norsk Hydro; Montedison's attempt to sell its half share in a Spanish polypropylene and acrylonitrile operation to the Spanish state company Enpetrol; the exchange of French and Belgian chemical shares between Phillips Petroleum and Petrofina on one hand and Rhone-Poulenc on the other; and BP's acquisition of certain of Union Carbide's and Monsanto's chemical properties in Europe, and its attempted purchase of a major part of Veba's downstream activities in West Germany (whose anti-trust authorities are unhappy with at least part of such a deal).

It is much harder to assess the impact of such deals than that of clear closures of plants. From this limited number of cases, however, one can see that certain companies are retrenching. American chemical companies tend to move back across the Atlantic, and badly over-extended European ones, such as Montedison, seek to chop off some of their less relevant branches. The fact that such deals are currently quite common is a clear indication that it is still cheaper to buy existing plants from struggling competitors than to invest afresh in new ones. Such acquisitions win an immediate and direct market share in the products concerned, while also guaranteeing markets for the acquired company's upstream products. As far as such deals replace new investment, they help reduce over-capacity in future years.

OECD-OPEC capacity transfers

As we noted in the previous chapter, it is still quite rare for OECD-based companies to sell excess capacity to investors from the oil-producing world. A good number of well-known cases (Libya and Fiat; Iran and both Krupp and Deutsche Babcock; Kuwait and Korf) are not strictly relevant, since the oil producers are buying technological expertise rather than surplus capacity. On the other hand, Petroven's interest in the Dutch Antilles' refineries, and the Arab investment in Montedison are more clearly attempts to secure excess capacity in the OECD world. Once again, it is difficult to assess the impact such deals will have, but clearly they will reduce the temptation for their investors to create competing capacity within the oil-producing world.

The big difference between the oil and petrochemical industries and those which have experienced Third World competition (such as textiles, steel shipbuilding, shoes and cutlery), is that the former possess a strong core of companies which are attuned to the fact that they must innovate and diversify to survive. The fact that the oil and chemical companies are relatively close to being genuinely multinational gives them a flexibility that more nationally-oriented competitors do not have. Their first defensive strategy is to improve existing processes by reducing their energy and capital intensity, and to build greater flexibility into plant operations. Given the state of world technology markets, there is no way of stopping the oil-producing states eventually purchasing these technologies as well, but at least the progressive company can build up its royalties' income and be sufficiently innovatory to stay a handful of years ahead of national petrochemical companies. The latter need time to build up their research strengths. Thus, Union Carbide, Dow and others have had considerable success in reducing the fixed capital costs of low-density polyethylene production, by reducing the production pressures over a hundred-fold. Similarly, ICI has a new low-pressure methanol process, and Shell and Halcon have been improving the processes for propylene oxide and styrene monomer.[2] Possibly the most interesting search for a process breakthrough is the work at present done by companies such as Union Carbide in developing a 'chemical refinery', whereby petrochemicals would be developed directly from crude — without going through the intermediate stage of producing naphtha and gas oil feedstocks. Although this is a process which will not be licensed before the mid-1980s, it will clearly start reducing the chemical industry's dependence on oil refineries for feedstocks.

The fact that so much effort is going into improving process technology and that no one is really expecting many new molecules or polymers with strong commercial value to be found is the sign that the petrochemical industry is rapidly maturing. It is following the refining industry where, with little exaggeration, any company with sufficient money can buy the best technology. In these circumstances, technological innovation may keep OECD-based companies one step ahead of their competitors from the oil-producing states. However, it is debatable whether there is any innovation in the offing which will seriously reduce the competitive advantage available to oil-producers willing to manipulate the prices of hydrocarbon feedstocks for their own plants.

OECD-based companies seek to move increasingly into areas in which the oil-producers will find it difficult to compete. Managers of a typical chemical company like ICI now stress that emphasis must be shifted away from plastics and fibres towards more specialised chemical markets, such as pharmaceuticals. At the same time, there is a growing acceptance that the chemical industry should begin planning for the era in which oil and gas feedstocks will become prohibitively expensive. After an initial phase of making better use of crude oil, there should be growing interest in coal chemistry and the use of more exotic sources of oil (shales and tar sands) leading to large-scale commercial utilisation of the biomass (plants, trees, etc.) as a source of chemicals.[3] We thus find chemical companies such as Dow moving into coal liquefaction technologies, and a number of companies are also moving into areas involving genetic engineering or the identification of plants such as the guayule plant, which could prove an interesting alternative source of hydrocarbons.

The strategies of the traditional oil majors are more complex since, over recent years, they have been moving into exactly those parts of the chemical industry (ethylene, the polyethylenes, etc.) which now interest the oil-producing countries. In refining, where they are most obviously vulnerable, the oil companies are actively moving into higher-technology areas, e.g. catalytic cracking, which allows them to produce increased quantities of light products, such as gasoline, from the increasingly heavy crudes which will be available. Looking further ahead, they are searching for ways of producing gasoline from feedstocks other than crude oil. Mobil, for instance, is developing a process which rests on the catalytic conversion of methanol.[4] However, whatever happens at the refining and base chemicals end of their industry, the oil companies have enough diversification projects under way to provide them with a future, should they really be squeezed out of their traditional activities. In 1977, for instance, the investment of the seven majors in areas other than oil, gas and chemicals exceeded $1 billion for the first time.[5] Much of this effort is going into coal, with a growing interest in other minerals such as uranium and copper. The course which these efforts are taking is perhaps best exemplified, not by Mobil's move into retail activities through its acquisition of Marcor, but by the fact that Exxon is building a strong presence in the venture capital business. Such investments are inevitably small in comparison with those in the company's traditional oil activities, and they include shares in subsidiaries involved with advanced forms of energy, of information systems and of materials.

The picture, then, is of a corporate sector in both the refining and petrochemical industries which has considerable flexibility, should the bottom end of these industries turn sour. The result is that these industries should be able to adjust themselves relatively smoothly, compared with other industries under pressure from Third World competition.

Demand creation

Before going on to look at some of the forces working against such a smooth adjustment, it is worth pointing out that traditional economic forces seem to be working at a more worldwide level as well. Obviously, the big jump in the price of oil during the early 1970s had an initial deflationary impact on the world economy, but the general construction boom within the OPEC world which then followed gave the OECD-based economies a chance to claw back a good part of the oil revenues by increased exports of manufactured goods. This has been particularly noticeable in machinery and equipment exports. In engineering products, the share of OPEC markets within the overall total of OECD's exports to the Third World rose from just under 20 per cent in 1970, to just over 40 per cent in 1976 — while the absolute size of the total market was boosted heavily by the boom in Third World commodity revenues during the 1972-73 period. In capital goods, the picture is much the same. By 1977, of all LDCs, Saudi Arabia was the most important market for OECD suppliers, closely followed by Iran. The next three most important countries were also OPEC members (Venezuela, Nigeria and Algeria); not until number six and below in the rankings do we see non-OPEC members such as Brazil, South Korea and Mexico.[6] It is this adjustment by the overall OECD manufacturing sector (similar developments took place in services) which explains why OPEC's current account surplus of $59 billion in 1974 could be turned to a slight deficit (−$2 billion) in 1978.[7] Admittedly, investment in refineries and petrochemical plants will not have been a major part of this increase in demand for manufactured goods, but developments in these two sectors will have reinforced the general trend.

What is not clear is whether those countries, industries and companies which will be most affected by Middle Eastern investment in refineries and petrochemical plants, will be able to compensate themselves by current exports of plant for future lost markets. On the widest level, the West European economy, which will be most affected by future imports of Middle Eastern products, has been doing reasonably well in exporting to the OPEC world (in 1978, the nine European Community members had just under 50 per cent of the OECD's share of the OPEC market).[8] Thus, the West Europeans should, in theory, be able to take a relatively calm approach to the potential competition from Middle Eastern refined oil and petrochemical products.

What is clear for countries and regions, however, is not so obvious for specific industries and companies. Some companies, particularly the oil majors, have adjusted quite well to the changed Middle Eastern economy. As partners in the proposed Saudi joint ventures, they will have an equity share in the new Middle Eastern capacity which may

177

threaten existing plants in the OECD world. Also, Mobil is picking up management fees for its role in bringing Saudi Arabia's East-West crude pipeline to completion, and the four Aramco partners will be earning similar income as a consequence of Aramco's heavy involvement in the Saudi gas-gathering scheme, and in the general development of the infrastructure within the Eastern Province. At another level, both oil and chemical companies will earn royalties from licensing their technology to Middle Easterners; for instance, any methanol plant built in the region is likely to use ICI technology, thus generating income for this company despite the fact that it has chosen not to invest directly in the area itself.

The traditional oil and chemical majors are not generally going into plant construction themselves. Of fifteen leading process plant constructors, we can only identify three in which oil or chemical companies have a significant share: these are Snam Progetti which involves ENI; Uhde, involving Hoechst; and Technip involving Elf-Aquitaine. The bulk of Middle Eastern industrial plants is being built by contractors such as Chiyoda, Fluor, Bechtel, Foster Wheeler, Davy International, Lummus, Kellogg, etc. Such companies will build plants involving processes licensed to them by the traditional companies but, in general, they keep themselves corporately distinct. This suggests that the bulk of the profits to be made from Middle Eastern investments in industrial plant is going to be made by companies other than those whose markets will be ultimately affected.

This generally confirms the picture we laid out in chapter 4, where we suggested that a large number of oil and chemical companies have chosen not to become seriously involved in the Middle East. The result is that such non-participants will inevitably be faced with declining profits from traditional commercial activities which are challenged by the new Middle Eastern investments. At the same time (ignoring the handful of companies which are winning themselves a share in this industrialisation process), they will have very little income from the Middle East to compensate for their losses. If such companies are confident of their ability to master new technologies and to diversify profitably they may stay out of the protectionist camp. As far as Europe is concerned, however, there are plenty of companies without the necessary dynamism. These can be expected to produce a protectionist lobby which cannot be totally ignored. To sum up, adjustment may be taking place at the macro-level. At the level of the individual company, vested interests may well suffer.

The protectionists: how strong?

One would not expect the petrochemical or refining industries to generate the sort of protectionist sentiments found in much more labour-intensive ones such as textiles. When Occidental closed down its 100,000 b/d Antwerp refinery, only 260 employees were laid off. In fact, on the assumption that one person is employed for about every 200 b/d of refinery capacity, West Europe could reduce its 1977 refinery capacity by 10 per cent at the cost of about 10,000 jobs — a moderate figure by the standards of traditional declining industries.

Even if job losses are relatively unimportant in the short term, yet there are those who argue that the migration of such industries needs careful control over the longer term. The argument here is that all industries have 'production chains' which are difficult to break at arbitrary points. In the textile case, it is argued, the fact that the very labour-intensive clothing industry has moved, in part, to areas like the Far East has meant that some artificial fibres plants have been attracted there in consequence; and this means that the petrochemical plants, which would once have been located close to the traditional OECD clothing industry, might also be tempted to move. To modify this argument for the petrochemical and refining cases, one could claim that, once new refineries and base petrochemical plants are built in the oil-producing world, the downstream processing industries will start clustering round them. So what might at first seem like a few plants involving a few thousand jobs will eventually become whole clusters of complexes involving tens of thousands of jobs.

There is some justification for this argument, but it should not be overstressed. Our analysis of the economics of these ventures suggests that their capital-intensity and the distances to OECD markets will make that kind of industrial relocation such a relatively slow **process** that the industrialised economies should be able to adjust relatively painlessly. However, people within the industry are not always convinced by this rebuttal. They see the petrochemical and refining sectors as distinctive from textiles. The latter is a labour-intensive industry which must inevitably move towards the Third World. Petrochemicals and refining, though, are seen as science-based, modern industries and, if the Third World starts eroding the OECD's hold on them, why should not other modern industries such as cars, aircraft or electronics start migrating too? Can we be certain that new industries will emerge to take up the role (creating employment and contributing to the balance of payments) which petrochemicals and refining have hitherto played?

The macro-economist always has great difficulty in answering such questions convincingly, because, although he will personally believe that declining industries have so far always been satisfactorily replaced

179

on an OECD-level of analysis, it is very difficult to draw up a list of industrial sectors which will prove most dynamic over the next ten or twenty years. In addition, the arguments become increasingly complicated by the fact that the developments within the electronics field are making the average up-and-coming industry significantly less labour-intensive than those it is helping to replace. It is still possible, however, to point to a number of industrial sectors where the OECD world seems pretty safe from Third World competition, such as industrial and scientific machinery, aircraft, medical equipment, computers and electronic components, nuclear plants, pharmaceuticals, agricultural machinery, and office equipment.[9] This is not to say that Third World companies will be totally excluded from such industries (Brazil, for instance, is manufacturing small aircraft), but rather that these are the types of industry which will provide the momentum for the OECD-based economies over the next ten to twenty years. When one adds the industrial world's strength in the service sector, there is no evidence that these industries will be unable to fill the gap caused by our two industries slowly moving towards the Middle East.

The world, however, is not made up of macro-economists, able to step back from the troubles of specific industries in order to point to the wider economic adjustments taking place, and to the relatively diffused economic advantages which general consumers may be gaining from cheap imports. Rather, economic policies emerge from the interplay of special interest groups, and there are few more powerful lobbies than the corporations and trade unionists directly affected by competition from non-traditional manufacturing centres. Whereas trade union pressures have not been particularly important in the case of the petrochemical and refining sectors (presumably reflecting their capital-intensity), corporate lobbies are well in evidence.

The protectionist (perhaps 'restrictionist' is a less emotive term) lobbies for these industries have been strongest in the United States, which will probably be least affected by Middle Eastern products. As far as such products are actually aimed at the US, however, it is unlikely that the lobbies which gave the world the oil import quota scheme of the 1950s and 1960s, and the American Selling Price scheme for benzenoid chemicals, are going to welcome competition from the Eastern Hemisphere. It would appear that, as we write, Washington is concentrating on how to encourage more investment in domestic refining — not on encouraging more product imports.

The two industries in West Europe have been more liberal in their approach to overseas competition than their American counterparts, but there are clear signs that concern is growing and that pressure is mounting for some form of 'restrictionist' measures against the eventual products from the Middle East. Of course, the main impact of such products will not be felt until some time in the mid-1980s, so we are here engaging in a certain amount of speculation. However, European industrial strategy has already been moving in a more 'restrictionist' direction during the 1970s, and we see very little on the horizon to force a major reversal of attitudes.

One key factor in the formation of West European attitudes has been the emergence of chronic over-capacity in both the petrochemical and refining sectors. The most spectacular initiative took place within synthetic fibres, when the EC's industry directorate under Vicomte Davignon actually gave its blessing, in the spring of 1978, for a 'crisis cartel'. Under this, the main West European fibres manufacturers signed a pact which committed them to cut back capacity by a given amount and to hold that new level to 1981. In the meantime, the producers would be expected to adhere to their supply patterns and market shares held in 1976. US companies (barred from joining by the US anti-trust laws) and manufacturers in other non-EC West European countries, were assumed to be willing to play a tacit part by not rocking the boat.

This cartel was narrowly blocked by other EC Commissioners, but the fact that it came so far (the competition commissioner helped draw up the crisis measures in an effort to get round the Treaty of Rome; the companies actually signed the agreement) pays tribute to the power held by 'restrictionist' forces within West Europe. In this case, the pressure came primarily from the Italians, who had over-invested in the fibres sector for reasons connected with Italian regional policy, as well as with the less-justified personal enrichment of certain politically powerful, industrial promoters. When the bubble burst, the weak Italian central government found itself politically unable to enforce a rationalisation programme which would both inflame important regional politicians and probably bankrupt a number of Italian companies. This latter consideration was very important; the battle to keep the financially-pressed chemical company Montedison out of the total control of the State is one of crucial importance to the credibility of the ruling Christian Democrat party.

Synthetic fibres are not the kind of product which are of immediate interest to the Middle Easterners, but this episode was used by some European companies to push for urgent action in plastics. For instance, French voices within the Association of Plastics Manufacturers in Europe started to call for similar collaboration between the EC Commission and the plastics manufacturers to overcome the over-capacity problem in that industry. Pointing to the fact that Eastern Europe's one per cent share of West Europe's markets was expected to start growing fast, they called for much faster anti-dumping procedures on the part of the EC Commission, and the erection of a 'dumping level price' for the most sensitive plastics. This was to be calculated from the manufacturing cost of the most efficient EC producer operating at full capacity. As soon as a certain quantity of product entered the EC market below that price, dumping would be deemed to exist (this is a version of the 'trigger price' mechanism now found quite widely in the world steel industry).[10]

In the refining sector, the calls for Brussels' intervention have come from companies of several countries. By the end of 1976, it was possible to identify a group of five European oil companies which led the way in pressing Brussels for action on the structural adaptation of the EC refining capacity. These companies were France's CFP and Elf, Italy's ENI, Belgian Petrofina and German Veba.[11] They actually had little impact for a number of reasons. Firstly, most recent EC initiatives in the energy field have come to naught: some have been blocked by the British, determined to defend their go-it-alone policies for North Sea oil, but also convinced that capacity problems are best left to the international oil companies; others have been blocked by countries like Italy which are unwilling to make any long-term commitments to take European-produced coal. Secondly, the industry has been split down the middle between the five companies mentioned above, and the international majors who have been financially strong enough to argue that the problem of excess refining capacity should be left to the play of market forces. Thirdly, the EC Commission has been powerless to do much, because of the German government's unwillingness to accept any tinkering with the free market mechanism in industrial sectors. In spirit, the EC's Energy Directorate has wanted to be interventionist. In early 1978, it unveiled a plan to set an annual limit to the expansion of the refining sector, to make an annual recommendation of desired refinery output, and to control refined product imports. The plan envisaged capacity being in balance with demand by around 1980-82. At that point perhaps one-third or one-half of the annual rise in the Community's needs might come in from the oil-producing world — at preferential tariff rates in exchange for crude oil supply guarantees. [12] Quite clearly, if this policy had been formally adopted (which it has not), the EC refining industry would have taken a big step towards the kind of cartel which nearly came to pass in the synthetic fibres sector.

Counterplays

There are various aspects to these West European reactions that the Middle Easterners will need to watch as they develop their export strategies. Firstly, all this activity has been triggered off when import flows were relatively low, compared with those faced by traditional, declining industries, such as textiles. There have been warnings that the one per cent of the EC's plastics consumption which comes from state-trading Eastern Europe is only the tip of an iceberg, justifying significant surveillance of imported plastics. In the case of refined oil products, the picture is much the same. All the mighty efforts to establish an activist EC refining policy were against a background of a mere 6 per cent of EC consumption coming from imports (of which about half was coming from East Europe).[13] This suggests that, when the inevitable rationalisation of capacity takes place (either with or without help from Brussels), European industrialists are likely to be sensitive to any new source of oil or chemical products, even if the flows are minuscule in relation to the total EC market.

Secondly, the Middle Eastern producers should be aware of some of the forces backing market intervention. These could well slide into a protectionist position regarding Middle Eastern products. The Italians, for instance, are late-comers to the European industrial scene, and have increasingly fallen into the trap of making political rather than commercial investments. This is best illustrated by the fact that their leading 'lame duck' is not the usual steel or shipbuilding company found elsewhere in Europe, but Montedison, the chemical company which currently has an accumulated debt of over $4 billion. The Italians are not likely to be happy about Middle Eastern competition in petrochemicals until they have put this company back on its feet. Next, there are the French, whose Prime Minister, Monsieur Barre, coined the phrase 'organised free trade' to describe the policy of resorting to sophisticated protectionist devices in an era in which the industrialised economies seem to be having trouble adjusting fast enough to structural economic change. The French are most likely to cause trouble in the refining sector, since they have traditionally run a tightly controlled domestic oil marketing and refining policy. Although they are now proposing to liberalise this sector, they are insisting that approval of future oil imports be conditional on compensatory purchases of French goods by the exporting country. At the very least, they will try to extend this condition to future imports of Middle Eastern products. In addition, the extremely tough position which France has taken at the GATT negotiations on reducing tariffs and controlling non-tariff distortions to trade, suggests that, whatever liberalisation may be taking place at the domestic level, it is against a background of increasing scepticism about any further freeing of international trade.

The Middle Easterners should also take account of those politically important European companies which have failed to adjust to the changed competitive situation of the 1970s. These are best exemplified by the five oil companies which led the demands on the EC Commission for action on the structural crisis in the refining industry. There is no convincing evidence that these companies will have been able to resolve their current difficulties by the time Middle Eastern products start to flow in the 1980s. If they have not been able to do so, they will be an important source of resistance to Middle Eastern ambitions. Perhaps they may also be given discreet backing by BP (say the company's enemies), which has over 40 per cent of its assets in Europe and has chosen not to acquire for itself a share in any of the Middle Eastern ventures which will form the new competition.

The Middle Easterners would also need to watch the schizophrenic attitude within the EC Commission about such issues. On the one hand, the External Affairs Directorate has proved relatively liberal on trade matters, generally seeing the political advantages to be won from trade concessions. It led the way on the key Mediterranean pacts with the Maghreb and Mashreq countries, paying little attention to the more narrow, sectoral worries of the Industry and Energy Directorates, which were considerably less enthusiastic about granting tariff-free access to these countries' industrial goods. The Industry Directorate, on the other hand, has veered heavily in the direction of backing rationalisation programmes which are operating in the case of the steel industry, and were narrowly avoided in the case of synthetic fibres. The latter scheme, which had all the characteristics of a Europe-wide cartel agreement, left liberal observers extremely uneasy about the Industry Directorate's philosophies. The Middle Easterners will want to watch how this directorate responds to heavy pressure, put on it by the petrochemical industry, to intervene against growing imports from Eastern Europe. Should some 'trigger-price' system be adopted, or should there be an even more intensive treatment of anti-dumping issues, then the free flow of Middle Eastern products will inevitably be affected in its turn. Again, the Middle Easterners should also watch the Energy Directorate which handles the refining sector. Although interested in keeping its communication channels with the oil-producing powers open, in early 1978 it was certainly of the opinion that oil-product imports into the EC should be kept at 1977 levels, and only liberalised as its proposed programme for refinery rationalisation progressed. The Energy Directorate seems ready to accept that after such rationalisation an increasing part of incremental product demand would be met by imports from producing countries, providing there are some reciprocal undertakings on crude oil supply.[14]

The Middle Easterners should also note that events during the 1970s have brought parts of the EC Commission much closer to the business lobbies than they have ever been. The abortive fibres cartel would never have reached the stage it did without a continued and extensive dialogue between the Industry Directorate and the European fibres industry. In fact, the monitoring of the scheme was due to have been left to the European Federation of Fibre Producers.[15] The Energy

Directorate has been carrying on a similar dialogue with the refining industry over the last couple of years on matters concerning capacity utilisation and price transparency. Within the Euro-Arab Dialogue, trade associations such as CEFIC (for petrochemicals) have been given an important role in producing the European side's statistics. In addition, the European delegations have included both civil servants and representatives from industry.

It would be unfair to suggest that this increased liaison between the EC and industry spokesmen is unknown in other quarters in Brussels. After all, an even stronger symbiosis of corporate and Community thinking has been established for some years in both steel and textiles. It would, however, be fair to suggest that events in both the petrochemicals and refining sectors show a major increase in the role of industry lobbies, and this means they will be in a better position to argue for import controls than they were in the late 1960s — and it is extremely unlikely that this will work in favour of encouraging Middle Eastern imports when these eventually start to flow in any quantity.

The 'restrictionist'-liberal trading balance

The last few pages have dealt predominantly with the West European situation. Can any more general conclusions be drawn about the likely balance between liberal and 'restrictionist' forces in the mid-1980s when Middle Eastern products will really start to flow? The fact that both the Japanese and European authorities have been partially drawn into the investment process in the Middle East should ensure that Middle Eastern products will not suffer too much interference when they seek markets in the OECD world. For instance, now that the Japanese have designated Mitsubishi's proposed ethylene complex in Saudi Arabia a 'national' project, how could the Japanese authorities bar the eventual products from the Japanese market? In the case of the EC, the picture is more complicated, because Brussels does not have as much influence over the behaviour of European companies as the Japanese have over theirs. But the EC does control tariff policies, and each time Brussels enters into an arrangement such as the Euro-Arab Dialogue, or the recently agreed twice-yearly meetings with OAPEC officials,[16] it becomes even less likely that the EC will increase barriers to Middle Eastern products or resort too quickly to safeguard procedures. In the case of the US, government involvement in the Middle Eastern operations of the two industries discussed in this book, is on a lesser scale than in the case of the EC or Japan (the US-Saudi Joint Economic Commission is probably the most important institution expressing the US government's formal relationship with the region's economy). The

US is not, therefore, putting itself into a position where it seems to be tacitly encouraging the Middle Easterners to expect reasonably liberal treatment for their products' exports in the 1980s.

Further support for the forces of liberalism will include foreign policy establishments around the world, since none of them will want to cause unwarranted offence to the Saudi Arabians and other leading oil producers. Partly, they will be concerned with maintaining future stability of oil supplies. There will be concern, particularly in the case of the State Department, to avoid driving the leading oil producers into radical positions on the Arab-Israeli dispute (we write this on the assumption that the Camp David accords have by no means settled this issue). These foreign policy establishments will thus see the dangers of taking restrictive measures against Middle Eastern industrial ambitions. On the other hand, foreign policy issues now count for much less in international economic policy than they might have done in the 1960s.

Again, on the liberal side, there are the plant constructors and a handful of multinationals which have decided to hedge their bets and take a share in Middle Eastern industrialisation. Once again, these are not particularly powerful advocates. For one thing, the plant constructors count for little in policy formation. For another, the influence of the multinationals, even when they are united, can be overstated, [17] and in this particular case, they are not even united. Some of them are willing to enter Middle Eastern joint ventures, but they are not showing the kind of enthusiasm which will make them effective advocates for the dismantling of access barriers against Middle Eastern products. Then again, these would-be investors will have their own corporate stakes in the industrialised world to sustain, thus giving them a relatively schizophrenic viewpoint about Middle Eastern ambitions. In any case those companies will be arrayed against other multinationals which have chosen to keep clear from Middle Eastern investments and which could align themselves with the more domestically-oriented, medium-ranking companies. These companies are likely to argue that national security and jobs are at stake if Middle Eastern products are encouraged to flow back to the OECD world. So, the multinationals entering the Middle Eastern ventures may well be able to side-step some of the worst trade barriers put up against the relevant products by finding a home for these within their corporate worldwide marketing network. On the other hand, these multinationals do not look as though they will be particularly effective lobbyists on the Middle Easterners' behalf.

Again, on the restrictive side is the probability that there will be growing resistance from the industrialised world to the excesses of 'state trading'.[18] This resistance will stem from the fact that the industrialisation of a growing range of non-OECD powers is being planned and funded by the state. Without the discipline of the market, which allows uncompetitive companies to go bankrupt, there will be a certain amount of arbitrariness about which industries receive state backing. When these countries decide to enter export markets in a substantial way, the scene is set for some bitter diplomatic wrangling, triggered off by OECD-based industrialists arguing that this new competition is 'unfair' as prices bear no close relationship to actual investment and production costs.

This issue is already emerging in the case of Eastern Europe's move into industries such as shipping and petrochemicals. It is due to arise in the case of the Middle Eastern and North African producers, unless the latter are very careful in how they manage their entry into refining and petrochemical markets. Obviously, countries such as Algeria, which are very much in favour of 100 per cent state ownership, will inevitably become embroiled in any widening of the fair-trading dispute. Despite the fact that they are bringing foreign partners into their plans, the Saudis could still be vulnerable to charges that their low feedstock and capital prices are unfair to OECD-based competitors.

This will seem unjust to the Middle Easterners, but the argument is that even the most ardent supporters of trade liberalisation may be forced to back some kind of restrictions against imports from state traders,[19] if these supporters are to keep the liberal trading tradition alive in other areas. There is a growing number of industrialists and trade unionists who once supported the idea of lowering barriers to trade, but who are now more doubtful as they see well-run companies being undercut by plants from the state-trading economies of Eastern Europe and (potentially) of the oil-producing world. These industrialists and trade unionists will see much of this competition as being 'unfair' and, unless there is heavy pressure on the most objectionable practices of the state-traders, there will be a steady drift of people away from the liberal trading camp into the protectionist one. Of course, one can argue that consumers will generally benefit from the lower prices that are the consequences of the subsidies offered by the state-traders, but this is very difficult to explain to a man who has lost his livelihood because a government in some distant land has declared his particular industry a national priority which must be developed and backed at all costs. The indications, then, are that a number of free-traders may back some restrictions on imports from state-trading parts of the world. Certainly, they will be tempted to back demands for registers of plant construction deals so that the OECD world can get advance warning as to the industries in which the state-traders are building up export-oriented capacity. Again, the free-trader may find it difficult to object to the setting of 'trigger prices' based on the most efficient plants.

Each similar initiative, however, is inevitably open to distortion. The surveillance register idea can be used as an argument that, as long as some part of the OECD world has a surplus of capacity in some industry, imports must be controlled and worldwide investment plans scrutinised even more closely. The 'trigger price' may be fixed in reference to relatively high-cost plants and thus become a barrier slowing down the relocation of key industries away from the industrialised world.

Possible initiatives

We reluctantly conclude that governments at either end of our two chosen industries will not just leave future events to the workings of the market system. At one end, the oil-producing governments will push investments ahead even if there is only a weak, or even negative, economic case for them. On the other end, consumer governments will be worried about the security implications of becoming over-reliant on Middle Easterners, and will also be susceptible to the blandishments of established indigenous companies which will cry for protection. The interesting questions are how far such intervention will go, and what forms any increased inter-governmental co-operation may take.

Much will depend on the scale of Middle Eastern competition in our two industries. Our conclusions are that the oil producers will not become significantly large industrial forces during the 1980s, but that the existing conditions in these industries mean that even their quite modest achievements will be enough to elicit defensive responses from governments in their preferred markets — particularly in Western Europe. Taken together, the aspirations of the two sets of governments (within the Middle East and the OECD world) are such that, unless there is some modification of either (or both) positions, existing conditions of over-capacity will continue well into the 1990s.

We believe that there are a number of factors encouraging some form of official, long-term dialogue about petrochemicals and refining. Protectionists in the industrialised world may well welcome such dialogues with the aim of influencing the oil producers' investment and marketing intentions; as the oil producers' plans initially seem to be uncompetitive or unrealistic, committed free-traders cannot object too strongly if this institutional innovation leads to the avoidance of the misallocation of economic resources. Again, as far as the industrialised world turns its attention to reducing non-tariff distortions to trade, it will find specific dialogues one useful way of extending the debate about what are 'fair' and 'unfair' practices in each particular sector. Nor should we feel that only the industrialised world can gain from such interaction, for the oil producers are only just starting to learn the market environment of these downstream industries, and can still use some technical assistance from the industrialised world. Regular interaction between the two ends of these industries can help the oil producers to identify areas in which the industrialised world can help. Again, should market access become a problem, then the Middle Easterners will gain from having an established institutional framework in which to make common protests.

Against these diffuse, but generally positive, potential results which should spring from a relatively formal interaction between the oil producers and their main customers in the industrialised world, there is the suspicion that — to adjust Adam Smith's famous remarks about conspiratorial tradesmen — 'Governments of the same trade seldom meet together but the conversation ends in a conspiracy against the public (particularly of the Third World) or in some diversion to distort trade.' Specifically, in an economic environment like that of the late 1970s, any dialogue on petrochemicals or refining is bound to be dominated by the industrial world's assertions about the scale of excess capacity, and then to lead to attempts to stop the oil producers investing in these sectors, whatever the comparative advantages involved. However, accepting that any dialogue or institutionalised negotiations between product exporters and importers are more likely to distort than to liberalise trade, we happen to believe that both sides are motivated strongly enough to want more interaction with each other rather than less. What form might this interaction take?

MFA model rejected

Clearly, these are not industries calling for the kind of framework which has evolved in the textiles and clothing industries as the Multi-Fibre Arrangement, a pact which lays down permitted annual growth rates for the exports of each Third World producer. Quite simply, the scale of the competition from the OPEC powers is nowhere so strong in petrochemicals or refining as Third World efforts have proved to be in labour-intensive industries such as clothing. In the case of our two industries, the new producers are considerably fewer in number; the number of significant projects is very small in comparison with the wildly competitive textile industry; the geographical distribution of the 'problem' is very much more narrowly defined for our industries (where West European markets are most affected) than for textiles where Third World competition is strong for the whole OECD world.

Regional approaches

Rather than on some worldwide, multilateral pact, we suspect that most diplomatic efforts will concentrate on a more regional agreement, with each of the three major OECD markets making their own deal with the most relevant oil-producing countries.

The Japanese

The Japanese will have the advantage of being able to bargain for themselves alone, and will have a relatively easy diplomatic time since they will primarily have to balance the interests of the Middle Eastern oil producers with those of one or two of the more ambitious East Asian economies. Since the latter will be dependent on Middle Eastern (and Indonesian) crude, they will not be in the strongest position if they choose to compete with Middle Eastern plants for access to Japanese oil product or petrochemical markets.

The United States

Because of the distances involved, the United States is not likely to be directly affected by large quantities of product imports from the Middle East. Probably of greater significance will be the ripple effect, as the greater competitive pressures on West European industries force these to look westward to US markets for export outlets.

There are signs that the combination of these direct and indirect pressures, along with the growing importance of Mexico in the hydrocarbon field, may mean the tacit emergence in the Western Hemisphere of a preference system for at least some of the products which interest the Middle Easterners. In the case of gas, there is now a clearly formulated US Department of Energy policy to discriminate against long-haul LNG deals, in favour of short-haul ones involving Alaskan, Canadian or Mexican gas. Whatever the LNG aspirations of the Saudi and Iranian authorities, they can clearly rule out the US as an importer of this product for at least the next decade.

In the oil-refining sector, it will need a revolution in official US thinking before all the administrative controls which currently favour domestic US refiners and some Caribbean ones are swept away. If controls are relaxed, it will probably happen only to encourage the Canadians and, particularly, that re-emergent oil power, Mexico, to help meet US energy needs. The Europeans and Middle Easterners will be left as marginal suppliers, whose refining industries will continue to suffer discrimination relative to the treatment given to those in the Western Hemisphere.

As far as petrochemicals are concerned, the picture is less clear. We are writing, not yet knowing the final outcome of the GATT Multilateral Trade Negotiations, where the US negotiators have been fighting extremely hard to maintain the high effective protection currently afforded to the US chemical market. At the moment, other countries in the Western Hemisphere do not receive any preferential treatment regarding the petrochemical trade, but the Middle Easterners should note that pressures are growing for the formation of a US-Canadian free-trade pact in petrochemicals, along the lines of the US-Canadian Automotive Pact. In June 1978, an industry task-force submitted to the Canadian Federal Government a report calling for such an initiative, and the idea is also publicly advocated by Zoltan Merszei, Dow Chemical's former chairman, who pointed out that his company's largest single investment is in Canada.[20] Any such proposal will be fought tooth-and-nail within GATT by other chemical-producing countries, but the idea is abroad and, with the growing importance of Canadian hydrocarbon reserves, it is not wholly inconceivable that the US might embrace such a scheme as part of a wider US-Canadian agreement on their respective energy policies.

Western Europe

Certainly, as must be clear from this book, there are strong pressures on the West Europeans to enter into some form of regional deal. The combination of existing excess capacity, the growing current problem of imports from Eastern Europe, and the potential problem of Middle Eastern products only serves to ensure that some West Europeans will seek political solutions to such problems. The Euro-Arab Dialogue is an interesting prototype of a regional bargaining institution. The Dialogue has had its uses for the West Europeans, but could well be usefully strengthened. For instance, the fact that the Arab League is the opposite number is not particularly satisfactory, and the decision to enter into discussions twice yearly with OAPEC, which is a much more logical representative body in the refining and petrochemical fields, is a step forward. However, there is still the problem of what to do with Iran. Can the country be ignored on the grounds that its main exporting strategy seemed to be directed eastwards into Asia, rather than westwards into Europe? Or would this leave it feeling diplomatically isolated, should the dialogue between Europeans and Arabs ever move to a stage in which investment levels in key industries are actually affected? Certainly, the Iranians are fully aware of Arab investment intentions in petrochemicals, and would presumably want to be in on any decisions to rationalise investment programmes around the Arabian/Persian Gulf.

The worries of non-Arab oil producers such as Iran that they might be excluded from the key dialogues with the EC, will be best met by the EC Commission's proposal to OPEC for twice-yearly EC-OPEC meetings to discuss the evolution of markets, information exchange and possible areas of co-operation.[21] On the other hand, this now leaves the EC discussing downstream investments issues with at least three widely overlapping groups (the Arab League, OAPEC and OPEC). Of these, the Euro-Arab Dialogue involving the Arab League shows the most dynamism, although Egypt's isolation after the Camp David talks has caused problems. Should this dialogue falter, then one suspects it would be replaced in effectiveness by the EC-OPEC relationship, particularly if the OPEC delegations are to consist primarily of representatives from countries whose downstream investments are most affected by EC policies.

The West Europeans also have the problem of what to do about the East Europeans. Logically, one can argue that the East Europeans need to be brought into any talks in which the EC discusses the future of the chemical and refining industries, because East European intentions are just as relevant to the discussion as those of the Middle Easterners. However, this brings about obvious problems. For one thing, the EC is extremely reluctant to recognise Comecon as its opposite number in Eastern Europe; hence any idea that the EC and Comecon might sit down at the same table to study each other's investment intentions in, for example, chemicals, is most unlikely. At the same time, the alternative of getting the individual East European countries to come together with the EC or the individual West European countries seems equally unlikely.

Thus, in the absence of any acceptable framework for discussing the East-West aspect of these industries (might the Economic Commission for Europe have a role to play?), we suspect that a gradually evolving Euro-Arab Dialogue will remain the most relevant body. Although some problems will be handled on a strictly bilateral basis, a number of them, such as EC tariff policies and the search for some form of complementary investment, will be discussed increasingly in such a multilateral body. At the moment, neither side in the Dialogue is constituted sufficiently formally for negotiations to be possible. However, as the present exploratory talks highlight serious problems on which negotiations are possible, we would expect both delegations to be constituted in a more formal way. Behind the West Europeans' thinking, however, must be the fact that the Middle Easterners are not the only claimants for EC markets and that any concessions made to them will have to be at the expense of the EC, East European or non-EC West European industries (might the European side of the Euro-Arab Dialogue be widened to include the Scandinavians?).

Worldwide approaches

Ultimately, though, issues such as conditions of market access would be best discussed on a worldwide, rather than regional level. After all, the investment intentions of any one region of the world will inevitably have an impact on petrochemical and refining industries throughout every other region. It would be far better to move towards a single, worldwide understanding about permissible subsidy practices than to allow regional or bilateral dialogues to come up with cumulatively contradictory formulae.

There are not many multilateral bodies which could qualify as the best forum for discussing such a range of issues. UNCTAD might put itself forward, because of its involvement in issues of North-South trade. This body, however, has lately tended to concentrate on commodity issues, and might be rejected by the industrialised nations, which distrust UNCTAD as being dominated by the Third World. UNIDO is positively studying the world petrochemical industry, but suffers from the same disadvantage as UNCTAD, as the industrialised world feels it to be too much under Third World control. Nor is it even certain that the oil producers would want to discuss such issues in institutions where non-oil-producing LDCs are in a majority. The oil producers might well be happier with a more restricted debate, such as a dialogue between OPEC and the OECD. OPEC members have already called for a limited version of this, when they proposed an OPEC-EC dialogue on downstream investment, and a series of such meetings with a membership expected to include other OECD members could make some sense. At the very least, an OPEC-OECD dialogue would have the mutually educative role that the rather more complex Conference on International Economic Co-operation (the North-South Dialogue) played in 1976-77. It would be considered manageable by both sides, as most of the countries involved have a real interest in the petrochemical and refining industries. Providing neither side entered such a dialogue with inflated expectations, no real damage would be done to either side's commercial interests, while some positive gains might be achieved.

The main disadvantage of such talks is that neither of the two logical representative bodies (OPEC and the OECD) is sufficiently involved with our two hydrocarbon-processing industries to make any initial dialogue between them more than exploratory. OPEC, for instance, has no policy for co-ordinating its members' investments in petrochemicals or refining. The fact, however, that it has held a conference on the issues at stake, shows that it will inevitably progress from considering oil production issues (pricing and perhaps pro-rationing) to downstream aspects of the industry. Similarly, although the OECD has been moving strongly in areas of industrial policy (export credits, industrial adjustments, and watching over developments in steel and shipbuilding), it has not been notably active in the refining and petrochemical sectors, nor on issues such as the terms of market access (in the latter case GATT is the relevant body). On the other hand, just as OPEC is starting to consider the issues surrounding our two industries, so also is the OECD, albeit in a slightly different way.

First of all, since 1974 the OECD has, via the creation of the International Energy Agency (IEA),[22] become the industrialised world's most important multilateral forum on energy issues. Much of the IEA's original work was purely defensive (e.g. setting up an emergency allocation scheme in case the events of autumn 1973 were ever repeated), but it has rapidly become more positive in its outlook. The most important work currently being carried out is the co-ordination of member country energy policies and energy research and development strategies.[23] There is now increasingly clear evidence that the IEA is willing to co-operate with leading Third World countries. As an example of this Mexico has recently joined an IEA R & D project involving small-scale geothermal technology. Another instance of this willingness is the workshop on energy data in developing countries which the IEA held in December 1978. Quite deliberately, the IEA aimed for a fifty-fifty balance of energy experts from member countries and the Third World (in the latter case both leading oil producers and LDC oil importers were invited). There is no doubting the importance of these developments. The Agency has shown that it is more than willing to enter a dialogue on technical issues with a leading cross-section of LDCs. If the IEA is willing to do this for energy statistics, whilst also opening its energy research and development programme to LDC participants, there is no reason why refining and petrochemical issues might not be dealt with in a forum involving both the industrialised and leading non-OECD countries.

The OECD can be expected to become further involved in areas such as the worldwide over-capacity within the steel and shipbuilding sectors. The Shipbuilding Working Party and the Steel Industry Committee already bring together most of the leading OECD countries which are involved in these two industries. Within these groups, the various governments are already discussing such issues as the provision of export credits, the removal of obstacles to normal competitive trade and the varieties of governmental intervention in these industries. Increasingly, in the case of shipbuilding, attention has switched to a mutual information system which makes it possible to follow trends in order books, new orders and ships completed.[24] In addition, there is now serious discussion about widening the membership of the steel committee to include some of the leading Third World producers of steel, and a limited number of invitations have gone out to countries such as India, Mexico, South Korea and Brazil.

So, one strategy the OECD might follow would be to create a similar sub-group for petrochemicals and refining, with the clear intention of also inviting the leading Third World powers within these industries. This would make it easier to invite non-oil-producing countries such as South Korea, which is already showing signs of becoming as much a force in petrochemicals as it is already in steel and shipbuilding. It may be, however, that our two industries pose problems on a more limited regional basis than, for example, shipbuilding, where the competition is genuinely worldwide. The North Americans, for instance, might be less interested in a sub-group for petrochemicals than in one for steel. If there is indeed a feeling of less urgency surrounding our two industries, it could be that sporadic talks between OPEC and the OECD on such matters would be enough for either side. Such talks could continue to identify the issues at stake, but would not lead to some permanent institution which might eventually prove unwanted.

However, before entering any such limited 'North-South' dialogue, OECD members should disabuse themselves of any belief that pressure for adjustment would be solely on the oil-producing countries. In fact, it is quite clear that there would be counter-pressures which could seriously embarrass some OECD members. For instance, the newly industrialising countries will have little patience with nations seeking to preserve over-fragmented, domestic industries from some sort of consolidation. Here one thinks of Japanese and European resistance to corporate mergers in industries plagued with excess capacity. Again, the new economic powers will be impatient with OECD governments which continue helping investment in domestic industries which should be gracefully making way for the former group's products. Finally, it is inevitable that tariff and market access issues would be raised at such a dialogue, however strenuously the industrialised countries stressed that these are issues best left to the GATT.

A disclaimer

We are only too aware that some readers will interpret this chapter as being protectionist in tone (some readers of an earlier draft certainly favoured this interpretation). We must, therefore, stress a few points we have specifically *not* been making. For one thing, we have not been dealing with institutional initiatives which we think are *desirable*, but with those we think are *likely*. Secondly, we nowhere argue that the effective ambitions of the Middle Eastern and North African oil producers are on a scale to cause any notable strains in a healthy world

195

economy.

However, the world economy is clearly not as healthy as it was in the period 1945-73. Growth rates have faltered, and the industrialised world's self-confidence has faltered. The result is that the automatic workings of the adjustment process are increasingly challenged, and protectionism is much nearer to the surface than it has been for decades. Faster economic growth would undoubtedly remove most of these problems, but are we going to see it in the coming decade?

On top of this is the fact that the governments of the newly industrialising powers, such as the oil producers, are playing an unprecedented role. Inevitably, this increasingly politicises trade relations with the OECD world, at a time when the latter is just starting to come to grips with the excesses of governmental intervention which show up as non-tariff distortions of world trade.

So, the reason why we have analysed various institutional initiatives within the refining and petrochemical industries is not because we necessarily welcome them, but because these industries have already become politicised, and will, in our view, remain so in the near future.

In a policy-oriented book such as this, we would be doing our readers a disservice by glossing over the full implications of our admittedly pessimistic view of the coming decade.

Conclusion

In this book, we have tried to set out both sides of the issues at stake, writing in a non-technical way for readers who, like Sir Alec Douglas-Home (the former British prime minister), find political problems insoluble and economic ones incomprehensible. There are some cross-disciplinary conclusions which need to be made.

Firstly, policy-makers in the OECD world should avoid becoming too absorbed by the fate of any one industrial sector or type of products. Instead, they should accept that we live in a world of interdependent trade and should be willing to step back and view the workings of the OECD economies at the broadest level. After all, the industrialised world has taken only about four years to come close to covering its tremendously inflated bill for crude oil imports by increased reverse flows of goods and services to OPEC nations. Changes in industries such as petrochemicals and refining will be on a much smaller scale than the great rise in oil costs with which the world system has roughly come to terms. Furthermore, change will come more slowly, because of both the considerable inertia in the planning and construction processes within these industries and the fact that the new producers will not be able to manipulate prices as the OPEC powers were able to do in the early

196

1970s.

Secondly, policy-makers should remember that a good number of the crises which have occurred in other industries (such as textiles, steel or shipbuilding) have been caused by the fact that most of the companies involved reacted in narrowly nationalistic and sectoral terms, refusing to diversify or advance their skills in order to compensate for losing parts of their traditional activities. In petrochemicals and refining, however, we are primarily dealing with giant multinational companies which are generally showing a willingness and capability to adapt and move away from the threatened areas. In these circumstances, no-one should show too much sympathy for badly-managed companies left stranded by competitive change. The jobs at stake tend to be both few in number and highly skilled so that redundant employees could be more easily re-employed than is the case with many redundant textile or ship-building workers.

One further aspect which policy-makers should bear in mind is that the faster world economic growth occurs, the easier it is to accept the strains and stresses of industrial adaptation. The trouble is that world growth now seems temporarily set at rates which are noticeably slower than those experienced between 1945 and 1973. Inevitably, this will make OECD governments more sensitive to demands for protection of industries under competition from Third World sources. So, we would urge world governments to push for growth rates which are rather closer to the pre-1973 average, even if this involves some inflationary risks for the OECD world. We would, in fact, endorse the EC study which, when analysing the strains likely to be caused by new, South European entrants into the Common Market, argued that if EC growth fell below 2 per cent per annum, the new social strains would probably be too severe for the existing EC membership — but that if growth rates were up around 4.5 per cent per annum, the new entrants should be easily absorbed. We feel that the same arguments hold good for the industries which we have been discussing.

Another conclusion is that not even a country as important as Saudi Arabia can create a New International Economic Order by decree. The economics of investments do matter and, despite the official liberal-trading philosophy of most OECD members, the latter will give market access to Middle Eastern products quite grudgingly. In this case, LDC statesmen must follow a twin programme of maintaining a drive for increased efficiency in any industry they hope to enter, while simul-taneously keeping continued pressure on OECD governments regarding market access issues. Finally, the oil producers' policy-makers must be aware of the arguments from development economists who suggest that capital-intensive industrialisation is not necessarily the best strategy for every oil producing economy. Nations such as Iran, Algeria and Nigeria have a more urgent need to create jobs than, for example, a country like Kuwait. For the former countries, money spent on labour-intensive industries may make a longer and more worthwhile contribution to their development than the 'cathedrals in the desert' discussed in this book.

This book has some lessons also for economists. For one thing, in some aspects of our analysis the institutional form through which the relevant investments should occur becomes extremely important. The fact that the Saudis have chosen to enter petrochemicals through joint ventures with multinational companies immediately means that the timing of investments in that country will be different than if it were following the Algerian or Libyan approach of totally national enterprises. Again, although we are not convinced that the industrialising oil producers will be faced with out-and-out protectionism, it is clear that the world into which they hope to launch their products is a complex one, far removed from any ideal espoused by Adam Smith. The relatively slow world growth we expect for the immediate future makes it quite likely that the concept of 'organised free trade' will be extended to include the types of products and Middle Eastern countries discussed in this book. The fact that a good number of the projects under analysis are really 'infant' export industries, which will not be sufficiently strong to stand on their own competitive feet, will play into the hands of the 'interventionists' within the OECD world.

Increasingly, then, a study of these industries leaves us with a picture of the world in which the industrialised countries will continue the struggle to purge each other of remaining 'impure' trade and investment policies, while simultaneously dealing with a new generation of 'graduating' economic powers from the Third World. The latter will be seeking to take their place in the world economic order, without fully accepting the range of obligations which the OECD members will increasingly impose on each other. So, the 1980s will see a series of skirmishes between the industrialised world and these newly industrialising countries, and some idea of the issues at stake emerged from the GATT negotiations which were continuing as we revised this book in February 1979. The industrialised world is asking for the right to use selective safeguards against the leading Third World countries. At the moment, in Geneva, most thought is being given to defending industries against 'super-competitive' countries such as Hong Kong, South Korea or Taiwan; the Middle Eastern oil producers will move into this particular category as their petrochemical and refining capacities increase. Also in the GATT negotiations there is discussion on LDC export subsidies, on the extent to which LDCs can promote industrial development through techniques banned in the industrialised world, on improved procedures for settling trade and investment disputes between

198

the industrialised and Third World, and on the conditions under which export controls will be accepted.

Whatever happens at the GATT negotiations, it is clear that the case of the Third World has been poorly represented (the *Economist* reported that the US had 40 diplomats alone working on trade issues in Geneva, while an unnamed LDC had only one diplomat, whose time was spent between trade and other issues).[25] We would, therefore, expect these issues to reappear at irregular intervals throughout the 1980s as different groups of LDCs emerge on the industrial scene. Undoubtedly, the oil producers will be one such group of countries, and it is unrealistic to expect them to consider themselves bound by any general principles worked out during the current GATT negotiations. Tensions will grow as specific institutions are created to handle the trade problems of particular industries (such as petrochemicals). The LDCs involved will seek to get the maximum gains out of each individual sector, while the industrialised world will be trying to maintain general trading and investment principles which are not too far out of line with the tougher standards which the OECD countries set themselves.

This study of two industries has also shown us clearly how far we have actually moved towards a truly world economy. On one level — the transmission of information and technology — there is now a distinctively worldwide industrial community in which geographical location is almost irrelevant. Policy-makers within the Middle East read exactly the same sources of trade information as their opposite numbers in Houston, Tokyo or London. Everywhere one finds copies of the *Middle Eastern Economic Survey, Petroleum Intelligence Weekly* or the Stanford Research Institute's analyses of the world chemical industry. Where there is a need to go deeper, the Middle Easterners have the money to hire the best of the world's consultants to improve their knowledge. On the other hand, decision-makers within much of the non-OPEC world are equally well informed about developments within key OPEC economies — and this holds for leading Third World countries such as South Korea, India, Brazil and Argentina which have been bidding for and winning contracts in OPEC countries at the less complex ends of the business. Variations in the diffusion of technical and economic knowledge around the world are now virtually irrelevant in analysing future industrial developments.

On the technological front, the picture is slightly more complicated — but not much. Naturally, there is the problem that key technological breakthroughs are normally dominated by a few key multinationals, which may restrict access to the new technology for a while. Once that technology is licensed to plant constructors (and this happens with greater rapidity than ever), any country with sufficient money can buy that technology. Certainly, whatever the problems faced by the Middle Easterners, winning access to the best of OECD technology is rarely mentioned. On the other hand, it remains true that no Middle Eastern companies are yet starting to generate their own advanced technology; they remain passive buyers from other countries. This sometimes reduces their bargaining power on matters such as price.

But if the markets for information and technology are virtually worldwide, this does not mean that geographical factors are of no importance in future decisions about the location of key industries. Transportation costs are still a barrier and will remain so in the absence of any major technological breakthroughs. In the case of refined oil and petrochemical products, the move to much larger product carriers will reduce costs somewhat, but will have to be accompanied by large-scale investment in import terminals. In transporting gas, there are greater chances of a major cut in costs, since so much of the expense here is connected with the pressure under which the gas must travel. Once again, however, the need for specific import terminals will slow developments. So, all this is very different from, for example, the development of the clothing industry in East Asia which has the flexibility of choosing between airfreight, shipping or overland transportation. It therefore needs no new investment in transportation infrastructure, since clothing can enter a country through any existing port, airport or railway goods-yard. Quite clearly, shifts in the centre of gravity of the chemical industry will take place much more slowly than has been the case with industries such as textiles and shipbuilding.

There still remains the cultural question of relative managerial and operative efficiencies. Western pessimists argue that industrial skills are developed only slowly over decades, if not generations — that a 25-year-old Middle Easterner with a PhD in chemical engineering just cannot compare with a 40-year-old from Houston who may have much inferior paper qualifications but can rely on the experience of a life-time dealing with everyday problems of the oil and chemical industries. There is much substance in this pessimism. In the case of other non-western countries which have made the transition to industrial powers (Japan, Hong Kong, Taiwan, South Korea, Singapore), it is striking how they have progressed steadily from labour-intensive industries (clothing, shoes, toys, etc.) to a second generation of more highly skilled and managerially-challenging industries (steel, shipbuilding, etc.). Middle Easterners are trying to bridge this gap in one leap.

This emphasis on the Middle East's industrial 'underdevelopment' can, however, be over-stressed. For one thing, this generation's industrial inexperience can be overcome by following the current Saudi policy of relying on foreign partners to provide the management and expatriate workers to fill those jobs for which Saudis are not yet qualified. Providing strong emphasis is put on training Saudis for as many future posts as they want to fill, then the jump to the second generation of technologies could be successful. Secondly, it should also be stressed that, in the course of two years' hard research for this book, we have met very few fools in positions of responsibility in the Middle East. Rather, we met a number of people who are just as sharp and well-informed as many Westerners in these industries. This does not mean that they will always make the right decisions. All but a handful of the Middle Easterners struck us as being production rather than marketing-oriented, which means that they are tempted to push ahead with new capacity despite uncertainties about operating costs and future marketing opportunities. It also means that, in all likelihood, they will learn from their mistakes, with the result that the second generation of investment which will be made in the Middle East should be quite widely competitive on world markets.

The picture, then, is of the OECD's (particularly West Europe's) economy gradually accommodating itself to industrial products from the Middle East and North Africa. During the 1980s, this accommodation will proceed by fits and starts; in the 1990s, it should be a fact of life within the world economy. This is a picture of evolutionary, rather than revolutionary change — a picture much less dramatic than some champions of a 'New International Economic Order' might desire, but an example of how the real world develops. Today's leading economic powers may be able to partially slow down the process of Third World industrialisation. But we are dealing with a tide which cannot now be reversed.

Notes

1   *Petroleum Economist*, March 1978, p.118.
2   *European Chemical News*, September 22 1978, p.13; September 1 1978, p.22.
3   *European Chemical News*, July 21 1978, p.30.
4   *European Chemical News*, July 21 1978, p.30.
5   *Financial Times*, August 29 1978.
6   An OECD source.
7   *OECD Observer*, January 1979, p.22.
8   *OECD Observer*, January 1979, p.18.
9   Donges and Riedel, 1977, pp 70-2.
10   *European Chemical News*, June 23 1978, p.6.
11   *Petroleum Intelligence Weekly*, November 15 1976, pp 4-5.

12   *Petroleum Intelligence Weekly*, January 30 1978, pp 2-3.
13   *Petroleum Intelligence Weekly*, January 30 1978, pp 2-3.
14   Brunner, 1978, p.66.
15   *European Chemical News*, May 5 1978, p.4.
16   *Petroleum Intelligence Weekly*, October 30 1978, pp 6-7.
17   Turner, 1978a, chapter 6.
18   Zysman, 1978.
19   We heard this argument first from Jan Tumlir, as staunch a defender of free trade as one can find. See his arguments in Blackhurst *et al* 1978, 1977.
20   *European Chemical News*, Supplement, October 13 1978, p.62.
21   Brunner, 1978, p.66.
22   Strictly speaking, the IEA is not directly controlled by the OECD, having a subtly different membership and voting structure. See Turner 1978a, pp 179-86.
23   Turner and Parry, 1978.
24   *OECD Observer*, March 1978, pp 16-7.
25   *Economist*, December 2 1978, p.94.

Appendix: Principles of petrochemical production

For the purposes of this book, we have deliberately kept the technicalities to a minimum. However, there will be readers who want to know more about the production processes involved and the end-uses of the various products we have mentioned. This is an attempt to give a thumb-nail sketch of what is actually an extremely complex industry. Those left dissatisfied we would refer to basic texts such as Waddams, 1978 or chapter 19 of British Petroleum, 1977.

At the heart of the petrochemical industry lies the fact that key chemical 'building blocks' (such as ethylene) can be derived from the processing of natural gases or of particular by-products from the oil-refining process. Some building blocks can be produced from either source.

Oil refineries produce a range of products including naphtha and gas oil which can be treated in plants known as crackers to produce building blocks such as *ethylene*, *propylene* or *butadiene* (generically, these are called *olefins*). Naphtha can also be put through a reformer to produce the major *aromatic* building blocks, *benzene, toluene* and the *xylenes*. These building blocks can then be processed further to produce a range of derivative products ranging from explosives to plastic films. The trouble with the refinery-based approach is that the more gasoline is needed from a refinery, the less naphtha is produced, thus forcing petrochemical producers into building expensive steam crackers to convert more difficult refinery by-products, such as gas oil, into the desired building blocks.

As far as the olefins are concerned, it is possible to take the alternative route of using natural gas. This can be broken down into the simplest carbon molecules, C_1 (methane), C_2 (ethane), C_3 (propane) and C_4 (butane). The methane can be processed into products such as *ammonia* or *methanol*. The other three feedstocks can be turned into varying proportions of the olefin building blocks (by weight, ethane yields 80 per cent ethylene, while butane yields proportionally less ethylene and more propylene).

Figure 1 gives a simplified impression of the various ways the basic building blocks of the petrochemical industry can be produced. It clearly shows that there is considerable flexibility as to how one

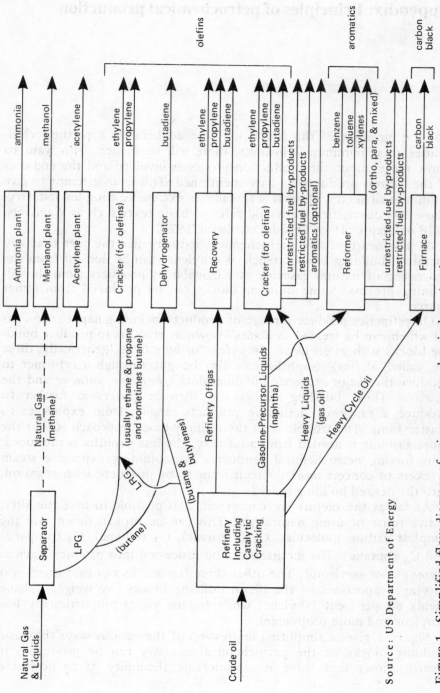

Source: US Department of Energy

Figure 1 Simplified flow diagram of primary petrochemical production

produces the olefins. Much of the debate on the comparative economics of producing these in the Middle East or in the industrialised world rests on the fact that one can start with either gas or crude oil.

Readers may well wish to know something about the end-uses of the derivative chemicals produced from the main building blocks.

Outlets for *ethylene* derivatives:
_____

Polyethylene — films, mouldings, pipes, cable covering, netting, etc.
Ethylene oxide — intermediate product in chain leading to anti-freeze, polyester fibres (Terylene) and detergents.
Styrene — polystyrene plastics and synethetic fibres.
Ethylene dichloride — step towards polyvinyl chloride (PVC) plastics, used for leather-cloth, piping, guttering.
Other derivatives — ethyl alcohol and acetaldehyde.

Outlets for *propylene* derivatives:
_____

Polypropylene — films, fibres and plastic mouldings.
Cumene — intermediate products for plastics, nylon and solvents.
Acrylonitrile — base for acrylic fibres; in chain leading to nylon.
Propylene oxide — intermediate for manufacture of plastic foams.
Other products are involved in detergent and resin manufacture.

Outlets for *butadiene* and other C_4 *olefins:*
_____

Butadiene's derivatives are heavily used in synthetic rubber production.
Other end-uses of butadiene and the other C_4 olefins include solvents, sealing compounds and the raw material for nylon.

Outlets for *aromatic* derivatives:
_____

Benzene

Styrene (also from ethylene) — polystyrene plastics and synthetic rubber.
Phenol — intermediate for resins.
Cyclohexane — intermediate for nylon production.
Other products are used for detergents, dyestuffs and polyester glass-fibre plastics.

Toluene

Derivatives used for plastic foams, resins, explosives (TNT) and paints.

Xylenes

Derivatives used for paints, lacquers, insecticides, polyester fibres and resins.

(Source: British Petroleum, 1977, pp 379-385).

Bibliography

Adelman, Irma and Morris, Cynthia Taft, *Society, Politics and Economic Development: A Quantitative Approach*, Johns Hopkins University Press, Baltimore, 1967.

Adelman, Irma and Morris, Cynthia Taft, 'Performance criteria for evaluating economic development potential: an operational approach', *Quarterly Journal of Economics*, May 1968, pp 260-80.

Algerian Ministry of Industry, *The Industrial Revolution*, Ministry of Industry, Algiers, 1974.

Allen, David, 'The Euro-Arab Dialogue', *Journal of Common Market Studies*, vol.16, no.4, June 1978, pp 323-42.

Amuzegar, Jahangir, *Iran: an Economic Profile*, Middle East Institute, Washington, 1977.

Bedore, James and Turner, Louis, 'The industrialization of the Middle Eastern oil producers', *World Today*, September 1977, pp 326-34.

Blackhurst, Richard; Marian, Nicolas and Tumlir, Jan, *Trade Liberalization, Protectionism and Interdependence*, GATT Studies no.5, GATT, Geneva, 1977.

Blackhurst, Richard; Marian, Nicolas and Tumlir, Jan, *Adjustment, Trade and Growth in Developed and Developing Countries*, GATT Studies no.6, GATT, Geneva, 1978.

Bradford, Peter Amory, *Fragile Structures: a Story of Oil Refineries, National Security and the Coast of Maine*, Harpers Magazine Press, New York, 1975.

British Petroleum, *Our Industry Petroleum*, 5th edn, British Petroleum, London, 1977.

Brunner, Guido, 'EEC policies and OPEC involvement in downstream activities: prospects for co-operation' in *Proceedings of the OPEC Seminar on Downstream Operations in OPEC Member Countries*, OPEC, Vienna, 1978, pp 55-6.

Buckley, Peter J. and Casson, Mark, *The Future of the Multinational Enterprise*, Macmillan, London, 1976.

Burchell, L.R., *Trends in Processing and the Petrochemical Industry*, Paper given to an OPEC seminar on 'The present and future role of national oil companies', held Vienna, 10 October 1977 (mimeo.).

CEFIC, *Survey on Olefins 1971-81*, CEFIC, Brussels, 1977b.

CEFIC, *Survey on Aromatics 1976*, CEFIC, Brussels, 1976a.

CEFIC, *Survey on Olefins 1976*, CEFIC, Brussels, 1976b.

CEFIC, *Survey on Aromatics 1971-81*, CEFIC, Brussels, 1977a.

Congressional Research Service, *Project Interdependence: US and World Energy Outlook through 1990*, printed for the use of the US Senate's Committee on Energy, US Government Printing Office, Washington, 1977.

Cooper, Richard N., 'US policies and practices on subsidies in international trade', in *International Trade and Industrial Policies*, ed. Steven Warnecke, Macmillan, London 1978, pp 107-22.

De Bruyne, D., *The Energy Outlook: Crisis or Myth?*, address to Dutch Ministry of Defence study centre, 20 October 1978, Shell Briefing Service, London, 1978.

Department of Energy (US), *The Role of Foreign Governments in the Energy Industries*, Office of International Affairs, Department of Energy, Washington DC, 1977a.

Department of Energy (US), *Trends in Desulfurization Capabilities, Processing Technologies, and the Availability of Crude Oils*, Office of Oil and Gas, Department of Energy, Washington DC, 1977b.

Department of Energy (US), *Technical Analysis of the International Oil Market*, Department of Energy, Washington DC, June 1978a.

Department of Energy (US), *Trends in Refining*, Department of Energy, Washington DC, 1978b.

Donges, Juergen B. and Riedel, James, 'The expansion of manufactured exports in developing countries: an empirical assessment of supply and demand issues', *Weltwirtschaftliches Archiv*, vol.113 (1977), pp 58-87.

Dunning, John H. (ed.), *Economic Analysis and the Multinational Enterprise*, Allen and Unwin, London, 1974.

Fellowes, Peregrine, 'OPEC, the Third World and international finance', *Optima*, vol.27 (1978), no.3, pp 2-23.

Fesharaki, Fereidun, *Development of the Iranian Oil Industry: International and Domestic Aspects*, Praeger, New York, 1976.

Franko, Lawrence G., *The European Multinationals*, Harper and Row, London, 1976.

Franko, Lawrence G., 'Multinational enterprise in the Middle East', *Journal of World Trade Law*, vol.10, no.4 (July/August 1976), pp 307-33.

Ghiles, Francis, 'Algeria', in *Middle East Annual Review 1977*, Middle East Review, Saffron Walden, 1976, pp 149-58.

Graham, Robert, *Iran: the Illusion of Power*, Croom Helm, London, 1978.

Hansen, Kurt, 'Investment and location policies of a transnational in petrochemicals' in *Proceedings of the OPEC Seminar on Downstream Operations in OPEC member Countries*, OPEC, Vienna, 1978, pp 67-84.

Jacoby, Neil H., *Multinational Oil*, Macmillan, New York, 1974.

Kitamura, Hiroshi, *Choices for the Japanese Economy*, Royal Institute of International Affairs, London, 1976.

Klinghoffer, Arthur J., *The Soviet Union and International Oil Politics*, Columbia University Press, New York, 1977.

Lichtblau, John H., 'OPEC as export refiners', *OPEC Review*, vol.2, no.4 (September 1978a) pp 43-7.

Lichtblau, John H., *Aspects of the US Crude Oil Entitlement Program*, statement to Sub-committee on Energy and Power, US House of Representatives, 15 June 1978b (mimeo.).

Looney, Robert E., *Iran at the End of the Century*, Lexington Books, Lexington, Mass., 1977a.

Looney, Robert E., *A Development Strategy for Iran through the 1980s*, Praeger, New York, 1977b.

McLachlan, Keith, 'Iran', in *Middle East Annual Review 1978*, Middle East Review, Saffron Walden, 1977, pp 203-14.

Middle East Annual Review 1977, Middle East Review, Saffron Walden, 1976.

Middle East Annual Review 1978, Middle East Review, Saffron Walden, 1977.

Mitsui, *The 100 Year History of Mitsui & Co Ltd, 1876-1976*, Mitsui & Co, Tokyo, 1977.

Morner, Aimée L., 'Dow's strategy for an unfriendly new era', *Fortune*, May 1977, pp 312-24.

Ochel, Wolfgang, *Die Industrialisierung der Arabischen OPEC-Länder und des Iran*, Weltforum Verlag, Munich, 1978.

OPEC, *Proceedings of the OPEC Seminar on 'Downstream Operations in OPEC Member Countries'*, OPEC, Vienna, 1978.

PIRINC (Petroleum Industry Research Foundation Inc.), *Outlook for World Oil into the 21st Century*, Electric Power Research Institute, Palo Alto, 1978.

Rostow, W.W., *The World Economy: History and Prospect*, Macmillan, London, 1978.

Sayigh, Yusif A., *The Determinants of Arab Economic Development*, Croom Helm, London, 1978a.

Sayigh, Yusif A., *The Economies of the Arab World: Development Since 1945*, Croom Helm, London, 1978b.

SIDF (Saudi Industrial Development Fund), *Annual Report: Fiscal Year 1396-97*, SIDF, Riyadh, 1978.

Smith, Geoffrey, 'Is time running out for the Shah of Iran?', *Forbes*, 10 July 1978, pp 68-74.

Spitz, Peter H., 'Outlook for OPEC member countries in downstream operations', in *Proceedings of the OPEC Seminar on 'Downstream Operations in OPEC Member Countries'*, OPEC, Vienna, 1978, pp 23-54.

Stauffer, T.R., 'Energy-intensive industrialization in the Arabian/ Persian Gulf', Paper presented to the Energy Seminar at Harvard University, April 1975 (mimeo.).

Tavoulareas, William P., 'A change in relationships', *Columbia Journal of World Business*, Summer 1977, pp 16-20.

Torii, Yasuji, 'Problems of technology and markets: an appropriate approach for OPEC', in *Proceedings of the OPEC Seminar*, OPEC, Vienna, 1978, pp 139-51.

Tovias, Alfred, *Tariff Preferences in Mediterranean Diplomacy*, Macmillan, London, 1977.

Tsurumi, Yoshi, *The Japanese are Coming: a Multinational Interaction of Finance and Politics*, Ballinger, Cambridge, Mass., 1976.

Tugwell, Franklin, *The Politics of Oil in Venezuela*, Stanford University Press, Stanford, 1975.

Turner, Louis, *Oil Companies in the International System*, Allen and Unwin, Hemel Hempstead, 1978a.

Turner, Louis, 'European and Japanese energy policies', *Current History*, vol.74, no.435 (March 1978b) pp 104-8, 129, 136.

Turner, Louis and Bedore, James, 'Saudi Arabia: the power of the purse strings', *International Affairs*, vol.54, no.3 (July 1978), pp 405-20.

Turner, Louis and Parry, Audrey, 'The next steps in energy co-operation', *World Today*, vol.34, no.3 (March 1978), pp 89-99.

Vernon, Raymond, 'The location of economic activity', in *Economic Analysis and the Multinational Enterprise*, ed. John Dunning, Allen and Unwin, London, 1974.

Waddams, A. Lawrence, *Chemicals from Petroleum: an Introductory Survey*, John Murray, London, 1978.

Wallace, David M., 'Saudi Arabia's building costs', *Hydrocarbon Processing*, November 1976, pp 189-96.

Warnecke, Steven J. (ed.), *International Trade and Industrial Policies: Government Intervention and an Open World Economy*, Macmillan, London, 1978.

Wells, Donald A., *Saudi Arabian Development Strategy*, American Enterprise Institute, Washington DC, 1976.

Yodfat, A. and Abir, M., *In the Direction of the Gulf: the Soviet Union and the Persian Gulf*, Cass, London, 1977.

Zysman, John, 'The state as trader', *International Affairs*, vol.54 (1978), no.2, pp 264-81.

Index

211

213

216

Qatar, CDF Chimie 66; NGL plant 90
Qusaibi, Dr Ghazi al- 22

Refining, Abadan 32; capacity 69-73; capacity in Africa 73; in Iran 28, 29, 30, 31; in Middle East 73, 111; in OPEC 69-71; in Saudi Arabia 69; in Western Europe 108-9, 134; reductions and adaptation of 173-9; location of 69, 91, 160; policies 160; in Iran 30; Ras Tanura 7; ventures, in Asia 29; in Caribbean 133-4; in Iran 27-31; in Latin America 133-4; in Saudi Arabia 15-16
Regional approaches (to trade policies) 190-2
Regional co-operation 163
Relocation, of downstream industries 2, 3, 200
Rhone-Poulenc 174
Riedel, James 180
Ritaco 41
Robinson, Charles 17
Rostow, W.W. 39
Royal Commission for Jubail and Yanbu 8

Sabah, Sheikh Ali Khalifah al- 167
SABIC 8, 9, 11, 12, 13, 14, 17, 18, 21, 22, 23, 27, 97
SAFCO 18, 49, 90, 163
Salzgitter 65
Saud bin Faisal, Prince 22
Saudi Arabia, aluminium in 8, 16, 19; crude oil in 7, 13, 20-2, 57, 139, 142; expatriate workers in 89, 140-1, 201; financing of projects 19; industrialisation 7-24; joint ventures policy 15-23, 90, 122, 162, 198; methanol 52; minerals 3; nationalisation 9, 129; petrochemicals 12-15; profitability 19, 23; refining 15-16, 69; second five year plan 7-8, 12, 22
Saudi Industrial Development Fund 19
Saudi Petrochemicals Development Company Limited 14
Sayigh, Yusif A. 4
Senegal, joint ventures with Iran 29
Service industries 158-9
Shah of Iran 4, 25, 38, 95
Shell 13, 21, 28, 29, 46, 49, 56, 57, 107, 130, 164, 175; international 15, 53; involvement in Saudi Arabia 47; Royal Dutch 13
Shipbuilding 62, 194, 200
Showa Denko 149
Siemens 40
Singapore, petrochemicals 66, 152, 200
Smith, Geoffrey 42
Snam Progetti/Anic 65
Snia Viscosa 65
Socal 47, 57, 129, 134
South Africa, joint ventures with Iran 29, 31; Iranian investment in 41
South Korea 198; expatriate workers in Iran 34; joint ventures with Iran 29, 31, 35; in Middle East 199; petrochemicals 64, 66
Soviet Union, EC trade balance with 123; interests in Middle East 141
Spain 119, 127